The Book of KALE & Friends

14 EASY-TO-GROW SUPERFOODS

The Book of KALE & Friends

14 EASY-TO-GROW SUPERFOODS

Douglas & McIntyre

Douglas and McIntyre (2013) Ltd.
Box 219, Madeira Park, BC, Canada V0N 2H0
www.douglas-mcintyre.com

Cataloguing data available from
Library and Archives Canada

ISBN 978-1-77162-014-7 (pbk.)
ISBN 978-1-77162-015-4 (ebook)

Editing by Sarah Weber and Carol Pope
Indexing by Iva Cheung
Cover and text design by Five Seventeen
Layout by Diane Robertson

CREDITS

All photographs by Christina Symons except as noted below.

Carol Pope: pp. 4, 12 (left), 13 (both), 14, 15 (all), 17, 18 (left), 19 (both), 20, 21, 22 (both), 23, 24 (both), 25 (both), 26 (both), 27, 28 (all), 30, 31, 33 (left), 36 (both), 38, 39, 40, 41, 42, 43, 45 (both), 46 (both), 47, 48, 49 (both), 51 (both), 52, 53, 54 (both), 55, 56 (both), 57, 58 (both), 59, 61, 62, 64, 72, 81, 85, 106, 110, 113, 114, 135, 145, 151, 164, 216 (bottom). Sharon Hanna: pp. 12 (right), 16, 18 (right), 33 (top right), 37, 163. hjschneider/Fotolia: p. 33 (bottom right). topeira/Fotolia: p. 34. Zoonar RF/Thinkstock: p. 3. Sean Nel/Thinkstock: p. 50. rickegrant/Fotolia: p. 65. Jill Chen/Stocksy United: p. 66. Harold Walker/Stocksy United: p. 69. Magmark76/iStock: p. 70. audaxl/iStock: p. 143. inerika/Fotolia: p. 154. Anna Comfort O'Keeffe: p. 216 (top).

Printed and bound in Canada

Distributed in the U.S. by Publishers Group West

We gratefully acknowledge the financial support of the Canada Council for the Arts, the British Columbia Arts Council, the Province of British Columbia through the Book Publishing Tax Credit, and the Government of Canada through the Canada Book Fund for our publishing activities.

Acknowledgements

First, we are thankful to readers of the first *Book of Kale* for their enthusiasm and appetite for even more kale. We are also grateful to the Taste Canada Food Writing Awards judges for their support of the first book. Big superfood bouquets to everyone at Harbour Publishing and Douglas & McIntyre for their tremendous belief in this book. In particular, kale kudos and bombastic bee kisses to Anna Comfort O'Keeffe for her enthusiasm, kale-chip acumen and talent in the kitchen that involved cooking up so many recipes for the photo shoots. Huge thanks to Annie Boyar, our marketing wizard, for her many miles walked on the kale trail.

Much appreciation to editors Sarah Weber and Lucy Kenward for such mindful, conscientious consideration of our manuscript. To our expert indexer Iva Cheung, big thanks, and the same to editorial assistants Megan Fergusen and Brianna Cerkiewicz.

We take great delight in the look of this book and are indebted to Five Seventeen, uber-talented designer, for his cover and text design, as well as to Diane Robertson for adeptly typesetting this volume and making all the recipes fit.

A very large acknowledgement goes to the mega-gifted Christina Symons of *everydayeden.com* for her magical food and garden photography taken in the studio at her very own Eden.

Once again, we thank Dr. Dean Adam Kopsell, "King of Kale" of the academic world, for his review of our nutritional information and for assisting with the answers to our many queries.

On a more personal note, Sharon would like to thank the following friends and family: "Karen Luke for her multi-level support, including regularly asking me if I 'need anything from the store;' Barbara Coward for walks, singing, recipes, birdwatching, and her unwavering commitment bordering on mania for growing food in the city; Iain and Heather for feeding me protein and for loving Pocky, letting her sit on chairs when their own dogs are on the floor. And, Deborah David of Courtenay for her unflagging long-distance enthusiasm. Bouquets to Roger for pruning my fig tree and helping me stay rooted; and to my sons, Jesse and Ted—thank you for being. Words cannot describe my gratitude to Carol Pope, co-writer and editor."

And from Carol: "Kale kisses to my super-supportive partner in the garden, kitchen and in life, Cliff Rowlands, who has grown kale, cooked kale and eaten kale—along with the other superfoods in this book—alongside me all these years, sharing inspiration and insight on a day-by-day basis, much of which finds itself in this volume. Also to Chris, Katherine and Elizabeth for their good-natured kale forbearance, for offering kale-recipe ideas and encouragement, and for helping in the garden just to hang around with their mom, even when it involved shovelling a mountain of llama manure on Mother's Day. Gratitude and love to Irene and

Continued from previous page.

Pat Pope, for their ongoing support and endurance of many a kale tale from their daughter. And, of course, hugs and love to my dear friend and kale comrade, Sharon Hanna."

Lastly, gardening and cooking are generally acts of generosity: we have received a bounty of ideas, recipes and inspiration from the gardens and kitchens of so many—most of whom are named in the forthcoming pages. To all of you who have so kindly contributed to this book, thank you—you have helped to make this a joyful journey, and for that we are deeply grateful.

CONTENTS

Why We Wrote The Book of Kale & Friends

Act as if what you do makes a difference. It does.

—WILLIAM JAMES

Planting a bit of kale is such a simple act. But what an extraordinary difference it can make: This is what we have learned over the years, and what became the experience of many readers of the first *Book of Kale*.

Like us, they discovered that kale is a miracle food, bursting with antioxidants and phytonutrients. And that when you pluck it straight from the earth, it's at its most healthful. Surprisingly easy to grow and lasting in most gardens right through the year—even sweetening after a winter's frost—kale is delectable raw or cooked, in salads, sides, soups and meal mainstays, and an unexpectedly good addition to sweet treats like cakes, cookies and ice pops. It is versatile, providing buckets of delicious buds through spring, edible flowers that support bees, and an almost infinite supply of lush organic greens. Plus, it seeds itself!

Like us, many readers have asked, what next? Along with kale, what other superfoods can we easily grow to add nourishment and flavour to our daily life *and* help sustain our struggling pollinators?

So…we asked ourselves *what* makes a plant a *super*food. We believe this extends to more than how healthy a food is—although, naturally, this matters too. As earth-advocate Wendell Berry puts it, "Eating is an agricultural act." When considering what might be a superfood, we went to the garden to evaluate how positively a plant impacts bees and our ecosystem in general, how easy it is to grow organically, in just a bit of earth or a few pots. In the kitchen, we asked whether or not it can help us to eat better for less. And can it be enjoyed with simple preparation, allowing us to slow down, spend time together and savour the meal?

All the garden edibles embraced in this book—kale in its many forms and 13 other picks—can be enjoyed every day in beautiful and wholesome ways, and we elaborate on this with dozens of quick meal ideas and over a hundred full recipes. Tucked into the garden together, these plants strengthen each other against pests and disease—making it easy to grow them organically—and support our pollinators while feeding us in the most life-affirming way. In short, these edibles are the ultimate superfoods for those who want unmatched flavour and the potent health benefits of fresh food, ease of care and growing, and the chance to do something extremely positive for this planet.

What we have learned, joyously and consistently, is that there are few things more satisfying than eating and sharing food we've grown ourselves in a way that nurtures the earth—and, we might add, there are few things in life that taste better.

Sharon Hanna   Carol Pope

Kale, the Easy-to-Grow Superfood

GROWING KALE IN A NUTSHELL

No, we're not telling you to grow kale seedlings in nutshells (although we *do* know of people who like to germinate kale seeds in eggshells). We're simply trying to say that growing kale is a snap, and we can sum it up pretty quickly. As the first book in this series, *The Book of Kale: The Easy-to-Grow Superfood* (which we call the first *Book of Kale* from here on), contains an extensive discussion of growing kale, we don't want to repeat ourselves…still, it's only polite to give new readers a bit of a summary.

The botanical name for kale is *Brassica oleracea acephala*, meaning "cabbage without a head."

PLANTING TWICE IS NICE

SPRING PLANTING FOR SUMMER

Kale is a lover of cool weather. Because of this, we start kale in February or March as indoor (or porch or greenhouse) seedlings for the spring/summer garden, planting it out by March or April. We also direct-sow into our garden in March. Both strategies work.

SUMMER PLANTING FOR WINTER

For winter eating, we seed Tuscan kale by mid-May and the rest in June. While the early-planted crop provides you with summer salads and kale chips, the June-planted stuff reaches a good height by fall and then slows and stops growing until mid-February.

If your garden is full come June—like gardens tend to be—grow new kale starts in pots (see Plant Some Seeds). As pest season is beginning then, we often protect these new plants while they are small, safeguarding them from cabbage butterflies and similar pests by keeping them inside or covered. Sometime in early fall, when there is room in the garden again, transplant each little potted kale to its new growing site. At this point, it won't hurt to throw in a handful of good, all-purpose organic fertilizer. The kale seedlings won't use much of the added nutrients right away, but will need them during the growth spurt in mid-February. Plant the kale seedlings a little deeper than they were growing in their pots, firm in and water well.

With a good group of plants, you can pick leaves until the stems are almost naked and keep yourself kale-fed for the next six months. For a family, a dozen good-sized kale plants can mean you never have to buy any of those limp salad greens in winter.

PLANT SOME SEEDS

THE SKINNY ON SEEDLINGS

Here's a sure-fire way to start kale from seed when it's still nippy outside in early spring. Fill a seeding tray with sterilized seed-starter mix. Warm the soil slightly, using a heating coil or heating pad on low. Or place the tray on the top of your nice warm fridge. Move seedlings to full-spectrum light as soon as they sprout to prevent them from becoming leggy.

Seedlings need bright light and excellent air circulation. Often it's better to wait until natural light levels are higher to seed in a cool greenhouse or outdoors. They'll catch up to indoor-grown plants and be sturdier.

Opposite: A rainbow of kale: so pretty in the garden and invaluable in the kitchen.

Typical of plants in the brassica family, the seed leaves of kale are double heart-shaped.

If you have access to a plug tray, use it. Water the cells every single day, or even more often if the growing environment is hot.

A fine-spray nozzle attachment for your hose is perfect for spritzing kale seedlings. Or use a watering can to water gently and sparingly when seed trays or containers feel light or seedlings look too relaxed. Don't let these seeds dry out, but be careful not to drown them. Use room-temperature water (ideally, water that has sat overnight to allow chlorine to dissipate, but don't fret too much if you have to use fresh tap water—kale's pretty forgiving).

Avoid fertilizing until seedlings have true leaves. If practical, add air circulation from a small fan. The movement will result in sturdier stems.

When the little kale plants are well rooted in their seeding tray or little pots, turn them loose outside on a nice day. If they seem a little spindly, tuck them into the soil extra deep. It's okay to plant your kale so the soil reaches partway up the stem; just don't bury any leaves. You can pick off the bottom heart-shaped leaves if necessary so that the seedling can be planted to a good depth.

SQUARE-INCH GARDENING

Are you wondering whether we mean square-foot gardening? Nope—this is square-inch...or actually half-inch gardening. Along with her friend Barb Coward, Sharon went cross-eyed in the greenhouse as she planted up tiny rows of kale, basil and other superfoods. In plant nurseries, an automatic seeder puts one seed in each little square of what's called a plug tray, which may have 36 by 18 squares (however many that is!). After growing the tiny plugs in a warm greenhouse, nursery workers then dump out the lot, the roots holding that tiny bit of soil together. The workers then pot the seedlings up in four-inch pots or hanging baskets by hand.

PLANTING SEEDS STRAIGHT INTO THE GARDEN

Direct-sow by planting three or four seeds in the same area, to be thinned out later. Or plant the seeds in organized rows, dropping a single seed every 2 to 3 inches (5–7.5 cm). These too will have to be thinned out. Your rows of kale should be at least 18 inches (45 cm) apart, but by planting more seeds than you need, you can favour (that is to say, leave to grow) the best and healthiest plants when thinning. And you can eat your thinnings.

Try to plant seeds deep enough to keep them from drying out. The general rule is to plant a seed three times deeper than its size.

Kale seeds sprout quickly in warm weather, usually in about four to five days. In cooler conditions, the seed may take much longer to germinate—two weeks or more.

Teenaged kale await transplant into the late-summer garden for winter harvest.

Kale will need to be thinned in order to grow large and produce lots of leaves. For big, healthy plants, give them an eventual spacing of 18 to 24 inches (45–60 cm).

BROADCASTING YOUR (KALE) LOVE

Sometimes we get lazy and just huck kale seed willy-nilly around our gardens, scratching it in a bit with a rake or our fingers. The results of broadcast seeding are always abundant—especially in the wet seasons when the seed won't dry out.

DON'T BE ASHAMED OF BUYING NURSERY STARTS, BUT...

We buy kale plants all the time when we see irresistible ones at the garden centre, but whenever possible choose those grown in coir or other biodegradable pots. From the horticulture industry alone, millions and millions of pounds of plastic pots are dumped into landfills annually—as consumers, we *can* say no to this.

TOUGH TO CHOOSE, EASY TO PICK

Here's a quick rundown on some of the key kale cultivars you will find as plants or seeds in nurseries, seed houses, at seedy Saturdays, in the gardens of friends and so on.

SUN MATTERS

Kale grows best with full sun spring through fall—the term "full" implies sun from morning through afternoon. Morning or evening sun alone is fine for some shrubs and flowers, but not intense enough for most edible crops. Areas receiving dappled sun because of some shade from trees will also work, assuming the shade is not too heavy. Plants situated against a wall may get enough reflected light to compensate for fewer hours of sun.

That said, August can be too hot for kale. Resilient as always, it will withstand the burning temperatures, dropping a few lower leaves in protest. Like us, you might feel sorry for it and shade it midday with a big umbrella, or cover it with a bit of shade cloth.

Portuguese kale ready for the soup pot: in Portugal, *caldo verde*, made from this variety, is sometimes called "the soup of the people."

DON'T AGONIZE

It doesn't matter what varieties you pick, just grow this wonder-veggie that contains over 45 phytonutrients, among them lutein, which is implicated in the prevention of age-related macular degeneration. Other kale compounds are thought to lower cholesterol, help protect the body from certain cancers, have an anti-inflammatory effect and supply other benefits. Considering it is so easy to grow year round in many climate zones, this superfood is a no-brainer in the garden and supplies nutrient-dense organic greens for mere pennies.

PORTUGUESE

More collard-like than the other kale types, this variety grows rapidly and has large smooth leaves that rinse off in a flash. Billed as being quite heat tolerant, this staple of Portugal has a sweeter taste than the other kales listed here.

RAINBOW LACINATO (A.K.A. RAINBOW TUSCAN)

A myriad of purples, pinks and greens that keep on coming, this gorgeous variety often reaches 6 feet (1.8 m) of glorious growth. We know of several gardens where Rainbow Lacinato is into its third or fourth year and behaves as a perennial, even though kale is regarded as an annual. You just cut it back a bit and it grows again.

REDBOR F1

The curly purple foliage of this kale variety is stunning in a container or front-entrance garden, and its leaves are equally gorgeous on the dinner table. It is a hybrid, though, so you can't save seeds.

RED RUSSIAN

We grow mountains of this tender kale with easy-to-rinse leaves, and it self-seeds like crazy. Red Russian grows anywhere—in sand, gravel, even between the cracks of a sidewalk—and you can simply tug out the little seedlings from wherever they pop up and plug them into the garden bed where you would like them to grow. Use all the seeds you collect from Red Russian to grow microgreens (see page 24). And we think this variety is the most generous when it comes to providing those amazing kale buds.

SCOTTISH

Curly and dramatic when planted in a cluster, this variety has fluffy light-green leaves that contrast beautifully with Redbor. While the leaves of Scottish kale are more time-consuming to wash than the flat leaves of other types of kale, we like this plant's hardy spirit.

TUSCAN (A.K.A. LACINATO, BLACK OR DINOSAUR KALE)

Elegant in the garden with long, textured blackish/greyish/green leaves, this kale is considered the best for drying into chips (see page 77). Tuscan kale is very cool looking because of its bumpy dinosaur-skin leaves—perfect for a stegosaurus or triceratops to chow down on, or at least you can

(Clockwise from top left) Rainbow Lacinato as tall as Carol; *hoot mon*—Scottish kale; Tuscan looking natty in a pot; Winterbor gearing up for winter; a rush of Red Russian volunteers in a giant container; a rapture of ravishing Redbor.

tell your kids that and get them excited about the kale garden. Plus, it sometimes looks like a palm tree. Tuscan kale is a little slower to get going than the other varieties, so plant your winter crop by mid-May.

WINTERBOR F1

Similar to Scottish kale, this curly variety is known for winter hardiness and, like Redbor, is a hybrid (F1). While all kale can hold its own through chilly weather, if you live in zone 4 or colder, add this variety to your kale mix for extra measure.

WHAT WE PLANT

Every kale type has its special strength, so we have learned that growing lots of varieties is the best practice:

· You will have more pretty colours and textures in the garden (and these will look best if you clump similar types together for maximum impact).
· If you do wind up with a garden pest on your kale, one variety is often more resistant than another, so growing a mix will increase your chances of having a continual harvest.

THE DIRTY DEAL

Growing kale can be a fast and furious business. Therefore, investing just a little bit of time in building up your soil will pay off with big (kale) dividends. "Organic matter" is what we're talking about.

What exactly is organic matter? Simply put, it's a formerly living plant or animal and can include leaves (brown or green), conifer needles and cones, bark, paper (egg cartons, newspaper, paper towels), wood ash, composted animal manure, kitchen compost, kelp, fish waste, even feathers—the list

IT'S A WRAP

The "brown," or carbon layers, in your compost provide aeration between the "green," or nitrogen layers. You may have run out of carbon in the form of dried leaves for layering, so to get things hopping in the heap, wrap veggie peelings and other compostables in newspaper, burrito-style, then add to the compost. This instant carbon-nitrogen layering will speed up decomposition and prevent odour.

is long. All these elements transform into rich, nutrient-filled soil as they decompose.

The easiest way to add organic matter is to put it on top of your garden bed or planter. This is called mulching—and it not only feeds your soil, but also holds in moisture and keeps weeds down. The very sensible Ruth Stout, author of *Gardening Without Work* (our favourite theme), advocated the no-dig method in the mid-1900s, pointing out that it was pointless to till or dig. Piling on organic material without digging became her modus operandi. She moved soil only enough to tuck in plants or seeds, allowing billions of microorganisms and other vital soil critters to work undisturbed.

You can also amend your soil occasionally by scratching in lightly or sprinkling on top a modest amount of organic fertilizer made from material such as kelp, alfalfa meal, greensand, rock phosphate, worm castings, glacial rock dust and other naturally occurring garden boosters.

Well-nourished soil produces more and healthier food that is resistant to garden pests and problems—and healthier for you.

CHEAP AND EASY

As big gatherers of organic matter, we are giant fans of composting, the cheap and easy way to give

Comfrey. Once you have it—you have it. The good news: this herb mines the soil for rich nutrients. Chop leaves and stems to add as a layer to your compost, and it will be superpowered.

our gardens what they need to grow—plus, it's a good "waste not, want not" use of garden scraps. And we like that.

There's a lot of talk about compost in the first *Book of Kale*, so here we just add a couple of cautions and some cleverness:

- Avoid the "dump and run" method of piling kitchen scraps into your compost. Keep a bag of leaves near your bin to use for layering—one layer of carbon (leaves), one layer of nitrogen (kitchen waste), one thin layer of soil—like making lasagna. The extra minute it takes to add leaves (or shredded newspaper) will give you better compost, more quickly. And it won't smell.
- Do not use fresh manure directly in your edible garden—compost manure first for a few months.
- If your compost is full and is not ready to be used, try "Russian composting." Being careful of the worms, gently dig 8-inch (20-cm) holes or trenches, fill to halfway with kitchen waste, cover with soil and tamp down. Trenches must be fairly deep so animals are not tempted to dig up the kitchen waste. Plant a few kale seeds atop your compost deposit.

LOVE THEM AND LEAVE THEM

Nothing drives us as nuts as seeing leaves bagged up for curbside pickup. Instead of tossing them, *use this free bounty:*

- Stuff pots halfway up with fallen leaves when planting edibles, then top with soil—you need only 10 inches (25 cm) of soil to grow kale. Chopping the leaves first will aid drainage. Run over them with your lawnmower or fill a plastic garbage can halfway with leaves and run a line trimmer through them.
- Use leaves to create a food-producing "lasagna garden" (see the first *Book of Kale* for more on this).
- Store a stash of fallen leaves (even the tough oak leaf is okay but just takes a little longer to break down). Pile them in an out-of-the-way area, or create a leaf compost bin—try stuffing leaves inside an easily fashioned cylinder of large-mesh chicken wire, waist-high. Broken-down leaves evolve into leaf mould, a valuable and nutritious mulch that will insulate your garden and decompose just like the forest floor. Or bag leaves in plastic, add two shovelfuls of soil, water well and tie. Poke a few holes for oxygen, store away from light—in a year, you'll have leaf compost.

Eating chickweed gives a new and much improved meaning to "weed and feed."

SUPERWEEDS

Carol says: Faster than the speed of light—or so it seems—chickweed sprouts and spreads through my kale gardens. Sometimes I roll up thick mats of it like grass turf, ripping out the roots, and use it to fill up the compost bin. Other times, though—particularly in the cool seasons of spring and fall when it's at its

most succulent—I nab this nutritious and abundant wild green for dinner.

Tender and slightly crunchy when freshly picked, chickweed is wonderful in salads, sandwiches and wraps. If you have masses of it, wash and freeze the excess for soup stock, blend it into a pesto or whip it into a dip or smoothie.

Naturally, when foraging it's important to know what you're eating. Do some research to ensure you can accurately identify chickweed (*Stellaria media*; *stella*, the Latin word for star, refers to its tiny star-like white blossoms). And it's imperative that you pick only from organic garden areas where there is no danger of pesticide poisoning.

Herbal "wise woman" Susun Weed writes extensively about the value of consuming chickweed in her classic volume *Healing Wise*, giving this "little star lady" full points for relieving inflammation, cleansing the liver, improving hepatic circulation, boosting digestion and cooling and alkalinizing the body.

A kale container garden is a beautiful thing.

Eli and Thomas hold down the kale fort—both boys love to eat their greens straight from the garden.

· Use leaves as a nutritious and insulating mulch—place a layer of chopped leaves on garden beds. Leaves provide great cold-weather protection and break down into organic matter, adding to the health of your soil.

Simply leave leaves where they fall to add nourishment to the soil as they break down (again, along with providing natural protection from the cold). And here is one of the most important reasons to leave leaves: many beneficial insects winter over in garden leaves and debris and areas left untouched, so it's vital to avoid over-tidying (and this can be your excuse to head indoors for a hot toddy by the fire instead of doing any more raking). Also, use a light hand when cutting back perennials: leave seed heads for birds, allow herbaceous grasses to remain standing and generally leave as much food and shelter for birds, bees and other beneficial bugs as you can.

> Did you know that the composted leaves of one large shade tree can be worth as much as $50 of plant fertilizer and humus, with twice the minerals of manure?

GOING TO POT

Kale, along with many garden edibles, grows well in pots. This means that anyone with a balcony,

back porch or any access to a little outdoor space can grow kale, along with the other superfoods we talk about in a bit.

These hardy veggies will be happy in pots, from which you can harvest bits of fresh organic greens for soups, salads or stir-fries.

Around Valentine's Day, your container kale will begin to leaf out (or up). It will require feeding every 10 to 14 days—since your plants are captive, you must fill their nutritional needs. We use organic kelp or fish fertilizer, liquid or granular.

Begin with a good potting mix. Don't use your garden soil, because it probably won't drain well. If you can find potting mix containing lots of good organic nutrients, so much the better.

There is no need to stuff your containers full of pricey soil right to the bottom, however; see our next section.

KALE IN CONTAINERS—WHAT WE'VE LEARNED

· Giant-sized containers don't need to be completely filled with soil; most edible plants require only 10 inches (25 cm) of soil at the most. Fill the bottom with dried leaves, wadded newspapers, the (seedless) weeds you just pulled

Portuguese and Red Russian kale starts looking smart with onions and lettuce.

Harvest buds and blooms as part of the bounty of beautiful kale.

out of the garden, broken-up egg cartons or an old cotton blanket or throw rug—anything that will fill the space. An upside-down three- or five-gallon plastic pot will take up lots of room.

· Include kale as a terrific thriller plant for small and mid-sized pots and fabulous filler plantings in giant containers.

· Use kale in hanging baskets for easy-to-reach snippings. Just remember to keep a hanging basket moist. If it gets dry, water may run out the sides rather than wetting roots. If plants wilt and the basket seems light, dunk it in a huge plastic muck bucket or other large container filled with water for an hour. Fertilize hanging baskets with balanced organic fertilizer every 10 days.

· Choose light-coloured containers for plantings in full sun; dark pots absorb sunlight and plant roots will bake. Kale really does not thrive if its roots are hot. Dark metal can become searing in bright sunlight, so use a plain plastic pot as a liner or place planted pots in semi-shade.

· Use almost anything to contain kale. Garage sales and thrift stores offer all sorts of containers at bargain prices, from battered pots to copper boxes to worn-out wheelbarrows— and don't forget old boots! If the container lacks drainage holes, use an electric drill to make

some. A coffee filter or some used teabags over the holes keeps soil in the pot.

· Dream up daring pairings, tucking bee-supportive flowers alongside your kale (see Mason Bees, page 23).

· Clean used containers inside and out before getting your potting soil ready. Vinegar will scrub off grunge, but sterilizing pots is a good idea. Use half a capful of bleach in a small bucket of water—dunk the pot in or use a rag to scrub inner and outer surfaces.

· Soak terra cotta pots in water overnight before you plant them up, to prevent them from drawing water out of the soil, away from plants.

SHARE THE GREEN

While you're planting up your kale, why not add one extra row? Our good friend Claude Ledoux, co-coordinator of the New Westminster Plant a Row, Grow a Row Program, reminds us that if every household donated one pound of produce during the growing season, food banks would have fresh vegetables for six months of the year. And what's better to share than garden-fresh kale?

And why not pass along some seeds to the local school too? Kale is a bountiful crop during the school year—September through June. Sharon says: Based on my stint as director of a school-garden

THE INCREDIBLE SELF-SEEDING POWER OF KALE

We thought it was very cool when David Catzel of Glorious Organics Cooperative in BC's Fraser Valley included kale in the list of "weeds" his team was harvesting along with lettuce for healthy salad mixtures. In addition to sheep sorrel, wood sorrel, shepherd's purse, dandelion, oxeye daisy, chickweed, peppercress, watercress, lamb's quarters and purslane, Red Russian kale is part of their wild-greens mixture because "it self-seeds like a weed."

Indeed, Red Russian proliferates like crazy. It withstands cold so well that it sprouts up in our gardens even in wintertime. And this volunteer kale often grows into carpets that provide snippings just like microgreens.

If kale sprouts where you don't want it, eat it or transplant it. Tug out the seedling very gently (preferably on a damp and cool day), poke a deep hole in the garden for the long root and pat the soil down around it. Or slide a shovel deeply under a swath and place it wherever naked soil needs coverage. Then water.

Did you know that an edible plant provides maximum nutrients when eaten soon after harvesting it? The faster it goes from the garden to your mouth the better.

program, I've learned that growing a food garden is a wonderful way to connect with children. As one of many projects, students laid down a 10-inch (25-cm) layer of maple leaves, topped with compost, and grew kale. The kids loved nibbling on buds and flowers in spring.

AVOID CLEAR-CUTTING

Pick as much kale as you want, even through the cold season, but always leave a few bits of green on the plant so that it isn't stripped. It's a good rule to take no more than a third in one go. That said, Carol has had deer eat her kale to the quick and it mostly came back, and Sharon has snipped her kale down to 6-inch (15-cm) stubs in an effort to tidy them up, and all grew back luxuriantly. It's hard to go wrong with resilient kale.

JUST WHEN YOU THOUGHT YOUR PLANTS WERE DONE FOR

Kale plants look wrecked after kale soup, kale cake, kale casseroles… But come March or even before, these pathetic half-naked plants burst forth with new foliage—and, gloriously, there's plenty of kale to pick again, just as you were worrying that you might run out.

BUDS TO NIP

By April, the overwintered plants are ready to seed a new generation, so in addition to fresh leaves, buds abound. Like little broccolini heads, they are delicious, and if picked every couple of days will keep growing for months (if you know the secret; see Bud Wiser, page 21).

AND IT GETS SWEETER

All the leaves and buds from this overwintered kale will be exceptionally sweet in flavour. Given a frost or two, this superveggie pumps "sugar" into its system to avoid freezing to death.

PICK, PICK, PICK

Pick the leaves, pick the buds and pick the flowers—just don't strip more than a third of your plant at one time.

PULL A QUICK SWITCH

By June or so, your kale will become gangly as it goes to flower and seed, so will not provide as much to pick for dinner. Some kale elders can be left to flower (for the bees) and then go to seed.

Let the buds begin! Every kale plant provides bowls of buds—if you keep picking them.

Others—to clear the way for new plantings—can be pulled out, rinsed and stored (stems and all if you wish) in the freezer as an ingredient for soup stock (see page 138).

CHANGE THINGS UP

Each type of veggie depletes the soil of certain key elements important for growth. Thus, repeatedly planted in the same spot your food will lose vigour. Rotate crop locations yearly and add organic material regularly; this will also help protect your plants from pests.

BUD WISER

Wanting to eat (a lot) from the garden every day but not work *too* terribly hard at it, we frequently find ourselves pining for that abundant spring season of kale buds.

Sometimes it seems too good to be true. After a long and hard winter of toughing it out in the garden—with us snapping and snipping off leaves through sleet and snow until our kale is almost naked—the plants supercharge into spring growth, with fresh tender leaves bursting out so profusely we can hardly grab them fast enough. Then—as if that weren't enough—each plant forms copious delicious buds (like broccolini heads). And because kale has endured a frost or two, every bud and bit snapped off is sweet and succulent due to the surge of "sugar" the plant generates to avoid freezing.

But there is a catch.

Some kale gardeners have noted to us that they can find no buds to pick. Instead, their kale plants have simply gone to flower by April.

The trick is that you need to keep your eye on your kale. You *must* pick all the buds every day or two if you want them to keep coming. If the kale buds, flowers and is now seeding, you've missed the chance.

And is this really a problem? Having to pick the buds off your kale plants every couple days is a perfect excuse to drop your deskwork or laundry

Let it bee: kale blossoms sustain bees; (above right) mason-bee houses tucked under the eaves shelter early pollinators.

A member of the kale clan, ornamental perennial *Erysimum* Bowles Mauve is a pretty provider of nectar for bees.

and head out for a meander in the garden, bowl and scissors (or paring knife) in hand...and maybe a glass of red wine in the other. With an every-two-days-or-so routine of picking, you can keep yourself and your household supplied with buds for three months or more, at least until those spring-planted new kale additions that are standing by in small pots have matured enough to take the place of the elders in your outdoor kale assembly line.

Just in case you are wondering if all this nipping of the buds is worth it...

We find it an easy pick to harvest a generous pound or two every second day from an average-sized raised bed of established kale plants. And to make it all the more exciting, kale buds are a gourmet treat not often seen in stores. The one and only time we did find kale buds for sale at a local supermarket, they were selling for an incredible $14.99 per pound.

THE BUDS AND THE BEES

Now that we've told you to pick every last bud, we're going to risk annoying you by advising the opposite.

In our gardens, we *do* pick every bud from the plants that are feeding us, *but* we always plant enough extra kale so that a few plants can flower right away. And when those plants finish blooming and go to seed, we let a couple more flower. Why? Because the bright-yellow kale flowers attract bees by the hundreds, and the flowers are our offering to these beloved and essential creatures. Nothing is sweeter to see than a kale blossom bouncing this way and that because a buzzing bee has burrowed its head deep in the flower to gather nectar.

As the bees cross-pollinate the plants, the sugars in the nectar give them what they need for life, and they return this same gift to our gardens—and to us—as their labours ensure that kale, along with *so much more* of our food, prevails.

Hollow stems from lovage and fennel provide an overwintering abode for beneficial insects.

BEE FRIENDLY

For more on how you can help the bees, read on. As organic gardeners, we can make a big difference to these threatened creatures. And every single flower helps, particularly a brassica bloom.

WATER WISE

Leave shallow containers (bowls, seashells, plant trays, etc.) filled with water around your garden for bees, butterflies, wasps and other beneficial insects. Be sure to add pebbles that rise up above the water level so that insects don't drown while trying to drink. Refresh the water daily to lessen opportunities for mosquitoes to breed.

MASON BEES

Hard-working mason bees are needed to pollinate our fruit trees, as environmental problems are negatively affecting other bees. You can buy special condos or houses for mason bees to attract them to your garden. Dandelions are an outstanding early source of pollen for mason and other small bees. Leave some of these weeds in the laneway, between your raised beds and in other spare garden corners—please! Other early-spring attractions for pollinators include crocus, hellebores, snowdrops, tulips, leopard's bane, rhododendron and heather.

KALE'S KISSIN' COUSIN

For a superbloomer that supports bees, sun-loving *Erysimum* Bowles Mauve manages to eke out a bloom or two even in the dead of winter. Named for British gardener Edward A. Bowles, this is a cousin of kale. Its sweetly scented flowers, like those of other members of the brassica family, are alluring to bees, butterflies and pretty much all winged beneficial insects, who will be kissin' it most of the year.

LET IT BEE

In autumn, honeybees huddle together for warmth around the queen. They gradually move around the hive, eating their honey stores. Native mason and bumblebee queens go through diapause, a kind of hibernation, until the warmth of spring awakens them.

Brian Campbell, certified bee master, wants us to know that many bees and other beneficial insects overwinter in dead twigs, herbaceous perennials and pre-existing cavities, as well as under leaf litter. Leafcutter bees make use of the hollow sections found in bamboo, raspberry and blackberry canes, lovage and fennel. Any plant that has a hollow stem is a potential nesting site. There are lots of good reasons to "let it bee" come fall and leave stems as sanctuaries for these tiny creatures.

GET SEEDY

If you've allowed your kale to go to seed after you've debudded it for weeks and months, save yourself some money: save the seed. Wait until seed pods have fully developed and look a bit crispy, then clip them off and stuff them into a paper grocery bag. A month or so later, scrunch the top of the paper bag closed and shake the dickens out of it, after which you'll find a gazillion little round seeds rolling about inside the bag, ready for future plantings or growing as microgreens. You might have to break open a few of the stubborn pods with your fingers to get them to release the seeds within.

Red Russian's seed pods proliferate in the garden when given the opportunity.

Gather kale seeds to grow microgreens like these under grow lights inside or on your back porch.

Other seeding kale plants can be left in the garden to allow their twisting prolific pods to burst open and drop seed onto the soil, resulting in potentially hundreds of offspring that can be transplanted or left as a "kale ground cover" to be snipped with scissors.

KALE MICROGREENS

Now that you know about the incredible self-seeding power of kale, particularly Red Russian, you may wonder what you're going to do with all that seed.

Once you have set aside some for next season and given some to friends and strangers, you might still have lots. At Carol's house, seeds are grown inside under grow lights as winter microgreens and snipped before meals to be enjoyed in soups, sandwiches, salads, omelettes and other dishes. In addition to adding nutrients, they are a fresh and tender green in the midst of dark and dreary winter. This is another way of enjoying kale in the cold season, along with grabbing leaves from the outdoor plants, and much appreciated on those slushy days when you don't feel like trudging through snow to gather a salad.

GROWTH EXPERIENCE FOR KIDS

Agrarian advocate and author Wendell Berry says it best: "Teaching children about the natural world should be treated as one of the most important events in their lives."

Why not invite a child to join you in planting one tree?

Explain to the child that this one tree will siphon more than a hundred pounds (45 kg) of carbon dioxide from our atmosphere every year and add back enough oxygen to sustain the two of you. This wondrous tree will also recycle water, reduce soil erosion, shelter birds and help shade our overheated planet. If it's a fruit or nut tree, it will hand over a bounty of food to those within an arm's reach and provide blooms for bees.

Below this tree, tuck in some of the superfoods we talk about in this book, all of which provide food for you and simple flowers to feed the bees.

KALE DINNER DIALOGUE

While you're sitting around the dinner table enjoying your Kale Cornbread with Bacon & Cheese, Garlicky Kale Zucchini Zuppa and Coconut Kale Cookies (see our recipes), don't be afraid to share these fun facts about kale, quite possibly the most-eaten and healthiest vegetable on the planet:

· Paleobotanists believe that a wild grass like kale covered the earth millions or billions of years ago, making kale quite possibly the food of dinosaurs.
· Fossilized ancient containers that date back to 4,000 BC, found in Shensi province in China, once held kale-like vegetables.

Elliott, Everrah and Chloe ready to plant overwintering kale in the summer garden.

Powdery mildew on Red Russian kale—it's not the end of the world.

- Wandering Celts brought kale from Asia to Europe around 600 BC because it is quick to grow and can withstand the cold.
- In 19th-century Scotland, "kail yard" meant kitchen garden and all kitchens featured a "kail-pot" for cooking. Family and friends asked, "Have ye had your kail yet?" when checking to see if a person had eaten.

COPING WITH THE ODD KALE CONUNDRUM

Our robust and resilient kale is pretty much free of pests and disease throughout the year. But we do experience the odd kale "problem," usually in late summer when kale is heat-weary and pests abundant. The solution? Generally, we don't worry, as the kale will usually outlast the pests. We also grow different types of kale and ensure that they have space around them so that if one patch is affected, the others probably won't be. And we rotate crops to keep pests puzzled about where their preferred foods are located—growing kale in a garden bed one year, for example, and then putting garlic or something else in the spot the next.

POWDERY MILDEW

Once in a while when you've pushed your plant to the wall by snipping it steadily for months of buds, you'll start to see a little bit of whitish powdery mildew show up on those very tired lower leaves, particularly on the Red Russian variety. At this point, apologize to the plant for overtaxing it, and remove it gently from the garden.

Don't put diseased kale in your compost bin because it's best to minimize this fungus in the garden by burying it deeply or making it vanish in an earth-friendly way. (And once you deal with the diseased plants, be sure to scrub your hands before you touch your healthy kale, because the mildew can be transferred from your hands to the plant.) If you're just not ready to part with these plants yet, milk mixed with water (1:9 ratio) is an excellent fungal control—give your plants a spritz and see if this does the trick.

…Or, if , like Carol, you feel too lazy to deal with this problem in the heat of August, you might just find, as she did, that come fall the kale provides new mildew-free leaves again. And perhaps you don't want to yank out those mildewy plants after all.

APHIDS

You might see a few of these green or black scamps hanging out on the underside of some of your kale leaves. Usually this happens more in the summer. It is generally agreed that aphids are naughty, spreading viral diseases and stunting plant growth. But did you know that aphids need to be present on your plant 10 to 14 days before appropriate predators (beneficial insects) show up to devour them? Be patient. Allow nature to take its course.

Remember—aphids are another creature's dinner just waiting to be eaten.

If, however, you are anxious to fix the problem and just can't stop yourself, snip the badly infected leaves into a bucket and put them in your food-scraps collection bin or leave them in your deer-snack pile. Use a garden hose to blast off leaves where just a few aphid guests remain.

The best way to minimize aphids is to grow fennel, lovage and some of the other superfoods we talk about, throughout the garden. These plants attract countless ladybugs, which settle into the garden on the plants they love and proceed to propagate prolifically. And ladybugs big and small love to eat aphids…and, well, you get where we're going here.

CABBAGE BUTTERFLY

The worst enemy of kale might be this brat, but don't let these loopers throw you for a loop. You'll know when they are around because you will spot white butterflies flitting around your garden patch. And chances are pretty good that they will lay a few eggs on the underside of some of your kale leaves.

But don't stress. These pests will arrive and then be gone just like that—you don't need to think about them from late fall through to midsummer of the next year. The eggs and wormy creatures can be rinsed or picked off. For that brief window of cabbage-butterfly multiplication, give your leaves a visual check before eating them.

If the teeny terrors are on your tender new seedlings, however, squish or pick off the yucky little green worms—they're tiny at first and almost always on the underside of the leaf, so you need to look closely.

Summer lightweight floating row cover can shield your kale crop from the cabbage butterfly if you tuck the fabric into the soil around the plants in May or earlier. Ensure the edges are secure enough to prevent insects from crawling in. You can also protect kale by interplanting it with flowers like alyssum or other strongly scented choices. Growing garlic and the other superfoods we suggest can be helpful too. Avoid monoculture, the planting

(Top) Aphids are a perfect lunch for ladybugs; (bottom) the cabbage-butterfly larva comes and goes.

of only one thing—plant diversity is the key to a healthy garden.

SLUGS

In the world of edible greens, kale is one of the more slug-resistant crops. You will agree with us if you attempt to grow lettuce, radicchio or any of those other feeble food plants that can become slug incubators.

Still, you *will* find the odd slug on a low-lying kale leaf. Like Sharon, you can consider it cute and simply let this little creature be; it will probably stick to that lower leaf you don't want anyway. Or, like Carol, you can pick off the leaf, slug and all, put it into your slug-gathering pot, then deliver it along with any others to a faraway area of the yard. In Carol's case, this is where a number of slug-eating

Once emptied, lightweight plastic plant containers like these can be used as effective slug traps. Simply leave one or two upside down in your kale garden. Check them every day and you may find—as Carol often does—several slugs, some very tiny, inside the pots.

garden snakes frequently can be seen soaking up sunshine on a balmy afternoon. The slugs have a chance to make a run for it and the snakes have a chance at dinner. Either way, nature can take its course outside of the kale garden.

Speaking of snakes, Carol's garden has a number of rock walls where other little snakes live. Very shy, they make themselves scarce when any human enters the garden, but when no one's looking (except maybe Carol, who knows to be still) they earn their keep by slugging down a slug supper.

BIGGER PROBLEMS
Pests come in all sizes—and some are even lovable—but, we'd prefer they not crush our kale, so here are a few hard-learned tips:

KITTIES, CANINES AND OTHER CRITTERS
If you have cats, kale-crashing dogs or raccoons in your neighbourhood, protect newly seeded areas by placing prunings from thorny roses, blackberries or other prickly bushes in a criss-cross pattern over them.

DEER OH DEER
Floating row cover can deter animals and has the double advantage of giving your plants some reprieve from too-intense summer heat and/or winter winds. And it can shield your crop from foraging deer—if they manage to squeeze under or through your deer fencing—as they sometimes do in Carol's garden. Take heart, though: if Bambi bamboozles his way into your garden to bolt down the kale, the stubby stems stripped of most leaves should resurge with fresh foliage in a few weeks.

Beneficial beauty: a syrphid fly (hoverfly) takes a break on a parsley bud.

MORE GOOD BUGS = FEWER BAD BUGS

Beneficial insects (that eat so-called bad bugs) need nectar to energize their airborne searches for prey, and help with pollination while they gather this fuel. Key plants that attract beneficial creatures to your outdoor space are California lilac, raspberries and other berries in flower, nepeta, veronica, verbena, yarrow, lavender, feverfew, fennel, lovage, mint, sage, thyme, oregano, chives, cilantro, parsley and other herbs in flower, annual alyssum, buckwheat, calendula, nicotiana, Victoria Blue salvia, sunflowers (with pollen) and zinnia. Such insects are particularly attracted to the flowers of kale, broccoli and other brassicas too.

Feverfew can help a neighbouring kale garden in two ways: its smell discourages new aphids from moving in, while attracting syrphid flies (hoverflies) that will gobble up those aphids that already happen to be hanging about.

Purple or green, kale provides a mega-punch of phytonutrients.

WHAT YOU GET WHEN YOU EAT KALE

A superfood? Absolutely. Here's a recap on what you get when you eat your kale:

- When kale is steamed or cooked lightly, it provides mega amounts of provitamin-A compounds, such as beta-carotene. This vitamin is critical for vision in low light and at night, as well as affording protection against certain types of cancer. The body uses vitamin A to keep mucous membranes—your first line of defence against infections—moist and supple. Vitamin A also converts to enzymes that destroy invading bacteria.

- One serving of (raw) kale contains 200 percent of the recommended daily allowance of vitamin C. This vitamin is critical for growth and repair of tissues, helps make collagen, heals wounds, maintains bones and teeth, and acts as an important antioxidant. While lightly steaming kale causes a small amount of vitamin C to be lost, doing so greatly increases the amount of available vitamin A.

- Kale is an outstandingly rich source of vitamin K: 3½ ounces (100 g) of kale provides seven times the daily recommended requirement. This vitamin promotes bone health and limits neuronal damage in the brain; its role has been established in treatment of people suffering from Alzheimer's and other age-related dementias.[1]

- Kale is an important source of calcium. Experts such as Dr. Annemarie Colbin, author of *The Whole-Food Guide to Strong Bones: A Holistic Approach*, believe that kale, along with other calcium-rich greens, is a better protector of bone health than calcium from dairy sources. The reason for this is the synergistic effect of iron, calcium and vitamins K and C, which when combined with protein allow the body to use calcium efficiently. Considering that more milk is consumed in North America than anywhere else in the world, yet this continent has the highest rates of osteoporosis, this view may not be far-fetched.

- Eating kale that has been lightly steamed has strong cholesterol-lowering benefits. Steamed kale binds to bile acids in the digestive tract, and thus they are prevented from being absorbed along with fat and are eliminated. The liver then replaces those bile acids, drawing upon stores of cholesterol to do so. As a result, total cholesterol is lowered.[2]

- Kale is a good source of copper, manganese, iron, potassium and phosphorus.

- Kale is low in oxalates, unlike other healthy greens like spinach and chard that are high in oxalic acid. This compound reduces the assimilation of calcium and magnesium in the body, so eating less of it is a good thing.

- Kale is not just packed with vitamins and minerals. Leading-edge research involves the area of phytonutrients ("phyto" meaning plant). While these nutrients occur in all plant-based foods, in kale they present themselves in particularly significant amounts:

KAEMPFEROL

- Prevents cancer by deactivating cancer-causing substances
- Is associated with reduced risk of heart disease
- Possesses anti-inflammatory and antioxidant properties[3]

QUERCETIN

- Inhibits LDL cholesterol (the bad kind) to promote good cardiovascular health
- Is effective at reducing the growth of certain cancer cells, such as non-estrogen-dependent breast cancers, leukemia and carcinomas
- Possesses anti-inflammatory and antiviral properties[4]

LUTEIN AND ZEAXANTHIN

- Are absorbed by the body and selectively sent to retinal tissues in the eye where they become macular pigment
- Protect your eyes from damaging ultraviolet light, helping to prevent age-related macular degeneration and cataracts[5]

A daily intake of 4 to 8 milligrams of lutein is recommended by the United States Department of Agriculture's dietary guidelines; 1 cup (250 mL) raw kale and cooked kale contain 26.5 and 23.7 milligrams of lutein, respectively.[6]

BETA-CAROTENE

- Supports maintenance of healthy cell differentiation, normal reproductive performance and visual functions
- Functions as a free-radical scavenger
- Enhances the immune response
- Protects eye tissues
- May suppress cancer development[7]

SULFORAPHANE AND INDOLE-3-CARBINOL

- Are found exclusively in kale and other brassica family vegetables
- Are implicated in the repair of DNA within cells
- Are effective at blocking the growth of cancer cells
- Possess antibacterial and antiviral properties[8]

CHLOROPHYLL

The association of increased consumption of fruits and vegetables with the prevention of chronic diseases has led to new investigations into the roles of chlorophylls as valuable phytochemicals. A recent review by Ferruzzi and Blakeslee (2007) characterizes potential health benefits associated with dietary natural chlorophyll and chlorophyll derivatives.[9] Chlorophyll may be associated with cancer prevention, and binds to potential mutagens and carcinogens in foods, aiding in their elimination from the body.

Additionally, kale is considered to be one of the best anti-inflammatory foods around. In short, kale may just be the most outstanding and efficient vehicle for getting vitamins, minerals and umpteen protective factors into you and your family.

The 10 Most-Asked Kale Questions

As you might guess, we have been the recipients of about a kazillion kale questions over the past couple years. Here are some that keep cropping up:

1 Is kale really a superfood?

Of all the vegetables (and foods), kale receives a whopping 1,000 out of 1,000 in the Aggregate Nutrient Density Index scoring system, catapulting it into the superstar category. This means it is one of the healthiest vegetables on the planet.[10] If you want to know more, check out our recap on kale nutrition on pages 28–29.

2 Is kale better raw or cooked?

Eaten raw, kale provides massive helpings of vitamin C and certain phytonutrients. Cooked, kale offers more vitamin A and other phytonutrients that become available to your body when they are heated. To reap maximum nutritional benefit from kale, eat it both ways!

3 Should I worry about eating too much kale?

Of course, kale should be balanced with other healthy foods, but eating too much is a concern only if you have one of two medical conditions:

Raw kale contains substances called goitrogens that can inhibit absorption of iodine. This may have a negative effect on people with hypothyroidism. If you have thyroid problems, check with your doctor about this, and stick to eating your kale cooked.

If you take blood-thinning medication, it is best to avoid kale due to its high content of vitamin K, which plays a key role in blood clotting. Not all blood thinners are the same, so again, consult your doctor. You can probably still eat kale, but you'll have to eat the same amount every day—your doctor will help you figure it out.

4 What is the best variety of kale?

This is one of those "favourite child" questions that a mother cannot answer. We love Tuscan kale for its dramatic presence in the garden and easy-to-wash leaves…Red Russian for its generosity—it is perhaps the kale that provides the most food, covering itself with tender salad-friendly shoots and buds and then hurling itself into a frenzy of self-seeding…Rainbow Lacinato for its beauty in the garden and tendency to live well beyond other kale types…Scottish kale for its fortitude…

5 When is the right time to sow kale for overwintering in the garden?

Plant Tuscan kale by May 15 because it seems to take longer to germinate than other types. They should be in by the end of June or squeaked in at the beginning of July but no later. Seed catalogues sometimes say July or even August, but this does not allow the plants to get big enough! June-planted kale reaches a good size for winter, and a dozen plants can provide a family with what they need from fall through to the next summer.

Opposite: Tuscan kale takes a bit longer to germinate than other types, so try to plant it by mid-May.

A verdant jungle of Tuscan, a.k.a. dinosaur kale: planted as seedlings in early summer, they provide organic greens all winter and burst into new growth in the spring.

6 What's the best time to sow kale for summer-through-fall eating?

You can sow kale twice in a year to ensure you have lots for year-round eating. Plant seeds inside in early spring in starter pots and put them out into your garden beds or containers once the ground has warmed up, probably in March in warmer regions and a bit later in colder spots. Or you can just direct-sow when the ground starts to warm up. Either way, kale should last through the summer and into fall.

7 How can I get my kids to eat kale if they think they hate the taste?

The thing about planting kale for winter harvest is that anyone (we think)—young or old—who doesn't yet think that kale is yummy will be blown away by how nice it tastes after being kissed by frost. Sweet, crunchy, tender and fresh tasting, a winter-grown crop is the crème de la crème of kale, and the plant's sweetness will remain for months. You might just find your kids nibbling buds out in the garden. If they grow their own and look after it, they'll eat it for sure. And you definitely won't have trouble getting them to eat Kale Fruit Freezes or Coconut Kale Cookies.

8 What is eating my kale?

This isn't a most-asked question, but it is an urgent one for those who find this happening in the garden. Some years, you will find cabbage-butterfly larvae munching on your kale. If this happens to us, we mostly just ignore the infested established plants until the critters move along. At that time, any rough-looking leaves can be composted or rinsed off for soup stock. Even if the plants look a bit worse for wear once the creatures are gone, they will quickly rebound with fresh growth. As for tender seedlings, pay attention, and if you see yucky green caterpillars, pick them off (you'll have to look closely to see them).

The other snackers you might stumble upon are aphids. If they are in your garden, wait for ladybugs or other aphid eaters to show up to devour them, or pull off infected leaves and do away with them, or blast the

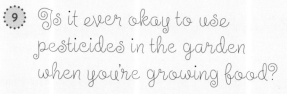

Help yourself: a daily dose of fresh greens direct from garden to kitchen.

(Top) Be on the lookout for teeny green munchers.

(Bottom) To protect your kale, attract beneficial insects by planting a few of the other superfoods we suggest—such as fennel.

intruders using a strong spray from the garden hose. Once aphids land on the ground, they will not climb onto your plants again. If you opt for the snip-off-the-infested-leaves approach, new foliage will spring back in days—you do not need to rip out the whole plant.

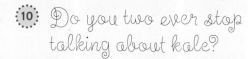

9 Is it ever okay to use pesticides in the garden when you're growing food?

When we are asked what to do about little kale invaders, we are sometimes asked if we think it's okay to use pesticide once in a while.

Eeeek…jumping up on a soapbox…we use no pesticides anywhere in our yards, ever. Why invite this health risk into the same gardens where we are growing some of the healthiest foods on earth? And just as important for us is the well-being of the birds and bees that trust our gardens enough to hang out.

When we say our gardens are organic, included are our bits of lawn, flowers and trees, much of which winds up in our compost and is reshuffled into the circle of life that is the food garden.

All this having been said, you don't have to worry much about "bad" insects if you plant the other superfoods we sneak in at the end of this section—you'll have so many beneficial insects bouncing around the garden that you'll never think about pesticides again.

(Off the soapbox now.)

10 Do you two ever stop talking about kale?

Uhhh…no.

But there are so many reasons to talk about kale: it's incredibly nutritious, a superfood…it thrives through winter and sweetens in the cold…you can snip it all year…it self-seeds…the flowers sustain bees…there are dozens of types, all pretty…it's so easy to grow you will feel like an amazing gardener…and if everyone planted it, think of the difference in our nutrition—you would have vitamin-loaded greens every day…for kale salad…kale soup…kale pesto…kale cake…kale cookies…kale chips…kale pizza…

We'll shut up now. For a little while.

Other Easy-to-Grow Superfoods

You know by now that we love kale, and why not? It's a superfood, it's delicious in so many ways, it's effortless to grow organically and it's super at supporting bees and other beneficial insects. We also started thinking about what other plants would qualify as garden superheroes. Basically, what plants are nutritious, easy and helpful in the garden *and* in the kitchen?

We bickered a little about which plants would qualify. Chervil was in, then out (see page 133). Carol voted for chickweed, Sharon did not (so Carol wrote a little about it anyway; see page 17). Sharon rejected chives but Carol jibed her into it (see page 112). Sharon thought tarragon was tops, but it's temperamental in Carol's garden.

In the end, we made the final cut—asking ourselves which edible plants from our garden feed us at almost every meal. Which ones boost our health and well-being? Which ones grow reliably and are no trouble, allowing us to feel successful as gardeners? Which ones are covered with bees come spring and summer? Which ones invite beneficial insects into our garden, thus protecting other plants, including our beloved kale? Considering all this, it was actually easy to pick the plants that we suggest you add to your garden.

ON HARVESTING HERBS

For maximum flavour and storage quality, harvest the herbs we recommend here on dry sunny mornings after dew has evaporated from the plants. The leaves secrete the most aromatic oils just before plants begin to flower, so that's the best time to cut for drying. Or eat them fresh. Harvest by cutting the stem and stripping the foliage off with your fingers—the leaves should come away easily. Or cut them off with a sharp knife.

ONE LITTLE WORD OF WARNING

Because of the powerful properties of some herbs, it's wise to not overdo eating any one of them at one time. Keep a good balance in what you consume. If you have health issues or are pregnant, please check with your doctor on the safe level of consumption for you.

What makes a superfood super? It's easy to grow organically, it's good for you and the bees like it too.

A member of the kale family, arugula rockets up—but treat it right, otherwise it can be resentful.

Arugula

Arugula—also called roquette, rucola or rocket—has rocketed to the top of food gardeners' must-have list. Arugula's nutty, peppery, mustardy flavour is amazing in salads, on pizza, in pesto and more. Use both the leaves and the pretty edible flowers. We debated adding this one to our super-foods recommendations as it can bolt pretty quickly in the garden, but—and listen up—it's akin to kale as part of the brassica family, and that means it's superhealthy. Plus, we love the taste of arugula, it's a prolific self-seeder—so if you leave a bit of it alone to reseed it will grow itself—and the bees adore it too.

PLANTING AND GROWING ARUGULA

Arugula likes it cool. Sow it in March *if you like*—but know that it will bolt (shoot up and go to flower and then to seed) when spring heats up. We sow arugula from late July through early September. It germinates very quickly and will mature within a month.

Do not seed arugula thickly—this causes bolting and a hot taste. To achieve large, mild leaves like those in organic markets, sow sparingly, then thin so that there is 6 inches (15 cm) between plants. Amend soil with organic matter, fertilize with kelp or fish fertilizer and water regularly.

If you prefer less work, just give arugula a little corner to live in, where it can seed itself. Once it's established, you may never need to worry about it again, except to add a titch of compost or other organic material. Snip away, but do leave some of it to flower and set seed so your supply doesn't run dry.

In spring heat, arugula produces flowers and goes to seed. Cut some of it back—side shoots will grow. Leave others to bloom for the bees and then set seed.

ARUGULA FAST FACTS

Generally, two seed varieties are available: *Eruca sativa*—the annual, which may self-seed, sometimes prolifically, and rustic arugula, a.k.a. 'Sylvetta', a perennial with small narrow leaves and strong flavour. Arugula

- grows easily from seed and self-seeds prolifically if you let it (and we suggest you do)
- thrives in cool weather
- can tolerate partial shade and needs rich, moist but well-drained soil

GOOD FOR YOU

Arugula contains high levels of phytochemicals and chlorophyll, iron, copper, calcium, folic acid, magnesium, folate, vitamins C and A, and—like kale—lots of vitamin K and lutein.

GOOD FOR YOUR GARDEN

Bees are attracted to the pollen-rich blossoms of arugula just as they are to kale flowers.

GOOD TO EAT

Eat both the peppery-sweet flowers and leaves, raw or cooked.

RESENTFUL PLANTS

Yes, it's true. Some plants are…resentful. Neither arugula nor cilantro respond well to being transplanted, so direct-sow them in a pot or (ideally) right in your garden soil. Given the right conditions, they'll self-seed and continue to do so. It is irksome to see arugula and cilantro sold as transplants in pots. The moment you separate each plant and tuck it in, they grow up immediately and bolt (flower and set seed), and you barely get to use a single leaf. This is most evident in spring as the sunlight waxes (gets stronger). For best results, plant both these herbs later in summer: after the solstice.

HOW TO EAT ARUGULA

- Pair it with fennel, pine nuts, garlic or other herbs.
- Use it as a pizza topping—just cover arugula leaves with cheese or tomatoes or mushrooms or any other ingredient that will prevent them from drying out in the oven.
- Combine pasta or potatoes with arugula pesto (see Arugula Kale Pesto, page 103).
- Add arugula leaves instead of lettuce to sandwiches or wraps.
- Snazz up omelettes or scrambled eggs with arugula flowers.
- Add arugula to cooked quinoa or couscous along with herbs and a tangy vinaigrette.
- Combine chopped arugula with cooked pasta, drizzle with olive oil and sprinkle with grated Parmigiano.
- Make a salad of arugula, chopped dates, toasted walnuts and feta.
- Pair with a milder green, such as lettuce or mâche (lamb's lettuce); add pecans or almonds (toasted or not), goat's cheese and a slightly sweet vinaigrette.
- Serve arugula with quartered fresh figs and a little Brie or Cambozola. Sprinkle with arugula flowers.
- Pair arugula with roasted bell peppers and/or slow-roasted or sun-dried tomatoes for a salad, or use the combination as a pizza topping or mix with pasta.
- Use arugula flowers in salads or as an edible garnish. They taste like honey-nectared arugula, much less tangy than the greens.

A doorstep planting—keep some basil close to the kitchen for quick snips.

Basil

It would be easy to assume that basil isn't particularly good for you, because it tastes so bellissimo. As Sharon likes to say, it's one of those herbs where whatever you make tastes like someone else—maybe somebody's adorable Italian grandmother—made it. But basil *is* very healthy for you, and if you let a few plants flower in the garden, you will also be helping bees.

PLANTING AND GROWING BASIL

When you can sit outside at night wearing a light sweater, it's warm enough to sow basil seeds.

It's surprisingly easy to grow basil right through the winter no matter where you live. Set up some indoor grow lights and watch it go! Pinch the tops off to make the plants bushier.

Basil—large-leafed and glossy—garners cachet nestled in a wine box. A bit of shabby chic, wine boxes drain naturally and are perfect containers for small herbs, baby kale or a plethora of parsley. Use well-draining potting mix with added richness from kelp and alfalfa meals and worm castings. A trio of thyme or other woody aromatics would also suit if sand and fine gravel are added to the soil mixture and less organic matter is used. Kept on a sunny porch and watered judiciously, your wine box will last for years. Ask at private wine stores for boxes.

Native to South Africa and India, basil needs heat and dryness; in clammy, cold conditions, seedlings succumb to "damping off" virus. Water sparingly, keeping your seedling just barely moist. If damping off occurs—seedlings die off at soil level—toss them. Reseed in fresh soil, avoid overwatering and ventilate. Knowing how much water is too much for basil is an acquired skill, so you might want to buy a few plants the first year as you also learn to grow them from seed.

Basil also grows well indoors under grow lights—snip and eat it while it's small, or transplant it into bigger pots or a garden bed when the weather is warm.

If your garden has slugs, grow basil in pots on a sunny porch or steps. Use a rich soil mix and space plants an inch or two apart; put containers in full sun. Frequent picking encourages lush growth and prevents flowering. Once the plant flowers, then seeds, it will stop producing leaves.

When your basil reaches a height of 6 inches (15 cm), start snipping off the top bits for kitchen use. This encourages branching. Grow lots so you can let a few plants bloom for the bees, and if you have blossoms to spare, nab a few for an edible garnish. Let some basil go to seed and you'll be able to collect it to grow as winter microgreens.

BASIL FAST FACTS

Basil (*Ocimum basilicum*) is available in a multitude of varieties, from Thai to cinnamon to compact to Genovese to red to lettuce leaf to lime…and the list goes on. Basil

- is grown as an annual
- grows easily from seed if not overwatered
- thrives in a hot and dry environment
- needs full sun and rich, moist but well-drained soil
- grows prolifically inside the house under grow lights all year round

GOOD FOR YOU

Like kale, basil offers a whopping serving of vitamin K; just 2 teaspoons (30 mL) provide more than half the vitamin K we need in a day. Basil is a good source of iron, calcium and vitamin A. Vitamin B_6, manganese, tryptophan, magnesium, vitamin C and potassium are all present too.

GOOD FOR YOUR GARDEN

Bees, butterflies and other beneficial insects are as attracted to basil as we are. Let some of your plants bloom for them.

GOOD TO EAT

Pick basil throughout its growing season and then, before temperatures drop and leaves darken, harvest it all. Eat leaves and flowers, and save tough stems for soup stock. Pesto is a snap to make in your food processor. Freeze pesto in small muffin tins, then store the frozen portions in plastic bags or glass jars in the freezer.

TRY THIS TRICK

Fill a large plastic plant tray or similar container (without holes) to within 1½ inches (4 cm) of the top with rich soil. Add an inch (2.5 cm) of fine seed-starter mix; carefully sow basil seed about an inch apart in all directions. Lightly moisten with a spray bottle and set in a warm, sunny place. If you keep the tray indoors, be sure that the air circulation is good. The result: a tray of basil which, though not tall, will be thick and bushy.

HOW TO EAT BASIL

- Basil leaves are meant to be eaten raw, as cooking can turn them black. But you can purée basil leaves with olive oil and keep this basil paste in the freezer (in cubes or in a canning jar). Add to soups, pesto and pasta, or spread it on pizza.

- Make aromatic basil "water" by adding basil, lemon slices and ice cubes to a pitcher of water—very refreshing, especially when served with Thai food.

- Heat crusty bread rounds, top with tomato sauce (cheese optional) and toast them in the oven. Add chopped basil before serving.

- Served as a pesto with fresh leaves strewn on top, basil is perfect with pasta.

- Throw together a classic Margherita pizza with crushed tomatoes, olive oil and basil leaves.

- Make basil oil to use on fish, chicken, eggs or just about anything else. Purée basil and oil in a blender, and heat mixture gently for an hour or so in a pot—don't boil. Strain through many layers of cheesecloth, a very fine sieve or a coffee filter. Keep basil oil in the fridge and use within 10 days.

- Buzz basil with butter; spread on fancy sandwiches topped with shrimp.

- Add basil to purchased tomato soup.

- Strew on sliced tomatoes and bocconcini with a little olive oil for a classic Insalata Caprese.

- Strew over Thai curries—especially good with Thai basil!

- Cook rice and combine with steamed green peas and some cheese. Let it melt in and serve the rice topped with chopped basil.

- Combine basil with watermelon and feta. Dress simply: a drizzle of olive oil, grindings of pepper and a dribble of balsamic vinegar.

- Use a vegetable peeler to make thin ribbons of green or orange melon. Toss with lime juice, a little oil and lots of basil (mint too).

Use chive flowers to make vinegar and toss into salads—but leave lots in the garden for the bees too.

Chives

There's no surer sign of spring thaw than chives starting to poke out of the ground. A patch of chive plants—with their ever-so-gentle oniony essence and edible flowers—will fancy up any omelette, baked potato or bowl of soup. Meanwhile, you will be getting disease-fighting goodness from this vitamin-rich, antiviral, antibacterial perennial powerhouse. And it will feed the bees and discourage bad bugs from attacking your kale.

PLANTING AND GROWING CHIVES

To grow chives, sow seeds or tuck in seedlings in the springtime after frost has passed. Or divide clumps in spring when barely emerging—they'll increase quickly. If you harvest regularly, you will have an ongoing and succulent supply for all of spring and summer, and into late fall, when these perennials die back for a winter's rest. Simply raze a clump to the ground with a snip of your scissors or swish of your paring knife, and then watch it grow back like mad. This is a crop that dies back come frost, so at the season's end—before they lose vigour—level your chives to the ground and freeze snippings for winter soups.

CHIVE FAST FACTS

Chives (*Allium schoenoprasum*) and garlic chives (*Allium tuberosum*) are both members of the onion family. These plants

- are perennials
- grow slowly from seed, are easily divided and sometimes will self-seed
- thrive in sun but can tolerate partial shade
- are deer resistant, although foragers are known to nibble them

GOOD FOR YOU

Rich in vitamins A, B, C and K, antioxidants, and antibacterial, antiviral, antifungal thio-sulfinites, chives are a natural caretaker of our health.

GOOD FOR YOUR GARDEN

Chive blossoms are compound flowers, meaning each consists of many, many tiny florets. Bees and other pollinators are attracted to them because they can gather a lot of nectar without having to expend energy flying to many different flowers. Meanwhile, the oniony smell of chives will help deter pests from some of your other edibles. Grow lots of chives so that you can let half of them flower

While some chives flower and bliss out the bees, others can be cut down to keep the greens tender and growing.

HOW TO EAT CHIVES

- Float a chive blossom on top of a gin and tonic.
- Make Chive Blossom Vinegar—see page 112. Make garlic-chive vinegar too. Use in vinaigrettes or in homemade mayonnaise.
- For easy-to-make chive oil, purée chives with oil in a blender, and heat mixture gently for an hour or so in a pot—don't boil. Strain through many layers of cheesecloth, a very fine sieve or a coffee filter. Keep chive oil in the fridge and use within 10 days; drizzle it on fish, scrambled eggs, pizza or salads.
- Make chive butter by blending butter and snipped chives, or whirl them together in a food processor. Garnish butter with tiny chive florets and chopped chives. Use on crostini or crackers, or slather on steamed or grilled potatoes, corn, carrots, asparagus...
- Try the classic combo of chives with potatoes— mashed, boiled, steamed, baked, scalloped...
- Snip chives over cottage cheese and tomato.
- Butter peas from the garden and top with chives.
- Try green beans with chive butter and chives and/ or bits of chive flower.

- Slather fillet of sole with chive butter and chives.
- Top toast with goat's cheese and snipped chives.
- Sprinkle leek and potato soup with chopped chives.
- Roll a log of goat's cheese in finely minced chives. Refrigerate, and serve with bread or crackers.
- Whip up a chive version of pesto.
- Make chive "cheese" with purchased or home-made pressed yoghurt. Add lots of chopped chives, and maybe some salt and pepper. Refrigerate, then mould into little blobs.
- Boil some buckwheat noodles (soba). Add sesame oil, lots of chopped chives and a little soy or Bragg Liquid Aminos.
- Mix chives into scrambled eggs and egg salad for sandwiches, or sprinkle on soft-boiled eggs.
- Barbecue potatoes or vegetables and then fling on masses of snipped chives with a speck of butter or olive oil and a grinding of ground pepper, and simple fare becomes fabulous. And beautiful...if you top it with some of the pretty pink and edible chive blossoms.

A volunteer cilantro plant with its dainty white flowers attracts many beneficial insects before going to seed. Collect the seed as coriander or let it self-sow. Cilantro seed is a schizicarp, meaning you'll get two seedlings per seed.

for the bees while cutting down others for use in your kitchen. They are an ideal edging for your kale beds.

KEEP THEM CLOSE

Chives are lovely in the garden, of course, but they're also groovy growing on a sunny back porch in plain terracotta pots near the kitchen for last-minute snips.

GOOD TO EAT

Enjoy eating the oniony greens and sweet mauve-pink blossoms of chives, as well as the broader-leafed garlic chives with white blossoms. For easy gourmet fare, fling masses of snipped fresh chives with a titch of butter or olive oil onto potatoes, vegetables and more. Dry, chop and bottle chives, or snip and store them frozen in ice cubes for winter soups.

Cilantro/Coriander

The cilantro/coriander plant provides us with not one but two harvests—the greens we call cilantro and savoury seeds we call coriander. A powerful natural body cleanser that binds to toxic metals within our systems and helps to flush them out, this herb is no doubt worthy of superstar billing. Plus, its dainty flowers attract beneficial insects to our gardens and support bees.

PLANTING AND GROWING CILANTRO/CORIANDER

Like arugula, this herb is a cool customer. You *can* sow it in March if you like, but it will bolt pretty fast. We sow it in late July through early September, and if you're wondering why, read the section about resentful plants (see page 35).

When you buy cilantro, it turns to brown mush awfully quickly. So, like us, you may want to grow some in a little corner of your garden. Snip away at your plants for tasty additions to salads and stir-fries, but leave some to flower and set seed. The spicy white flowers are a boon to beneficial insects. And if you let it go to seed, it will make more plants—or you can harvest this seed (coriander) to use as a sumptuous spice.

CILANTRO/CORIANDER FAST FACTS

Cilantro (*Coriandrum sativum*) is fast growing and a worthwhile addition to any garden. Cilantro

· is an annual
· grows easily from seed and self-sows prolifically if you let it (and we recommend that you do)
· thrives in cool weather
· can tolerate a little partial shade, but basically needs a sunny spot
· needs rich, moist but well-drained soil

GOOD FOR YOU

Cilantro helps to clean the body of toxic metals, and both the foliage and seed are rich in antioxidants. Like kale, the leaves are surprisingly rich in vitamins K and A, as well as minerals and even B vitamins.

The whole cilantro plant is edible—root and all.

HOW TO EAT CILANTRO AND CORIANDER

- Make cilantro butter by blending butter and minced cilantro leaves, or whirl them together in a food processor. Garnish butter with tiny cilantro florets and chopped leaves.
- With a pulse or two of your blender, add cilantro to tomatoes, peaches, nectarines or strawberries for fruit salsa. Add minced jalapeño and chopped sweet onions or scallions.
- Slice tomatoes and top with a drizzle of olive oil and chopped cilantro.
- Fry cubes of potatoes with garlic, and garnish with a few handfuls of chopped cilantro.
- Use lots of chopped cilantro leaves in cabbage slaw. Add orange juice to the vinaigrette.
- Garnish tomato soup or roasted red pepper soup with chopped cilantro.
- Mix thinly sliced cucumbers with cilantro, chives and yoghurt—serve with curries.
- Make cilantro pesto using oil, peanuts, garlic, salt and pepper. Serve on rice or over Asian noodles, or make salad rolls stuffed with shredded veggies and cilantro pesto.
- Use cilantro flowers as a garnish on salads or anything you fancy.
- Drink coriander-seed tea—it sweetens the breath.
- Add a spoonful of crushed coriander seed to the fruit in any crisp or cobbler.
- Use in homemade curry powder.
- Marinate raw mushrooms in olive oil with lots of coriander seed, orange zest and a little balsamic vinegar.
- Toss sliced cauliflower with crushed coriander seed, olive oil, salt, pepper and orange zest—squeeze the orange juice over it as well; roast at 425F (220C) until browned, turning cauliflower slices a couple of times. Garnish with cilantro leaves.
- Make coriander vinegar: add a handful of lightly crushed seeds to light-coloured vinegar, strain after two weeks, and sprinkle over apple and celery or Waldorf-type salads.

GOOD FOR YOUR GARDEN

Cilantro attracts bees, syrphid flies (hoverflies), ladybugs and parasitic wasps, all of which provide you with free pest-control services for your whole garden.

GOOD TO EAT

Cilantro's leaves, flowers, roots and little round seeds (coriander) are all delicious.

When collecting seeds, snip the seed heads into a paper bag. When they dry, gently thresh them into a bowl. Bottled and kept in a dry and cool place, coriander seed lasts for years. It is best freshly ground, either with a mortar and pestle or in a clean coffee grinder.

Architecturally statuesque, fennel stands tall and wafts its licorice-y fragrance into the garden, luring a bounty of beneficials.

Herb Fennel

Why do we consider herb fennel to have superstar status? Because this perennial grows like a weed and brings a tantalizing gourmet flavour to the kitchen, and because it is a huge supporter of digestion, key to good health. Plus, from July through September, fennel blazes upward, a mass of feathery garden architecture culminating in mustard-yellow crowns of blossoms followed by star-like webs of green and yellow seeds. Whether you plant green or bronze fennel, prepare to be dazzled by this wonder herb. Lastly, it is a magnet to bees and other beneficial insects—another reason to love fennel.

PLANTING AND GROWING HERB FENNEL

Sow seeds or tuck in seedlings in the springtime after frost has passed. You can also allow a mature plant to self-seed in a barren area of the garden—just don't let it get carried away (see sidebar below). Herb fennel returns every spring after dying back for the winter. Cut it down in the fall to harvest the seeds and foliage—but leave a few of the hollow stems partially intact for beneficial insects to hibernate in.

> Yes, there is a difference between herb fennel and bulb fennel...to learn more, go to our sidebar on page 125.

HERB FENNEL FAST FACTS

Green herb fennel (*Foeniculum vulgare*) and bronze herb fennel (*Foeniculum vulgare* Purpureum) are both similar in size and stature; the colour is the only notable difference. Herb fennel

· is a perennial
· grows easily from seed and self-seeds prolifically
· reaches a height of 7 feet (2 m)

DON'T LET FENNEL GET CARRIED AWAY

Herb fennel—and sometimes lovage too—is so hardy and prolific that it can be a problem in some gardens and even a bit invasive in warmer climates. With regard to our Pacific Northwest gardens, our response to concerns about the overzealousness of fennel is similar to what we say about parsley, kale and other eager edibles: if it's overrunning the garden, just eat more of it or share it with friends!

Before forming into this starburst of fennel seeds, each and every tiny blossom was pollinated by a gaggle of good bees and bugs.

- is suitable for a garden bed or deep container
- thrives in sun but can tolerate partial shade, and needs well-drained soil
- is drought tolerant due to its long taproot
- is deer resistant

GOOD FOR YOU
Magnesium-rich, digestion-enhancing fennel has been used for centuries to improve human well-being.

GOOD FOR YOUR GARDEN
The anise swallowtail butterfly is very strongly attracted to fennel, along with other members of the Apiaceae plant family, such as lovage and parsley. If you want to support butterflies, grow fennel, and you will find the green, yellow and black butterfly caterpillars chomping down the lacy foliage. Once they move on, the fennel will spring back quickly wherever it might look a bit depleted. And here's the best news of all: bees too are attracted to fennel and will flock to its gorgeous golden umbrella-like flowers. Other beneficial bugs that flock to fennel for its nectar are syrphid flies (hoverflies) and lacewings, both of which help control aphids, and tachinid flies, which can keep the cabbage butterfly in check. Ladybugs also can be seen in all life stages from egg to larvae to adult on the lacy leaves.

WATCH OUT FOR THE GOOD GUYS
Before you grab some seeds or chop a chunk of foliage from your fennel—or lovage, parsley, cilantro or any other aromatic member of the Apiaceae family (also called Umbelliferae, because the flowers are in umbels)—STOP. Look closely to ensure that the seeds or foliage are not hosting beneficial insects. You don't want to harm the very insects you've been trying earnestly to attract. Maybe grow two or three plants to increase your opportunity to both harvest from this plant through the year and also support the good guys that naturally protect our gardens.

GOOD TO EAT
Herb fennel's foliage, flowers and seeds are all useful in the kitchen. In late fall, when the seeds have mostly turned brown, snip the fennel stems and place them upside down in paper shopping bags (but before you do this, watch out for the good guys; see sidebar). Come winter when the seeds are dry, gently thresh the seeds into a bowl and bottle them for culinary use. Foliage can be air-dried or chopped finely and frozen in ice cubes.

HOW TO EAT HERB FENNEL

- Steep fennel foliage or a teaspoon of seeds in boiled water for a soothing licorice-laced digestion-enhancing tea.
- Top any seafood, particularly locally harvested shrimp or spot prawns, with finely chopped foliage.
- Infuse oil with foliage for a licorice-flavoured gourmet drizzle.
- Finely chop foliage and sprinkle over roasting potatoes or vegetables, then top with a few fennel seeds too.
- Use a mortar and pestle, or a food processor, to grind fennel foliage with oil, salt and garlic into a pesto, and slather it over seafood or vegetables.
- Sprinkle finely chopped foliage over summer cucumber salads.
- Strew seeds over bread dough before baking.
- Add foliage, seeds or even some of the fennel stalk to fish stock.
- Wrap salmon or any other seafood in foliage before steaming or baking.
- Add finely chopped foliage to egg dishes and potato or green salads.
- Add seeds and chopped foliage to salmon or crab cakes. Decorate with pretty yellow fennel flowers.
- Sauté seeds with slices of turkey sausage to add to a tomato-based pasta sauce.
- Add the licorice-tasting seeds to sweets…fennel-seed blackberry quinoa cobbler or almond fennel-seed biscotti, anyone?
- Chew green or brown fennel seeds for an effective breath-freshening digestion booster.

Garlic

There are so many reasons to embrace garlic as a superfood. Incredibly easy to grow, garlic deters pests from your kale and the rest of your garden. Among the healthiest foods we can eat, homegrown garlic is antibacterial, antiviral, anti-inflammatory and antioxidant, and can be gathered in three wonderful forms—as bulbs, scapes and greens. If you let a few of your garlic plants flower, the stunning spherical blooms will become the nucleus of a frenzy of bees.

PLANTING AND GROWING GARLIC

Buy locally grown organic garlic from a farmers' market, nursery or seed supplier for seed. Avoid imported garlic as it may not be suitable for your growing conditions and has often been treated with sprouting inhibitors.

You can plant garlic for as long as the earth can be worked in the fall, although aiming to have it in the ground before Halloween is a good goal. (Sharon likes to plant it by October 15.) Gently separate garlic bulbs into cloves *just before* planting, leaving the skin on the cloves. Plant 2 inches (10 cm) deep and 8 inches (40 cm) apart with the pointy tip up. Don't bother planting the smallest cloves—save those for supper. Big cloves grow into big bulbs and are your best bet for a good crop.

Garlic is a heavy feeder since it grows for such a long time. Lean soil results in tiny garlic—not a judicious use of garden space for nine months. Improve the soil with abundant organic matter, adding an all-purpose, organic fertilizer when planting. As green shoots emerge, feed biweekly with kelp or fish fertilizer.

Mulch your garlic crop with chopped leaves or straw—it's going to be in the ground a long time and will look much nicer with a layer of mulch to keep it snug and weed free.

There are four opportunities to harvest garlic.

1. In early spring, snip a few of the green strappy leaves or tug out some of the young scallion-like bulbs.
2. In June, pick the scapes (see sidebar page 45).
3. By July 1, it's time to stop watering your garlic so that the bulbs mature a little in the ground. In midsummer, gardeners have differing ways of deciding exactly when it's bulb harvest time. Some people wait until two-thirds of the plant has yellowed; for others, seeing three discoloured strappy leaves is the signal to harvest. Either way, don't leave garlic bulbs in the ground longer than that, as they might begin to split and won't store well. To cure garlic, hang your bulbs out of the sun in an airy spot for three weeks.

Both garlic cloves and bulbils can be planted in the fall—cloves will produce a bulb in nine months; bulbils require longer.

GREAT SCAPES

While most gardeners choose hardneck garlic over softneck garlic, both yield fantastic returns. Hardneck garlic sends up a rigid central stock; softneck, on the other hand, remains pliable and is suitable for braiding; it is also considered the best choice for storing. One softneck clove planted in fall produces a sturdy bulb of up to 24 cloves. And each hardneck clove can multiply into 12, with the added bonus of a scape—the curly stem that leads to the newly developing seed head—which can be snapped off for salads and stir-fries. In fact, you can use the crunchy, curly scapes anywhere you'd use garlic—the flavour is a little milder so add a little extra if you like. Harvest scapes around mid-June when they have formed one loop or two; removing them from the plant helps it to direct energy to the bulb below.

These scapes flourished in Carol's container garden. In a good-sized plastic pot (that came with an apple tree), she planted 10 bulbs that grew into garlic plants that looked smartly architectural amidst the potted kale. When the scapes formed, they were left to develop into giant globular flowers that had the bees dizzy with delight. In late fall, Carol cleared away the fading flowers and foliage to find fresh new garlicky greens coming up just in time for winter soups and stir-fries.

Garlic can be gathered in three wonderful ways—as greens, bulbs and scapes (shown here).

You don't need a pot to put pluckings in—simply pop each scape onto your wrist like a bracelet. Invite a child to join you in the fun!

4. Resist snapping off scapes or harvesting bulbs from just a few of your garlic plants: they will bloom spectacularly—supporting the bees. Then seeds called bulbils will form and can be planted; they require two years in the garden to form bulbs. Lastly, the thick stems will die back by September. Simply pull this debris away, and you will find a chive-like growth of garlicky greens coming up for fall snipping.

Planting garlic, with its large, silky-smooth pointed cloves, is a tactile and fun experience to share with children. Don't forget to let them do the harvesting nine months later!

GARLIC FAST FACTS

Many varieties of garlic, *Allium sativum*, are available to home gardeners: Evans, Music, Spanish, Red Russian, Roja, Korean, Sicilian Gold (a softneck type, perfect for braiding), Persian Star

HOW TO EAT GARLIC

- Put garlic cloves on top of winter squash pieces, drizzle with oil and bake. Everyone gets some roasted garlic on their squash.

- Surround a chicken with heads of garlic and roast as usual. Spread the garlic on bread or smush it on the chicken.

- Roast heads and squeeze the soft garlic onto soft Brie or Camembert on good bread—an old favourite that never goes out of style.

- Add garlic bulbs and scapes to pestos, stir-fries, soups, hummus and other bean dips. Many of our recipes in this book contain garlic.

- Chop scapes to add to salads.

- Pitch scapes into the food processor with fresh basil, olive oil and pine nuts, filberts or pecans and a nip of salt to make unforgettable pesto. Other herbs, such as parsley, can be used instead of basil.

- Use garlic greens anywhere you'd put chives.

- Whiz together scapes, white beans, lime juice, mint leaves and olive oil. Serve on crackers or as a dip for veggies.

- Buzz scapes with a little oil and salt to smear on bruschetta. Top with a slice of tomato, a little grated Parmigiano, and bake.

- Make scape butter, spread it on bread and bake in the oven just enough to toast it up.

- Add the greens to any Asian-inspired cuisine—with noodles, stir-fries and rice dishes.

- Mince garlic greens and add with goat's cheese to baked or steamed or mashed potatoes.

- Add garlic greens to potato soup or potato leek soup.

- Mince garlic greens and add to vinaigrettes.

- Mandoline carrots in long thin shards and stir-fry with garlic greens.

A generous giant: the aromatic leaves and seeds of lovage taste of celery, but are much easier to grow.

and more. Plant large cloves in fall for a summer harvest of bulbs. Garlic

- · is a perennial but is usually treated as an annual
- · thrives in sun and needs rich, well-drained soil
- · is deer resistant

GOOD FOR YOU

Cooked and raw, this miracle food has natural anti-bacterial, antiviral, anti-inflammatory and antioxidant properties, and is a good source of manganese, tryptophan, selenium, calcium, phosphorus, copper, protein and vitamins B_6, C and B_1.

GOOD FOR YOUR GARDEN

Bees go mad for the strikingly architectural flowers of the Allium genus. And more good news is that, whatever form it's in, garlic planted anywhere in the garden will help deter pests from your all-important kale crop.

GOOD TO EAT

Enjoy garlic scapes, bulbs and greens in all kinds of dishes.

Lovage

Edible from root to leaves to seeds, this perennial garden superstar tastes like celery and is a strong attractor of beneficial insects. Giant, deer-resistant lovage towers in the ornamental or edible bed as yet another offering to the good bees and bugs. A nip of fresh or dried foliage is a powerful celery substitute, so use just a little. The seeds are useful in the kitchen too. Lovage enables you to harvest the taste of celery without resorting to this pesticide-saturated vegetable, high on the list of the dreaded "Dirty Dozen" if not organically grown.

PLANTING AND GROWING LOVAGE

Sow seeds or tuck in a couple seedlings in the springtime after frost has passed. Or allow a mature plant to self-seed in a barren area of the garden—just don't let it get carried away (see the sidebar on page 42). Perennial lovage returns every spring after dying back for the winter—cut it down in the fall to harvest the seeds and leaves,

Collect seeds for kitchen use in fall, but allow a few seed-laden stems to remain standing in the garden for feathered friends through winter.

but leave some of the hollow stems intact to provide hibernation spots for beneficial insects.

LOVAGE FAST FACTS

Another useful member of the Apiaceae plant family, lovage (*Levisticum officinale*) deserves a place in every garden. This herb

- is a perennial
- thrives in partial shade and needs rich, well-drained soil
- is drought tolerant due to its long taproot, although it will droop if growing conditions become too dry
- grows easily from seed and self-seeds prolifically

- reaches a height of about 7 feet (2 m)
- is deer resistant

GOOD FOR YOU

Like fennel, lovage is an excellent booster of digestion.

GOOD FOR YOUR GARDEN

Bees and other beneficial insects are strongly attracted to this member of the Apiaceae family and will flock to its giant cartwheels of greenish-yellow flowers.

GOOD TO EAT

The leaves and seeds of lovage bring the taste of celery to the kitchen—use it sparingly because it is strongly aromatic. In late fall, when the seeds have mostly turned brown, snip them into a paper shopping bag (but before you do this, watch out for the good guys; see the sidebar on page 43). In winter, when the seeds are dry, gently thresh them into a bowl and bottle for culinary use. Foliage can be air-dried or chopped finely and frozen in ice cubes.

LADYBUGS, LADYBUGS

Planning to trim this giant perennial down for a second flush of growth one August in her garden, Carol received a "stop-work order" from the universe when she discovered it had become a nursery for dozens of developing ladybugs. Always give lovage a good look before cutting down any foliage!

HOW TO EAT LOVAGE

- Add chopped lovage leaves to shepherd's pie, salsa, turkey stuffing and rice.
- Spiff up vegetable soups with a couple of chopped lovage leaves.
- Substitute a pinch of lovage for salt or grind lovage seeds with salt.
- Make lovage vinegar. Harvest, wash and dry leaves. Pack loosely into very clean jars. Cover with white wine vinegar, seal and store in the dark for a few weeks. Strain out solids before using. Try with rice or cider vinegar too.
- Use hollow stems of lovage as straws to drink or stir mixed drinks like Caesars—anything that uses vegetable juice. Make sure there are no overwintering insects hiding in the stem before you sip!

Mint with Red Russian kale—pick both to make Sharon's favourite salad, Minted Kale with Peas & Blue Cheese (see page 122).

The strong scent of mint helps to camouflage Redbor kale from the cabbage butterfly.

Mint

This herb's "rambunctious" quality is of mythological proportion. Literally. Pluto, married to Proserpine, fell in love with a nymph named Menthe. In a jealous rage, Proserpine stomped Menthe to the ground. Some scholars say Proserpine turned Menthe into a plant; others speculate it was the inspiration of Pluto, who wanted Menthe near him forever. In this second version of the story, he gives Menthe an irresistible fragrance to further annoy his spouse. Either way, mint remains a legendary edible—supereasy to grow and useful beyond measure, repelling bad bugs and luring good ones,

NAUGHTY OR NICE?

We believe mint has the undeserved reputation of being "vigorous" (a nice way to say invasive). Lowly mint cannot be compared to the vigorousness of such botanical bullies as goutweed, lamium or bindweed. In fact, bergamot, apple and pineapple mints are practically tidy and well behaved. In any case, all mint is easy to manage. Just pull it out where you don't want it—share pieces (anything with a bit of root will grow) with friends and neighbours.

To contain it, you can also plant mint in buckets or plastic nursery pots at least 10 inches (25 cm) deep and with the bottoms cut out; simply sink the whole works into the soil. That naughty mint will mostly stay put, with escapees easily captured.

sweetening our digestive health and, all the while, making us happy with its scent.

PLANTING AND GROWING MINT

Mint can be planted any time the ground isn't frozen solid. It thrives in dampish soil in part shade, with protection from very hot sun. Utilize small-leafed varieties like Corsican mint between stepping or paving stones too.

Mint can get a bit straggly, so give it frequent haircuts. And after you finish gardening, what better way is there to reward yourself than a soak in a hot herbal bath liberally laced with freshly gathered mint snips?

MINT FAST FACTS

Mentha is available in many varieties—try them all! Mint

· is a perennial
· can be grown from seed or, more easily, from divisions or root cuttings (see page 55)
· thrives in partial shade or shade and dampish soil
· is deer resistant

GOOD FOR YOU

Mint has long been used as a medicinal and aromatic herb. Ancient Egyptians used it to cure digestive upsets and freshen breath. The ritual of after-dinner mints carries on to this day; the inclusion of mint as an antispasmodic and calmative in modern-day pharmacopeias worldwide is testament to its efficacy.

GOOD FOR YOUR GARDEN

Mint attracts a plethora of beneficial and pollinating insects when it's in bloom. These critters include bees, syrphid flies (hoverflies), lacewings and butterflies. And there is anecdotal evidence that mint—particularly peppermint—repels aphids and cabbage butterflies.

GOOD TO EAT

There is a mind-boggling array of mint. Available almost year round in the garden and usually always at the market, mint adds unexpected and surprising dimensions, taste-wise, to a wide variety of foods. Why bother with packaged herbal tea when a simple sprig of fresh mint—or a handful of crushed dried leaves—is invigorating for the body and abundant in the garden? And mint is also magical—fresh or dried—in many culinary creations.

Whether fresh or dried, mint makes the perfect cuppa all year round.

HOW TO EAT MINT

- Make a calming tea with spearmint.
- Or use spearmint to make a perfect mint sauce.
- Add bergamot mint to herb butter and lather on lemon loaf, or toss into fruit salads.
- Add ginger mint leaves to hot apple cider.
- Use the fuzzy leaves of apple mint (a.k.a. French mint) for cool drinks.
- Brew washed, chopped fresh mint leaves as you would regular tea—steep for about 5 minutes. In India, mint leaves are often mixed with black tea for a refreshing cuppa.
- Mint is made for iced tea. Add mint leaves to the ice cubes. Or add to a pitcher of juice or water at the dinner table.
- Make Persian Mint Elixir: combine water with fresh mint leaves, lemon slices and a dash of rose water. Serve over ice in the nicest tall glasses you have.
- Melon + mint = magnifique. Combine cubed firm watermelon with mint and a little crumbled feta; drizzle with olive oil.
- Variation on above: add halved tiny tomatoes in all colours.
- Punch up fresh pineapple with chopped mint.

- Boil or steam new potatoes with a smattering of mint leaves; drizzle with butter and add chopped baby mint leaves.
- Ditto fresh green shelling peas.
- Steam baby carrots. Sauté a little butter and a spoonful of honey for a few minutes. Add the carrots, toss them around to coat with sauce and add chopped fresh mint.
- Make mint raita: mix finely chopped mint with yoghurt, shredded apple and a little chopped onion. Serve with curry.
- For a quick salsa, chop a ripe mango, and add the juice of a lime, chopped fresh mint, and a little minced ginger and jalapeño. Serve with warm tortilla chips.
- Make tabbouleh with a ton of mint; add parsley too.
- Whip up some briam—Greek ratatouille: dice potatoes, onion, zucchini, eggplant and peppers, sprinkle with olive oil and lots of chopped fresh mint, and bake until sizzling.
- Gussy up warm French potato salad with chopped mint and freshly snipped chives.

A luminous ground cover, golden oregano is gorgeous in the garden and pretty on the plate.

There's a buzz in the air: oregano blossoms hum with happy bees.

Oregano

Remarkably rich in antioxidants, oregano is gorgeous in the garden and a super supporter of bees and other pollinators, including predacious good guys that protect our kale.

PLANTING AND GROWING OREGANO

Sow seeds or tuck in seedlings in the springtime after frost has passed. Try growing oregano in a terracotta pot, hanging planter or rock garden.

OREGANO FAST FACTS

Origanum comes in many varieties—try lots. *Origanum vulgare hirtum* (a.k.a. *Origanum heracleoticum*) is the real Greek oregano and the most intensely flavourful. Most cultivars grow from seed, cuttings (see page 55) or divisions. Oregano

· is perennial
· thrives in sun and needs well-drained lean soil
· self-seeds prolifically in good growing conditions
· is drought tolerant once established
· is deer resistant

GOOD FOR YOU

Oregano is reportedly 40 times more potent than a fresh apple as an antioxidant. Vitamin K abounds in this antibacterial herb too, along with minerals and omega-3 fatty acids.

GOOD FOR YOUR GARDEN

When oregano blossoms open, bees and other pollinators will be abuzz, along with other beneficial insects that will help protect your plants from predators. And—hurray—oregano also helps repel the cabbage butterfly from your kale.

GOOD TO EAT

The ultimate addition to Mediterranean cuisine, oregano is fabulous fresh, frozen in ice cubes for soups, or dried. Drying is one way to maximize its flavour for cooking. Oregano is most pungent just after buds form but before blossoms open.

HOW TO EAT OREGANO

- Make oregano tea or mouthwash when you have a cold or sore throat.
- Throw chopped oregano into vinaigrettes. Try Arlene's Husband's Favourite Vinaigrette (see page 114).
- Marinate olives or small button mushrooms in chopped fresh oregano, olive oil, wine vinegar and a little garlic.
- Halve ripe tomatoes. In a food processor, combine oregano leaves, a handful of bread crumbs, garlic and grated Romano or Parmigiano. Spread onto tomatoes and roast in a medium oven until tops are browned.
- Add lots of chopped fresh oregano to meatballs—whether they be lamb, turkey, chicken or whatever meat substitute you might be using.
- Oregano perks up anything cooked in a roasting pan or on the barbecue.
- Throw extra oregano into Mediterranean soups and stews.
- On a baking pan, cover a good-sized piece of feta with chopped oregano leaves and garlic. Slice tomatoes and place on top. Anoint with olive oil, salt and pepper. Bake in a medium oven until cheese collapses. Serve with amazing bread.
- As above—but use Greek cheese like kefalotyri, or goat's cheese.
- Freshen up frozen pizza with chopped fresh oregano.
- Add chopped oregano to thinly sliced cucumbers. Drizzle with olive oil whisked with balsamic vinegar, a pinch of sugar, salt and pepper.

LAYERING

Layering is even easier than taking root cuttings (see page 55). Select a gangly (long) stem on your oregano, rosemary, sage or thyme, leaving it attached to the plant. Scoop a little soil over the stem, put a rock on top to keep it in place. Water and wait for a month or so. Chances are that the stem will root, and then you can snip it from the mother plant, gently dig it up roots and all and move it to wherever you wish.

Super-nutritious curly parsley self-seeds in the garden with little fuss, attracting the good guys when it blooms.

Parsley

Invaluable as a garden-fresh green for myriad menus, parsley is a year-round source of vitamin C along with other nutrients, and a superstar to bees and other beneficial insects.

PLANTING AND GROWING PARSLEY

Even though it's a two-year plant, or biennial, parsley usually bolts in the spring of the second year, so we suggest you plant it every year to have a continual supply. That said, some people swear that their parsley is perennial—so be open to it! Sow seeds or tuck in seedlings in the springtime after frost has passed. Position parsley so that it has some shade in summer and sunshine through winter. Space plants 6 inches (15 cm) apart for best growth.

PARSLEY FAST FACTS

Petroselinum crispum is available in flat- and curly-leafed varieties, and we love both. For fun, grow the variety usually called Italian Gigante. Parsley

- is a biennial
- grows from seed and self-seeds if you let it (and we suggest you do)
- thrives in sun but can tolerate partial shade and needs rich, deep, moist soil

GOOD FOR YOU

Parsley is a big supplier of vitamin C, iron, chlorophyll and antioxidants, including beta-carotene.

Italian parsley can grow several feet high, providing massive amounts of greens throughout the year; like kale it sweetens after a frosty winter.

GOOD FOR YOUR GARDEN

Bees and other beneficial insects are strongly attracted to this member of the Apiaceae family and will flock to the creamy-white flowers in flat umbels of second-year parsley.

GOOD TO EAT

While you can dry parsley, we don't. Biennial parsley grows like a perennial in our gardens because just when it's on the out, it self-seeds and produces a fresh crop to last another two years. Harvest directly from the garden year round, snipping stems (and chopping them for crunchy salad or throwing them into soup stock) in year two to hold plants back from going to seed until the next generation stands tall. As with other members of the Apiaceae family, watch out for the good guys (see page 43) when you're cutting parsley.

HOW TO EAT PARSLEY

- Double or triple parsley amounts given in recipes—it is one of the most vitamin-packed greens (outside of kale, of course). Eat lots of it raw to get maximum benefits. Toss with impunity into any salad.

- In its second year, biennial parsley goes to seed. Just before that, the thick stems are sweet and delicious. Chop like celery to add to salads, soups, omelettes and more.

- Strew any grilled vegetable, chicken, fish or meat with heaps of chopped parsley before serving.

- Toss parsley onto soups and stews as well.

- Purée parsley, kale and garlic to add to mashed potatoes.

- Make tabbouleh—a ton of finely chopped parsley mixed with bulgur, quinoa, freekeh, rice or whatever carb you like. Add chopped onions, tomatoes, mint too.

- Make Pasta with Parsley Pesto (see page 105).

- Purée chickpeas and lots of parsley with olive oil and lemon juice to use as a dip for veggies, kale leaves, crackers or bread.

- Make parsley oil—purée parsley with oil in a blender, and heat gently for an hour or so in a pot—don't boil. Strain through many layers of cheesecloth, a very fine sieve or a coffee filter. Keep in the fridge and use within 10 days.

- Whiz up parsley vinaigrette: tons of parsley, garlic, olive oil and good white wine vinegar. Drizzle on salads, new potatoes or yam fries, or serve in a shallow dish with warm freshly baked bread.

Snip, snip, snip—take cuttings of your rosemary for culinary capers to help the plant stay full and luxuriant.

Child's play—rooting rosemary is easy, especially in the summertime.

Rosemary

In a heartbeat rosemary's earthy aromatic scent whisks us to Mediterranean climes. With a little TLC it's a wonder crop for temperate climes too, offering us antibacterial and antifungal protection when we eat it. All the while in the garden, it discourages the cabbage butterfly from laying eggs on nearby kale crops.

PLANTING AND GROWING ROSEMARY

Rosemary grows well in climate zone 6 and above, but needs excellent drainage to survive the winter. Position it on a south-facing slope if possible, where it will have some winter protection. Mulch with leaves or straw. If you grow it in a pot, remember that in effect you are losing two climate zones. Not that you can't overwinter rosemary in a pot, but we suggest you bring it inside when the mercury dips very low.

Snipping rosemary for culinary use should keep the lower branches bushy. Go easy on taking cuttings in fall and winter though, as this can set the plant back or even kill it. Pinch off just enough for your culinary needs.

ROSEMARY FAST FACTS

Gloss-green gorgeous rosemary (*Rosmarinus officinalis*) is versatile in the garden, working well as a hedge, feature or container plant. Rosemary

- is a perennial
- grows best from cuttings or layering—see sidebars on page 52 and 55
- thrives in sun and must have well-drained soil
- is drought tolerant once established
- like most woody herbs, does not react well to fertilizer or compost
- is deer resistant

GOOD FOR YOU

However you relish rosemary, you and your dining companions will benefit hugely from its antioxidant properties, multiple vitamins and minerals. Also anti-inflammatory, iron-rich and a remedy for colds, this herb deserves a place of honour in your garden and on your plate. Feeling a little out of it?

Prostrate rosemary grows prettily in a pot that can be kept inside during cold snaps.

Snip a little sprig of rosemary and rub the leaves. Sit down, stop what you are doing and inhale…for five minutes. You'll be good to go.

ROOTING CUTTINGS

Don't be intimidated by the idea of propagating by cuttings—you can grow dozens and dozens of new herbs for your garden in this fun and easy way.

Root softwood cuttings from the new growth in the spring—they should "take" easily. Use gritty, fast-draining soil mix such as two parts sterilized potting soil to one part each coarse sand and perlite, *barely moistened*. Plant six or eight 3-inch (7.5-cm) cuttings per clean 4-inch (10-cm) plastic pot—cuttings seem to do better if they are not planted alone in pots. Carefully remove all but a few top leaves and bury the cuttings halfway, tamping the soil lightly. Place in a sheltered location; bottom heat speeds rooting. Covering the pots with a closed plastic bag is a good measure (although we seldom bother with this last step and our cuttings grow just fine). Just *don't* overwater them.

Root hardwood cuttings in July and August.

HOW TO EAT ROSEMARY

- Feeling worn out? Cut a couple of sprigs of rosemary. Add one to a pot of tea and, while it's brewing, squeeze the leaves of the other and inhale the scent deeply. Or add rosemary to your bath while you sip the tea. You should feel calmer, fresher and more alert.

- If you have a sore throat, add a sprig of fresh rosemary to the teapot, along with sage and/or oregano.

- Cube potatoes and put them in a bowl with some olive oil, chopped rosemary, salt and pepper, and toss. Bake in a hot oven, and stir often. Or wrap in foil and barbecue. Variation: half potatoes, half sweet potatoes.

- Add chopped rosemary to yam fries.

- Stuff a chicken with sprigs of rosemary, a head of garlic and half a lemon. Roast as usual. Remove the "stuffings" and enjoy a flavour-filled meal.

- Steep rosemary in olive oil; use the infusion as part of the marinade for lamb and chicken.

- Chop rosemary leaves together with lemon zest, salt and pepper until finely minced, or grind in a spice grinder. Use as a not-quite-dry rub for chicken or lamb.

- Make your favourite shortbread recipe and add finely minced rosemary.

- Add rosemary to white bean soup with lemon.

- Put a couple of sprigs of rosemary in grape, raspberry or blackberry jelly or jam—or make rosemary jelly on its own.

- Infuse honey with rosemary; drizzle on chicken before baking or onto ricotta on toasted English muffins. Use to sweeten tea or add to vinaigrettes.

GOOD FOR YOUR GARDEN

Ravishing in a pot or garden plot, rosemary is thought to repel the cabbage butterfly from brassicas, including kale. And when rosemary flowers, bees will be blissed out and flock to it in droves.

GOOD TO EAT

For stews and roasted meals, rub the lovely fresh rosemary leaves off the stem, then chop and sprinkle on your food; it will be redolent with Mediterranean flavour. Or dry rosemary and store it. Use its woody stems as skewers to add interest and flavour to barbecued foods.

Pineapple sage grows a mile a minute in the heat of summer, culminating in dramatic maraschino-red blossoms in fall.

Salvia officinalis thrives in terra cotta; like all the sage family, though, when potted it prefers to spend winter inside a greenhouse or other protected place.

Sage

Salvia ("salvation" in Latin) has been cultivated for millennia. An important medicinal herb in the garden, sage also attracts beneficial insects while repelling the cabbage butterfly, so is the perfect friend to kale.

PLANTING AND GROWING SAGE

Sage can easily be grown from seed: sow mid-spring indoors, in loose, sandy starter mix. It thrives in poor soil and must have good drainage. Snip it for kitchen use all spring and summer—it will benefit and bush out after being pruned. Don't cut it back hard in the fall, as this can kill the plant. In cold zones, protecting sage plants in winter is wise. Berggarten sage is particularly hardy and has large oval leaves.

SAGE FAST FACTS

With soft blue-grey leaves, handsome sage (*Salvia officinalis*) adds architectural interest to your garden and is a substantial foundation plant. Sage

· is a perennial
· grows from seed, cuttings or layering (see pages 52 and 55)

· thrives in sun, and can tolerate poor soil but it must be well drained
· is drought tolerant once established
· is deer resistant

GOOD FOR YOU

Like kale, sage provides a lot of vitamin K. It also contains flavonoids, has anti-inflammatory antioxidant properties and is billed as a memory enhancer. Not to mention that it's highly recommended as a tea to soothe a sore throat.

GOOD FOR YOUR GARDEN

An attractor of bees and other beneficial insects, sage also pumps out a "stay back, cabbage-butterfly" scent. Yay!

GOOD TO EAT

There are lots of sage varieties available, so don't be shy about trying them—but also don't forget the reliable zone-5-hardy plain-Jane *Salvia officinalis.* Fresh sage tastes more lemony than dried. Dried store-bought sage, especially ground sage (eeek), bears little resemblance to fresh sage. Delicately flavoured, sage is best added at the end of the cooking process.

A sage cluster: variegated and Berggarten sage happily share a pot with thyme.

HOW TO EAT SAGE

- Try sage leaves brewed into tea (add a little honey too) for upset tummies, coughs and sore throats. Brain fog? While you make sage tea, breathe in the scent of the leaves; you should feel rejuvenated.

- Use the charming blue sage flowers in steamy drinks—hot lemon and water, mulled wine or apple cider.

- Make Browned Butter & Sage—see page 111.

- Caramelize loads of onions. Add chopped sage leaves for the last five minutes of caramelizing, then fresh-ground pepper and a squeeze of lemon. Pair with pasta, boiled potatoes or mashed rutabaga, or use as a pizza topping. If you like, top with Romano or Asiago. Or strew in layers with thinly sliced potatoes in a gratin.

- Make pesto with sage and toasted hazelnuts. Serve with pasta, roasted sweet potatoes or butternut squash, or use as a pizza topping with aged Provolone.

- Make sage jelly to have with cheeses, turkey, chicken or meats.

- Walk on the wild side: dip perfect big sage leaves (like Berggarten) in batter and deep-fry, tempura style; drizzle with a little honey.

- Rather than dried sage, which tastes old and musty, use fresh chopped sage leaves in stuffings for turkey and chicken.

- Add chopped sage to your favourite corn-bread recipe.

- Ditto cheese scones to serve with hearty winter soups.

- Make risotto with chopped pears or apples (pancetta too, if you like), using the fruit as you would any other addition to risotto. Crisp a lot of sage leaves in butter or oil, chop and toss in toward the end. Divine.

- Crisp some sage in a frying pan with a little butter, then top baked squash of any kind with it, and drizzle with honey and butter.

- Add a few sage leaves to apple or grape jelly.

Lemon thyme: rub the little leaves off for kitchen use and savour the citrusy scent.

Divide and conjure—it's easy to make more thyme for gardening friends; just slice mature plants into two, or more.

Thyme

Time after time, we wax on about thyme. And why not? This garden superhero is bountiful, bee-friendly, beneficial to health, beautiful and a boon in the kitchen—plus, you almost can't kill it.

PLANTING AND GROWING THYME

Sow seeds or tuck in seedlings in the springtime after frost has passed. Thyme is a perennial and a gorgeous "spiller" for containers, rock walls and hanging baskets. In our gardens, carpets of thyme line the front of rockeries, hug the trunks of trees in a weed-free expanse of pink blossoms and spill over the sides of raised food beds, as well as being tucked in between pavers on Sharon's patio. We trim it regularly to keep it tidy, gladly using the clippings in the kitchen.

THYME FAST FACTS

Thyme (*Thymus vulgaris*) withstands drought and rain, and holds its own through the winter. Thyme

- is a perennial
- grows from seed or cuttings, or by layering (see pages 52 and 55) and division, and sometimes self-seeds
- works well as a rock-garden plant or ground cover
- thrives in sun, needs well-drained soil
- is drought tolerant once established
- is deer resistant

GOOD FOR YOU

Every time you enjoy thyme with your meal, you are topping yourself up with antioxidants, minerals, vitamins B_6, C and A, and disease-fighting thymol oils.

Just run your fingers up the stem to roll off thyme's flavour-filled little leaves, and enjoy the aromatic experience while you are at it.

GOOD FOR YOUR GARDEN

Resplendent in pastel-pink blossoms, thyme is much visited by bees throughout the summer.

Flowering thyme will have bees abuzz with joy.

GOOD TO EAT

Thyme is fabulous fresh, and the tiny thyme leaves can be pulled off the woody stems and strewn into wraps, sandwiches, oven roasts and soups. If you're thinking of the taste of dried thyme purchased in the supermarket, don't! Fresh thyme is more aromatic but in a subtler, simpler way. Use three times as much fresh thyme as you would dried in any recipe. Harvest fresh thyme from the garden all year long, although you *can* dry it if you wish to avoid having to get it from the garden in winter.

THYME FOR TEA

You've created your own tea garden by planting mint, fennel, rosemary, sage and thyme. The last three herbs in particular can work wonders when you're fighting a cold or flu.

HOW TO EAT THYME

- Use thyme to make a soothing tea when you're fighting a cold or flu.

- Toss clouds of tiny thyme confetti onto anything to be cooked on the barbecue or in a roasting pan: tomatoes, peppers, onions, salmon, veggie burgers...

- Sprinkle thyme leaves over cream cheese on crackers or goat's cheese on toast, or into toasted cheese sandwiches.

- Scatter thyme leaves into scrambled eggs.

- Add thyme leaves to any and all Mediterranean or Greek-style food.

- Toss sliced cauliflower with thyme, olive oil, salt, pepper and chopped lemon pieces; roast at 425F (220C) until browned, turning cauliflower slices a couple of times.

RECIPES

Kale in the Kitchen

Kale leaves tolerate more time in the pot than thinner greens like chard and spinach, which can easily be overcooked. You can also steam kale lightly for a few minutes and drizzle it with a little olive oil or butter, or serve it plain. Toss it into almost any soup or stew, and add it to pasta dishes.

Enjoy kale raw by adding a few leaves, buds or flowers to your favourite salad. Buds are great for dipping and easy for kids to handle.

HARVESTING FROM THE GARDEN

Though cooking with kale isn't rocket science, if you grow your own kale—we hope you will!—be aware that older leaves are suitable for use in soups and stews, kalekopita (like spanakopita, but made with kale), kale chips or anything with longer cooking times. Newer, tender leaves from the top of the plant or side shoots are best for quick cooking and salads.

In winter and early spring after kale has frozen and thawed a few times, the stems become edible, even delicious. Thinner, tender stems can be chopped and used along with the leaves in any recipe. Thicker ones can be peeled like a carrot, chopped up and thrown into soups or stir-fries.

STORE-BOUGHT KALE

If you are buying kale, look for organic and preferably locally grown. Unfortunately, as kale becomes more and more popular, conventionally grown kale has made it onto the "Dirty Dozen" list of foods contaminated by pesticides.

Organic specialty markets and farm markets usually carry decent kale, often the Tuscan (a.k.a.

CHIFFONADE?

Many recipes indicate that kale leaves should be "in chiffonade." The technique comes from the French, and is also commonly used with other leafy vegetables and herbs such as basil. It refers to a way of rolling a few leaves at a time tightly together, the way tobacco leaves are rolled into a cigar. After rolling the leaves, a sharp knife is used to slice the roll into thin sections as you would slice a baguette, straight or on the diagonal. When unrolled, the "chiffonade" method yields thin pieces that cook quickly or are perfect for salads.

Of course, it makes sense to roll the flatter-leafed or slightly curled kales, and not the very curly ones that would be difficult to roll up tightly. If curly kale is to be chopped, just grab it with one hand firmly, squeeze it a little, and cut it as you would chop parsley—roughly for stews and stir-fries, finer for other dishes like salads and slaws.

Curly Redbor kale (facing page) is stunning in the garden and on the plate—cut it roughly for cooked dishes; finely for the salad bowl.

Carol uses an outdoor sink to wash her garden greens—catching the water in a bucket below and using it to water kale growing in containers.

DRYING KALE

4 cups (1 L) packed, chopped fresh kale = ½ cup (125 mL) dried, ground kale

Harvest your kale—any type is fine—and rinse it, allowing the water to drain off for a couple of minutes. Remove any tough stems and ribs, as they become as hard as sticks when dried. Chop or chiffonade the kale and spread on an ungreased cookie sheet.

If you're not in a rush: Place the pan of kale in the oven set at 170 (80C) or whatever the lowest setting is (the convection setting works best if your oven has one), and let it dry for about 20 minutes. Then turn off the oven. Leave the pan of kale in the oven overnight. In the morning, turn the oven on again, as above, and allow the kale to dry for another 20 minutes. Turn off the oven, and leave the kale there to dry for a few more hours in the residual heat. (Alternatively, use a dehydrator, following the manufacturer's directions.)

If you want that dried kale now: Preheat the oven to 325F (160C), and place the rack in the middle of the oven. Bake kale for 10 minutes and then check how dry it is; continue to check every 5 minutes until the bits are crispy enough to shatter.

Place the crispy kale bits in a food processor and pulse them for a minute or so until they are at the desired consistency. The larger the dried kale flakes, the more noticeable they will be in your recipes; the finer they are, the more sneaky you can be if you have any kale-nervous nellies at your house.

Black, Dinosaur or Lacinato) variety, currently the darling of cooks. Increasingly, produce managers at these markets try their best to find local growers.

Choose fresh, sturdy leaves and get them into the fridge as soon as possible. Or eat them right away—nutrients are lost once the leaves are picked, as with all vegetables, so the quicker they find their way to your table and into your mouth, the better!

WASTE NOT

You can count on us to harp on about not discarding the water used for cooking kale, and we apologize in advance should you find this tedious. The water is just too good to pour down the drain. Let it cool and drink it like herbal tea or mix it with tomato or vegetable juice. If you have a large jar or plastic container that fits in your freezer, use it to collect and store small amounts of kale broth for later use in soups or for cooking quinoa, rice or pasta.

And, speaking of broth—nothing equals homemade stock or broth of any kind, be it vegetable, meat, chicken or even just kale. Carol goes on quite the tirade about making stock and not wasting any

kale cooking water or even a solitary kale leaf. Sharon agrees that the soup made from garden scraps is pretty fantastic and basically costs almost zilch. Some stores sell sort-of homemade stocks as well; some are better than others, but they all tend to be on the pricey side.

MEASURING KALE

When you buy kale, it's usually sold in a bunch. However, these bunches can vary in size and amount. We have measured kale every which way and here are our calculations:

1 BUNCH OF KALE (ABOUT A DOZEN LARGE STEMS)
= 300 grams (just over ½ lb) with stems
= 250 grams (½ lb) without stems
= 2 L (8 cups) loosely packed
= 1.4 L (6 cups) tightly packed

Wash leaves before using, and save any hard or fibrous stem parts for the soup pot (or compost bin).

= 1 L (4 cups) tightly packed in chiffonade
= 250 mL (1 cup) cooked and packed
And one thing's for sure: you can always go ahead and use a little extra, because more is a good thing when it comes to kale, and virtually all these recipes could accommodate a titch more of the Queen of Greens.

AS YOU BEGIN COOKING

The recipes assume washing all vegetables before using, and removing any hard or fibrous stem parts. When cutting away kale ribs and stems, try to find a use for them. Toss them into the freezer for when you're making broth. Or feed them to your chickens or someone else's—chickens love kale and eating it contributes greatly to the quality of their eggs.

A few other thoughts: When we mention pepper it's freshly ground, and if a recipe calls for olive oil, we mean extra virgin. Organic would be nice too, but it seems that many olive-oil manufacturers in Europe would shudder at the use of pesticides on their precious olive trees, so the term may be at least partly redundant—let's hope so, anyway.

Unless we say otherwise, we always mean fresh herbs, not dried. And we're hoping that lots of them will come from your garden, or if that's not possible then from the local farmers' market.

And, lastly, along with using locally grown organic herbs, vegetables and fruits, it's nice to lean to free-range eggs and poultry and locally caught wild seafood whenever available and within the food budget. And by growing the supereasy, super-healthy foods that we talk about in this book—and focusing meals around these garden stars—we find we do wind up with a bit more to spend on the foods that are produced in ways we want to support and encourage.

We've done our best to note which recipes are gluten free, or gluten free with substitutions, but please do double check the labels of your ingredients to ensure your meal is safe for you to eat.

Bon appétit!

ABOUT THE SYMBOLS

These symbols help identify recipes suitable to your (or your guests') dietary preferences:

VG Vegetarian   **VE** Vegan   **GF** Gluten free

* = Gluten free, vegetarian or vegan with modification

Kale Quickies & Other Superfast Meal Ideas

KALE QUICKIES

This book has lots of recipes with ingredients precisely laid out. A few got a little fancier than we had planned—life's like that—and we hope you might even like to do a little special cooking now and then.

Still, we have mostly tried to keep things simple: we want you to have fun with kale and our other superfoods and not feel burdened by too many must-do's or rules. After all, a recipe is just something someone made up—it ain't written in stone.

Our good friend Diana (of Pea & Lettuce Potage with Mint fame) is a by-the-book cook—everything is measured and pretty precise. She likes to do that perhaps because she majored in math. We are more casual. We huck stuff into a pan and cook it up. We open the fridge or mosey about the garden to see what needs to be used, and use it.

Whichever type of cook you are, we hope this section will inspire you. It might seem like a contradiction, but we're aiming for "slow food" that's fast…as in simple to prepare and flexible in ingredients so that you can use what's in your garden and fridge and what suits your mode of eating…as in little stress and not much fuss.

It's our wish that even on a busy day you feel empowered to whip up simple slow food, using your wits and a little know-how about what works well together. It's our intention that cooking and eating

Opposite: Kale has more staying power than lettuce and resists getting soggy in salads. When using thicker, more mature kale, massaging it a bit will soften the leaves and allow the dressing to adhere.

be fun, relaxing, joyful, life-affirming and spontaneous. That with a bit of a garden and a few basic odds and sods kicking around in the fridge, good cooking can happen fast, leaving time for the meal to be a slow-down celebration. Silence your cell phone, let a candle shimmer, savour each bite and sip on something nice—tea made from just-snipped fennel or mint, or maybe a splash of Chardonnay—and seize this simple moment to nourish yourself, body *and soul.*

KALE'S BEST FRIENDS

Oils, Butters & Sauces—Olive oil, butter, sesame oil, chili garlic sauce, almond butter, peanut butter, peanut sauce, miso butter (half miso, half butter).

Nuts, Raw & Lightly Toasted—Pine nuts, walnuts, almonds, pecans, filberts (a.k.a. hazelnuts).

Citrus—Lemons, limes, oranges, blood oranges, clementines, mandarins, grapefruits.

Fruits—Apples, avocado, cherries (dried or fresh), pears, tomatoes (sun-dried or fresh), dried cranberries, currants, raisins, dried apricots.

Savoury Flourishes—Squash, sweet potatoes, yams, potatoes, peppers, onions (caramelized or not), garlic, leeks, shallots, bacon/pancetta/prosciutto.

Cheese—Kale is great with all cheese; try goat's, Parmigiano, Asiago, Romano, Cambozola, Gorgonzola, Stilton, Emmental, Gruyère, Jarlsberg.

Greens—Other flavourful greens like arugula, bitter endive/escarole/radicchio types, chickweed, sorrel.

Soft Herbs—Especially basil, chervil, chives, cilantro, garlic greens, mint, parsley.

Woody Herbs—Oregano, rosemary, thyme, or browned butter and sage (see page 111). Try lemon thyme or pineapple sage for extra flavour and fun.

FAST (BUT NOT FURIOUS) KALE SALADS

The Salad—Chiffonade kale or chop it the way you like it. Garnish with a few kale flowers if you like. Check out Kale's Best Friends for ideas on what else to toss in, and anoint with your choice of these simple dressings:

Heather's Avocado Moose—Mash an avocado with 2–3 Tbsp (30–45 mL) buttermilk. Mix in the juice of a lime, a little olive oil, salt and pepper.

Sharon's Standby—Buzz a little goat's cheese, juice of half a big orange or a whole small one, a small clove of garlic, a dash of balsamic vinegar, a glug of olive oil, and salt and pepper.

Chive Jive—Basically the same as Sharon's Standby, but substitute lime juice for the orange and add lots of chopped chives and a little buttermilk or yoghurt to make it creamy.

Kale Capers—Buzz a spoonful of capers with a little olive oil, white wine vinegar (half vinegar to oil), pepper (no salt—capers are salty enough) and the zest of half a lemon.

Miso Tired—This'll wake you up: a little miso, olive oil, rice vinegar, a small piece of chopped fresh ginger, a spoonful of honey, juice of an orange and a dash or more of Sriracha or other hot sauce. Buzz until smooth.

KALE FOR BREAKFAST

Quick Kale Quinoa—Put quinoa on to cook; chop some kale. About 5 minutes before the quinoa is done, throw the kale on top to steam. When it's done, toss on chopped avocado, douse with lemon juice and add a dab of butter or miso butter (half miso, half butter). Phytonutrients in kale are more available to your body when eaten with a little fat.

Kale Butter on Toast—Buzz kale and butter (or miso butter, see above) until smooth and green. Spread on toast, and add thinly sliced radishes and/or slivers of cheese.

Herbed Kale Quinoa Fritters—Add chopped kale (cooked or raw) to leftover quinoa. Stir in a beaten egg, a little flour (regular or gluten free), salt, pepper and chopped herbs. Form into patties and fry. Serve with salsa or ketchup.

Kale Noodle Fry—Use up leftover cooked pasta: In a frying pan, sauté chopped kale briefly in oil or butter; toss in the pasta and eggs beaten with a little cold water. Fry until done on the first side; flip over, add Asiago or other cheese, or not. Top with fresh herbs if you like.

Scrambled Kale Eggs—Sauté kale leaves/buds briefly, then add beaten eggs to the hot frying pan. Top with a little cheese or salsa or both.

Smooth Move—Add kale to any breakfast smoothie: apple, banana, blackberry, pineapple and/or lemon, plus yoghurt, make it extra yummy.

KALE FOR LUNCH

Bread Spreads—Combine minced kale with one or more of these ingredients, then spread on bread, crackers or kale leaves:

- Mayo
- Chives
- Shredded cheese
- Cottage or ricotta cheese
- Goat's cheese
- Grated apple or pear
- Avocado
- Lime juice
- Finely chopped nuts (walnuts, almonds, pistachios, pecans)

Sub Butter or Quick Dip—Toss kale, a small can of chickpeas (drained and rinsed) and a little mayonnaise into the food processor. Use as a green submarine or sandwich spread or butter substitute, or as a tasty dip.

Tasty Tuna—Add fine chiffonade of kale to tuna sandwich filling; if you have any pineapple, mince a little and toss it in too. Great on rye bread. Ditto salmon sandwiches: add kale in chiffonade, lots of chopped chives and a few minced capers.

Opposite: Toasted bread topped with a quick kale spread and leftover roast vegetables makes a colourful lunch.

In the garden, combine kale with colourful companions like calendula; in the kitchen, it goes well with just about everything.

Kale & Chive Egg Salad—Add finely chopped raw kale to egg salad, with snipped chives and parsley, and perhaps minced red or orange bell pepper for colour.

BKT—Toasted bacon, kale and tomato sandwiches with mayo…need we say more? Add sliced egg, avocado too.

Forbidden Rice Roll—Use a Vietnamese rice wrapper to roll up a few spoonfuls of leftover black rice (see page 169) a handful of tender young kale leaves and herbs, plus a chopped hard-boiled egg.

SWIFT KALE SUPPERS

It's a Wrap—Use your favourite wrap, roti or tortilla, warmed or not. Or toast it in a frying pan and melt a little cheese on it. Pile on chopped avocado or chicken, chiffonade of kale, other chopped veggies (raw or sautéed), such as peppers, tomatoes or onions. Now add chopped herbs: chives, garlic greens, cilantro, parsley, a titch of thyme, oregano, basil…whatever you have. Drizzle on a bit of peanut sauce for an Asian theme or spoon on salsa

to go Mexican. Roll 'em or fold 'em and wolf 'em down. It's fun to create a make-your-own wrap smorgasbord for kids—with bowls of stuff and a few sauces to choose from—for lunch, dinner or family movie night.

Kale Leaf Rolls—Wrap any filling in a kale leaf in the style of conical sushi. This is a good use for leaves that have gotten big, generally Red Russian, Portuguese or Rainbow Lacinato kale. Rub the leaves a little so they don't break or snap when you roll them. Possible fillings: any mixture from Kale for Lunch (page 68): tuna, salmon, chicken or egg salad; hummus or thick yoghurt or cottage cheese mixed with chopped radishes and herbs. Roll, sushi or burrito style. Or simply wrap the kale leaf around a spoonful of tabbouleh or a hunk of soft cheese with chives…you get the idea.

Kale Cheese Balls—Add chopped steamed or raw kale to cooked seasoned rice (Arborio works well) and cheese. Form into balls with wet hands. Serve with a simple tomato sauce or make little ones for appetizers.

Pizza to Go—Grab your favourite frozen pizza (we love Rocky Mountain Flatbread's, made with mostly organic ingredients). Top with chopped kale leaves or buds, then cover with more cheese, mushrooms and/or tomatoes. Bake as directed on package.

Almost Instant Noodling Around with Kale Buds (kids love this)—Boil water, throw in quick-cooking noodles from Asian markets (often in individual-serving "blocks" that take about 2 minutes to cook), and throw kale buds in for the last minute of cooking time. In a frying pan, sauté a little onion and some small squares of tofu, maybe a little garlic and fresh ginger—anything is optional! Add the cooked noodles and kale buds, along with chili garlic sauce, sesame oil, a little soy and peanut butter if you like. Garnish with a lot of chives or garlic greens.

CHICKEN ON THE RUN

Here are a dozen easy meals made in minutes with a takeout rotisserie chicken and you know what…

1. **Kale & Chicken Fasta Pasta**—Cook whatever pasta you like, adding chopped kale leaves or buds (as much as you want) during the last 2 or 3 minutes of cooking. When pasta is cooked the way you like it, drain, then combine with a little pesto and chopped chicken. Add grated Asiago or Parmigiano. If you use spaghettini or angel-hair pasta, you can "ciao" down in less than 10 minutes.

2. **Kale Chicken Alfredo**—Cook linguine or fettuccine (or any other pasta) as above, adding chopped kale leaves or buds during the last part of cooking. Drain, saving a teacup full of cooking water. Add chopped chicken, then toss with freshly grated Parmigiano, as much butter as you have the nerve to use, and the cooking water. If you like, add chopped parsley, chives, gratings of nutmeg, or all three.

3. **Udon Soup with Chicken & Kale**—Cook packaged udon or noodle soup (or cook your own noodles and heat your own stock). Add kale leaves or buds to the soup for the last few minutes of cooking. Add chopped chicken (tofu too, if you like). Sprinkle with chopped cilantro.

4. **Tortellini with Kale Soup**—Cook spinach or cheese tortellini for half the indicated cooking time, drain. Heat chicken or veggie broth, add the tortellini and a couple cups chopped kale leaves or buds. Simmer until kale is wilted and pasta is cooked through. Add chicken; let it heat a little in the soup. Toss in chopped fresh herbs. To make it even better, grate cheese on top and add a splash of olive oil and freshly grated pepper.

5. **Chicken Chili with Kale**—Pick up some frozen or canned vegetarian chili; there are many healthy and organic kinds. Add chopped chicken and lightly steamed kale. Heat through; accompany with cornbread.

6. **Curried Chicken Kale Salad**—Toss chopped chicken with kale in chiffonade. Add a handful of halved seedless grapes (red is nice but green is fine), chopped almonds or walnuts, toasted or not. Mix a little curry powder into some mayonnaise, and toss with the salad.

7. **Kale Cobb Salad**—Lay chiffonade of kale on a platter. Add chopped chicken, hard-boiled egg, chopped tomato, bacon if desired, minced chives and Roquefort or other blue cheese. You can add lightly steamed asparagus spears and kale buds, though the result is not traditionally cobb-ish. Dress with your favourite vinaigrette and chow down.

8. **Niçoise-ish Kale et Poulet**—Prepare a bed of chiffonade kale (Tuscan looks nice) on a large plate or platter. Arrange lightly steamed green beans and kale buds, chopped chicken, chopped anchovies, hard-boiled eggs and Niçoise olives atop the kale. Julia Child–ize it: add cooked new potatoes, artichokes and red peppers, and other barely steamed veggies (including kale buds if you have them).

9. **Kale Chicken Gado Gado**—Prepare a bed of chiffonade kale in a wide shallow bowl. Add steamed potato chunks, raw or fried tofu, sliced cucumbers, chopped cilantro, bean sprouts, tomatoes and steamed veggies like kale buds and green beans. Dress with peanut sauce,

Toss olive oil and herb confetti liberally over zucchini or any other veggies prior to throwing on the grill.

and sprinkle with chopped peanuts if you like. Squeeze a little lime or lemon juice over everything.

10. **Kale & Chicken Tacos**—Whip up a quick kaleslaw: combine finely chopped kale, mayonnaise or salad sauce to taste, minced chopped scallions (or red or sweet onions). Warm corn tacos briefly, until soft, in the oven or microwave, or on a cast-iron pan. Top with chopped chicken, some kaleslaw and chopped tomato. Add salsa and chopped cilantro, and maybe sour cream.

11. **Cheesy Baked Spuds with Kale, Chicken & Chives**—Bake potatoes the way you usually do. Remove from oven, cut lengthwise in half, scoop out potato and mash, adding chopped kale, chicken and chives. Pile mixture back into potato skins, and top with a little cheese.

Return to oven for 10 minutes or until the cheese bubbles. Serve with salad or soup.

12. **Herb Stuffed Tomatoes**—Cut the top off 1 large tomato per diner. Scoop out the interior of each tomato and lightly sprinkle with salt. Chop the insides, combine with minced chicken, olive oil, a little balsamic vinegar, minced kale and lots of herbs like chives, parsley, cilantro, chervil and/or tarragon. Put the filling into the tomatoes and serve on top of kale in chiffonade and other greens. If you want to go vegetarian, skip the chicken and use cooked rice, quinoa, bulgur or any other grain. **Variation: Baked Stuffed Peppers**—Cut the tops off bell peppers and remove membranes and seeds. Stuff like the tomatoes, adding a little of your favourite cheese. Bake at 350F (175C) for 20 to 25 minutes until peppers are tender. Serve on rice or quinoa.

MORE SUPERFAST SLOW FOOD

Asparagus Eggstasy—Poach eggs, serve over steamed asparagus and kale buds. Strew with chopped parsley, basil, chervil, chives or any other "soft" herbs. Top with cheese if you're inclined. Garnish with kale blossoms.

Pasta Herb Heaven—Toss lots of finely chopped mixed herbs with a few tablespoons of olive oil in a medium-hot frying pan. Cook angel-hair or other skinny pasta, tossing in a little chopped kale for the last 2 to 3 minutes, saving a little cooking water. Dilute the herb mixture with some of the cooking water (or a splash of white wine if you want to). Add the herb mixture to the pasta and sprinkle with grated Parmigiano and freshly ground pepper.

Thyme for Beans & Prawns on Kale—Drain and rinse a can of white beans, and combine with olive oil, salt, chopped prawns, minced garlic and thyme leaves in a frying pan. Cook gently for 1 to 2 minutes, ensuring shrimp is properly cooked if raw is used (or choose pre-cooked shrimp instead). Garnish with fresh basil, parsley, chives or whatever combination of herbs you like. Serve on a bed of baby kale leaves.

Asian Tomato & Egg with Cilantro—Cook minced garlic in oil until lightly coloured. Add chopped tomatoes and kale and, a minute later, beaten eggs, along with salt and pepper. Scramble with a little soy sauce and serve with lots of chopped cilantro and garlic chives or garlic greens.

Pasta Toss with Tomato, Garlic & Basil—Cook pasta and toss in a little chopped kale for the last 2 or 3 minutes. Meanwhile, combine a couple of cups of chopped tomatoes, a tablespoon of minced garlic and olive oil. Toss with pasta, salt, pepper and grated Parmigiano. Garnish with garlic chives or garlic greens and a whole lot of basil.

Herbed Chicken on Kale—Dredge thinly sliced chicken breasts in lightly salted flour or cornmeal; fry for about 2 minutes a side in hot olive oil until cooked through. Serve on a bed of kale and other greens. Top with lots of chopped herbs—chervil, chives, parsley, basil, a teeny bit of lovage—and a big squeeze of lemon juice.

Turkey Grind—Brown ground turkey or chicken with minced garlic and chopped onion. When the meat is thoroughly cooked, add chopped kale and a splash of water, and sauté until kale wilts. At the last minute, stir in 2 beaten eggs along with grated Parmigiano and salt and pepper. Top with lots of chopped fresh herbs—chives, basil, parsley, oregano, and a little rosemary and lovage too.

Herbed Garlic Zucchini—Sauté shredded zucchini in olive oil, adding garlic and lots of chopped herbs and kale. Season to taste. Serve over pasta, rice, quinoa, farro (also called emmer, an ancient cereal grain), buckwheat or whatever you like.

Kale Pasta with Pine Nuts—Cook pasta, adding chopped kale for the last 2 or 3 minutes of cooking. Meanwhile, in a skillet, cook pine nuts in as much butter as you like on medium-low heat until nuts are lightly browned. Combine with cooked pasta and kale, and add chopped herbs, grated Parmigiano and freshly ground pepper.

Zippy Herb Omelette—Make an omelette, adding lots of chopped herbs and kale, and a touch of cheese—try goat's, cheddar or whatever strikes your fancy. Even better with some sautéed sweet onion (sauté onion first and then add the beaten eggs and toss in the herbs and cheese).

Herbed Seafood Salad Sandwich—Combine crab meat or chopped shrimp with mayonnaise, a touch of grainy mustard, snipped chives, tarragon and basil if you have it. Put filling into a wonderful bun or between good heavy bread, along with a handful of kale in chiffonade.

Garlicky Olive Pasta—Pit and chop a cup (250 mL) or so of different types of olives, or buy them pitted. Heat in a little olive oil with chopped garlic and parsley, serve over pasta and sprinkle with chopped parsley and kale, as well as basil and chives or garlic greens.

Tomatillo Garlic Roast—Toss halved tomatillos with chopped peppers (ideally fresh poblano, but red is fine), coarsely chopped onions and whole peeled garlic cloves. Roast at 425F (220C) for about 15 minutes, stirring occasionally. Serve with tortillas, fish tacos or over rice; sprinkle with chopped kale and oregano, cilantro, basil or parsley—or a combination of them.

Quick Herb Couscous—Prepare couscous as usual. Add chopped mint, parsley and basil if you're going for a Middle Eastern flavour, or oregano, basil and parsley for a Mediterranean one. Add chopped veggies, including kale leaves or buds (raw or lightly steamed). Top with kale flowers.

Kale, Swimmingly—Combine cooked chickpeas with lots of chopped kale, bell pepper and fresh herbs like parsley, cilantro, chives and basil. Toss gently with good quality, oil-packed tuna (and as much or as little of the oil as you like). Drizzle with lemon juice and season with salt and pepper. Serve with crackers or flatbread—perfect for a picnic lunch.

"To eat with a fuller consciousness of all that is at stake might sound like a burden, but in practice few things in life can afford quite as much satisfaction."

—MICHAEL POLLAN

STARTERS & LIGHT MEALS

Kale Chips Several (Million) Ways

¼ cup (60 mL) cashews, hazelnuts or walnuts

1 tsp (5 mL) kosher or coarse sea salt

2 Tbsp (30 mL) olive oil

1 Tbsp (15 mL) crema di balsamico (see sidebar below)

8 cups (2 L) mature kale leaves, ripped into 2-in (5-cm) pieces

Save those tender greens for salads—for the most satisfying and crunchy chips, use mature leaves of flatter, thicker kale varieties like Tuscan or Rainbow Lacinato. This is one of our favourite flavour combinations, but the possibilities are infinite (see sidebar on next page for ideas). Whatever variation you try, make sure the leaves are washed and completely dry before tossing with the dressing.

Grind nuts and salt into a coarse dust using spice grinder, or crush with a rolling pin. Set half the dust aside and whisk the rest with olive oil and reduced balsamic.

Toss leaves in the dressing mixture until evenly coated. Arrange on parchment-covered trays, a plate or dehydrator trays, according to your preferred cooking method below and sprinkle with remaining nut dust.

OVEN METHOD

The main advantage to the oven method is that most kitchens have an oven, but it does require some attention to ensure the leaves dry evenly without scorched bits.

Preheat the oven to 275F (135C). Place rack in the middle of the oven. Arrange kale leaves on a large parchment-covered baking tray (cook in two batches, if necessary—the kale should have enough room to bake in a single layer). Bake for 15 minutes, rearrange to ensure the leaves are toasting evenly, then continue baking, checking for doneness every 5 minutes or so. The leaves should feel crispy, but not scorched. Serve immediately.

If you can't find crema di balsamico, cook down ½ cup (125 mL) regular balsamic vinegar (white or dark) or very good white wine vinegar with 2 tsp (10 mL) of sugar until thick.

Over

Continued from previous page.

DEHYDRATOR METHOD

A dehydrator with a strong heating element and fan is best for this method—otherwise the mood for kale chips will have long passed by the time they're ready to eat.

Preheat dehydrator on high setting. Arrange leaves in a single layer on the dehydrator trays. Dry for 1 to 2 hours or according to the manufacturer's directions, until crispy. Serve immediately.

MICROWAVE METHOD

The microwave technique is fast for small batches, and chips become drier before scorching than with the oven method, so they keep longer. A microwave with a turntable works best.

Arrange leaves in a single layer on a plate. Microwave for 3 minutes. If leaves are crispy, transfer to serving platter; if not, flip leaves and continue to microwave in 15-second bursts until done. Repeat with remaining leaves. Chips can be stored in an airtight container for up to a week.

WEST COAST CEDAR–PLANK METHOD

Just kidding.

MAKES 4 SERVINGS

AMAZING KALE CHIP FLAVOUR COMBINATIONS

There are a million possibilities when it comes to dressing up your chips. Here are a few ideas to get you started…

Tropical = Coconut cream + dried pineapple or banana (shredded with a microplane)

Sesame = Tahini + miso + lemon juice + sesame seeds

Thai Curry = Peanut oil + Thai curry paste + cashew dust

Pizza = Olive oil + Parmigiano + dried basil + diced sun-dried tomato

Kitsilano = Hemp oil + nutritional yeast + grated onion

Cracked Pepper = Olive oil + Bragg Liquid Aminos + black pepper

South Asian = Peanut butter + fish sauce + sambal + sesame oil + Kecap Bentang (thick soy sauce from Indonesia)

Sweet = Coconut cream + shredded coconut + honey

Keen for Green Kale Hummus

19-oz (540-mL) can chickpeas, drained and rinsed

2 garlic cloves or about 2 garlic scapes, chopped

Juice of 1 lemon (or more)

3 Tbsp (45 mL) tahini

½ tsp (2.5 mL) ground cumin

½ tsp (2.5 mL) salt

Water

1 cup (250 mL) chopped kale, packed

A drizzle of olive oil

½ cup (125 mL) chopped parsley

We shriek when we see others buying hummus for six bucks per piddly container. It costs less than two dollars to make double that amount, and, if you have a food processor, takes less time than it does to read this introduction—unless you make hummus the old-fashioned way. A Lebanese gentleman told Sharon that his mother pops the chickpeas out of their skins to make hummus, a surprisingly easy and strangely satisfying task, but that does take time. Sharon did it—once. The hummus is smoother, she notes. If you are using dried chickpeas, cook about 1¼ cups (300 mL). For not-so-green hummus, fold in the minced kale at the end. If you are as keen about the green as we are, just throw the kale into the food processor with everything else.

Throw everything up to and including the salt into the food processor. Pulse a few times, add a little water, then turn the processor full on. Continue to drizzle in more water until the desired consistency is reached.

Add the kale (if you want very green hummus) now, and pulse a few more times.

Add a little olive oil and pulse again.

If you didn't put the kale in, transfer hummus to a bowl, finely mince the kale in the processor and fold it into the hummus.

Refrigerate for at least 2 hours to allow the flavour to develop.

Scoop the hummus into a nice bowl, drizzle with olive oil, toss on the parsley and serve.

MAKES ABOUT 3 CUPS (700 ML)

Kale, White Bean & Caramelized Onion Dip

2 Tbsp (30 mL) olive oil

2 cups (475 mL) thinly sliced onions

2 pinches salt

2 tsp (10 mL) brown or Demerara sugar

2 cups (475 mL) finely chopped kale

2 garlic cloves, crushed

¼ cup (60 mL) pine nuts

19-oz (540-mL) can white beans, drained and rinsed

Juice from 1 large lime or 2 small

½ cup (125 mL) minced parsley

A small handful of mint leaves, finely chopped

A few grindings of pepper

There are two variations…one for green and one for not as green. If you can find cannellini beans, use them—they seem more rich and flavourful than navy or other white beans. This dip is delectable with raw veggies, especially radishes, young radicchio leaves, cauliflower and bulb fennel.

Heat oil in a large skillet on medium heat. Add onions, salt and sugar. Sauté, stirring fairly often, for about 15 minutes until onions begin to caramelize.

Add the kale, garlic and pine nuts and continue to stir-fry for another 5 minutes or so.

If you want green dip, put the kale mixture, along with the remaining ingredients, into the food processor and process until smooth. If you prefer a more homogenous look, first process the beans until puréed and then add everything else, combining well.

Refrigerate in the processor bowl for at least 1 hour to allow flavours to blend. Taste for salt now, adding a little if necessary; because you are using canned beans, which have salt added, it's best to go easy on it.

MAKES ABOUT 3 CUPS (700 ML)

COOKING DRIED BEANS

Instead of using canned beans, you can cook dried beans to use in this recipe. You'll need a scant ¾ cup (180 mL) dried beans to make 2 cups (475 mL) ready-to-eat beans.

There is no need to soak dry beans overnight—just rinse them well a couple of times, then transfer to a medium-sized pot. Cover the beans completely with water—lots of water! Bring to a boil, lower heat to medium, cover the pot halfway, and cook for 45 to 90 minutes. Add water as needed and ½ tsp (2.5 mL) salt after the beans have been cooking for 35 to 40 minutes. If the beans are relatively fresh, they'll take less time to cook; older ones may take up to 2 hours.

When soft, drain the beans before using them, or keep them in their liquid in the fridge for up to 3 days.

Cannellini Purée with Caramelized Fennel & Garlic

1 smallish fennel bulb, (about ½ lb/225 g), trimmed

8–10 garlic cloves (with skin), smacked with the side of a knife (see sidebar on page 158)

About 1 Tbsp (15 mL) olive oil for baking

1 Tbsp (15 mL) Fennel Huckleberry Shrub (see page 97), sambuca, Pernod or ouzo (optional)

1–2 pinches of salt

A few grindings of pepper

19-oz (540-mL) can cannellini beans, drained and rinsed (see sidebar on page 80)

2 Tbsp (30 mL) lemon juice

A small handful of parsley

½ tsp (2.5 mL) thyme leaves

A few herb fennel "umbrellas" (with pollen) for garnish

Kale blossoms for garnish

Combined with the roasty sweet smoothness of the fennel and garlic (ameliorated by the liqueur if used), the little crunch from the raw fennel is *very* good! And it's simply smashing with still-warm-from-the-oven Rosemary No-Knead Bread (page 87), as a veggie dip, or scooped when still slightly warm onto a plate, alongside something just roasted…or to just eat with a spoon. Use large white beans if you can't find cannellini beans, but do try to locate them, as they seem to have more richness and depth of flavour. You'll never guess when tasting it, but this recipe contains almost no oil—imagine that!

Preheat oven to 450F (230C).

Halve, then quarter the fennel bulb. Remove the hard core (usually small). Cut each quarter into 3 or 4 sections. Reserve about a quarter of the fennel for later.

Put the fennel and garlic in a heavy ovenproof baking dish. Drizzle with olive oil and liqueur (if using), and sprinkle with salt and pepper. Bake for about 20 to 25 minutes (depending on how hot your oven is), stirring and shaking the pan occasionally, until veggies are lightly caramelized.

Remove from oven; transfer fennel and garlic to a plate. When garlic is cool enough to handle, remove the skin.

Place the fennel, garlic, beans and lemon juice in a food processor and process until smooth. Add the remaining chopped raw fennel and the parsley and thyme. Pulse a few times only, as you want to have little pieces of crunchy fennel in the dip.

Garnish with fennel umbrellas and serve.

This preparation keeps for a few days in the fridge, but it's unlikely you'll have any left to store.

MAKES 2 CUPS (475 ML)

Carol's Favourite Guacamole

3 ripe but firm avocados

Juice of ½ lemon

¼ tsp (1 mL) sea salt

1 garlic clove, minced

Pinch each of ground cumin and coriander

1 tsp (5 mL) Sriracha or other hot sauce—or more if you like

1–2 tomatoes, chopped (some seeds and juice removed)

⅓ cup (80 mL) chopped cilantro

Carol adores cilantro for both its flavour and abundance in the garden. The plants are continually self-seeding and pop up here and there. Snip the fresh leaves for salad or salsa…and then, before you know it, the plants are going to seed, and these seeds are what we call coriander.

Mash avocados with a fork and turn into a bowl. Add the lemon juice, salt, garlic, pinches of spice and hot sauce. Blend well.

Fold in the tomatoes gently, as well as half the cilantro.

Garnish with remaining cilantro. If you aren't eating the guacamole right away, put the avocado pit into the guacamole to keep it from turning brown. Serve with tortilla chips or what have you.

MAKES ABOUT 1½ CUPS (350 ML)

Kaleamole

3 ripe but firm avocados

1 cup (250 mL) finely chopped kale

¼ cup (60 mL) finely minced cilantro leaves, stems and roots

2 garlic cloves, minced

½ tsp (2.5 mL) hot sauce (or more to taste)

Juice of 1 lime

¼ cup (60 mL) minced red onion

Salt and pepper to taste

1 small tomato, diced

Cilantro leaves for garnish

If you grow cilantro and can spare a plant or two, or your plants have bolted, chop up the cilantro root to add to this guacamole. It adds a certain something…Don't worry about exact measurements, just throw in what you have.

Mash the avocados in a medium-sized bowl. Add everything but the tomato and cilantro leaves, and mix well.

Fold in the tomato gently at the end, and garnish with cilantro leaves.

MAKES ABOUT 2 CUPS (475 ML)

KALE NACHOS

Try tossing a few handfuls of kale in chiffonade with the tortilla chips when making nachos—then pile on the grated cheese and other toppings per usual. The edges of the kale crisp up nicely and add a nutritional boost.

Tunisian Zucchini Kale-Leaf Spread

3–4 small to medium zucchini (about 1 lb/454 g)

1 garlic clove, minced

2 Tbsp (30 mL) olive oil

2 tsp (10 mL) Green Harissa (see page 108) or 1 tsp (5 mL) purchased harissa paste (or less to taste)

1 tsp (5 mL) ground coriander (see sidebar on grinding, page 101)

½ tsp (2.5 mL) ground caraway seed

Juice of 1 lemon

A few grindings of pepper

½ cup (125 mL) chopped cilantro leaves, tender stems and roots

About ½ cup (125 mL) crumbled feta (optional)

*vegan if optional feta is omitted

A meze from Tunisia, this spread is another way to use up zucchini that has run rampant. Try making your own Green Harissa or purchase harissa paste in a Middle Eastern food shop or deli. Start with a little; allow the zucchini to mellow for about 10 minutes and add more heat if you like. To serve, spread on crisp Portuguese kale leaves or young Tuscan kale leaves, or smear onto sangak (Persian flatbread), heated in the oven for just a few minutes and drizzled with butter. Or pita, if you can't find the flatbread.

In a large saucepan with lid, cover the zucchini with water. Bring to a boil, then turn heat to medium and keep at a low boil for about 20 minutes until zucchini is tender and cooked through. Transfer to a colander and allow to drain. Mash the zucchini in the colander so that more of the liquid drains, then transfer to a medium mixing bowl.

In a small bowl, whisk together all remaining ingredients except the cilantro and feta. Pour mixture over zucchini and mix well. Fold in half the cilantro, then transfer to a wide low serving dish such as a pasta bowl. Garnish with remaining cilantro, and distribute crumbled feta over the top.

Serve the dish barely cooled; it keeps for a day or two in the fridge but tastes the best the day it's made.

MAKES 4 TO 6 SIDE DISH SERVINGS

Veronica's "Green But Good" Kale Pâté

4 cups (1 L) kale in chiffonade

1 cup (250 mL) pecans

¼ cup (60 mL) pitted Kalamata olives

14-oz (398-mL) can coconut milk

Himalayan pink salt to taste

Sharon's dear friend Veronica Smith recently became a raw-food enthusiast and had this story to share:

I come from a large family. They gather every Friday for Happy Hour. One person is responsible for cooking the meal and up to 20 arrive promptly at five o'clock with a beverage in hand, in eager anticipation of food and gossip. As I live in another city and only get to attend these gatherings when visiting, I take the time to cook something special. This summer, it was a raw-food feast. I made all kinds of cool things...well, cool to me, but in fact it didn't go over that great...except for one dish—the kale pâté. It was, as my nephew said, "green but good." The best thing about it: it was simple to make and...so good for you, especially if you dip carrot sticks into it. My family opted for tortilla chips, which somewhat defeated the raw-food objective, but at least they ate the pâté.

Put the kale, pecans and olives in a blender or food processor and purée. Add the coconut milk and salt, and process until the mixture is smooth and pudding-like. Transfer mixture to a covered container and refrigerate for about 1 hour. The consistency will become more like that of pâté, because the coconut milk acts as an emulsifier when the mixture is cooled.

MAKES ABOUT 3 CUPS (700 ML)

Majid's Goat's Cheese with Herbs

½ lb (225 g) goat's cheese

1 large tomato, seeded and fairly finely chopped

2 Tbsp (30 mL) finely snipped chives

1 Tbsp (15 mL) minced oregano leaves

3 Tbsp (45 mL) olive oil

¼ tsp (1 mL) salt

A few grindings of pepper

Majid is a special man who loves to cook and does it very well—including many lovely dishes that reflect his Lebanese roots. This was one of the mezes we had sitting in his floriferous backyard sipping wine. So simple and so good! Present on a bed of kale in chiffonade and sprinkle with kale blossoms.

Remove goat's cheese from fridge at least 1 hour before. With a sturdy wooden spoon, cream together all the ingredients in a bowl. Drizzle a little more olive oil over the top before serving with warm pita bread or sangak.

MAKES A VERY GENEROUS CUP (250 ML)

FRESH FINES HERBES!

Late April through mid-May is probably when you'll have all the requisite elements of fines herbes in your garden—last year's parsley won't have gone to seed, and the other herbs are abundant.

Combine equal amounts of chervil, parsley, tarragon and chives. Mince finely…and that's it. Use fresh fines herbes on French-style potato salads, with beans, eggs, fish, chicken or what have you.

If you have a dehydrator, you can dry the herbs well, powder them up with your hands and store in a jar with a tight-fitting lid in a cool dark place. A great gift from your garden.

Rosemary No-Knead Bread

VE

3 cups (700 mL) unbleached (preferably organic) white flour

1½ tsp (7.5 mL) salt

¼ tsp (1 mL) fast-acting (not regular) yeast

2 Tbsp (30 mL) finely chopped rosemary leaves

3 Tbsp (45 mL) olive oil

About 1½ cups (350 mL) water*

*The amount of water needed to make this dough will depend on factors such as the freshness of the flour and the altitude of your location.

A variation of the dead-easy recipe from Jim Lahey of Sullivan St Bakery in New York. It's astonishing that his bread is so good but requires so little work. Your kitchen will smell divine…be prepared for friends asking for the recipe. We've made changes to it—we do *not* bake this bread at the very high temperature Lahey suggested, nor for as long, as doing so can result in a very brown (and tough) crust. The olive oil makes a difference, and the bread slices like a dream. As for variations, the sky is the limit: add up to half whole-wheat flour if you wish and the bread will be much denser, although just ½ cup (125 mL) whole-wheat flour will give the bread a rustic feel. Or skip the rosemary and add thyme, or add both, or oregano or tons of chives.

This bread is usually baked in an enameled cast-iron covered pot, but glass or ceramic ovenware works too. In addition to the superexpensive French enameled cast-iron pots, other just-as-good knock-offs are available. To prevent the bottom crust from getting very dark, place several layers of parchment paper under the dough when you throw it in the pot—yes, you practically throw it in!

In a medium-sized bowl, mix together the flour, salt and yeast—use your hands, a whisk or a pastry blender to combine. Add the rosemary and drizzle the olive oil around the dry ingredients. Add most of the water and stir. The easiest way to stir the dough at this point is with a knife—you can cut into the dough, and a knife is much easier to clean than a wooden spoon or other stirring implement. If the dough is still very dry and a lot of flour remains at the bottom of the bowl, add a little more water, just enough to make a very raggedy dough (with some flour visible). That's it. If you really must, you can fold and knead the dough a little in the bowl.

Over

Continued from previous page.

Cover the dough with plastic wrap or a plate that fits and will keep most of the air out, or use both the wrap and the plate. Leave the dough somewhere it won't be disturbed for 18 to 24 hours.

Transfer the dough to a floured board or cloth. Gently fold the edges in and knead very lightly. Shape it into a round, making sure there's enough flour underneath and on top of the dough to prevent it sticking. Cover it with a towel and let it sit for 30 to 60 minutes.

About 15 minutes before you wish to bake the bread, move the oven rack up to as high as it can go and still allow the covered pot to fit into the oven. Slip the empty pot in, covered, and turn the oven up to 475F (245C). When the oven has reached the required temperature, set the timer for 15 minutes.

When 15 minutes is up, carefully—wearing very good oven mitts—remove the very hot pot from the oven and place it on the stovetop, remove the lid and place the dough in the centre of the pot. Cut an X with scissors or a knife in the middle of the dough. Cover the pot, carefully place it back in the oven and set the timer for 35 minutes.

Bake for about 35 minutes. If you prefer the top to be darker in colour, remove the cover and bake another 5 minutes. Remove bread to a rack and allow to cool for at least 30 minutes before slicing.

MAKES 1 LOAF

Kale Cornbread with Bacon & Cheese

1 cup (250 mL) cornmeal

1 cup (250 mL) flour

1 Tbsp (15 mL) sugar

1 tsp (5 mL) baking soda

½ tsp (2.5 mL) baking powder

½ tsp (2.5 mL) salt

¼ tsp (1 mL) cayenne

½ cup (125 mL) chopped raw bacon (about 3 rashers)

2 cups (475 mL) packed kale leaves

1 large egg

1 cup (250 mL) buttermilk

3 Tbsp (45 mL) oil or bacon grease

1 heaping cup (250 mL) grated aged cheddar and/or Asiago and/or other sharp cheese

1 small red bell pepper, chopped

1 cup (250 mL) minced chives

Coarse salt (optional)

A small handful of rosemary leaves

This was a big hit with tasters—and, yes, you can leave out the bacon if you like. Or, if you really want to go Paleo, you can add both the bacon and some of the bacon grease instead of oil. But don't skip the cheese too…otherwise it's basically just cornbread with kale, right? The cheese needs to have some bang so we suggest using half Asiago and half cheddar, or at least something relatively strong-tasting so it doesn't get lost in the corn.

Preheat oven to 375F (190C).

Combine cornmeal, flour, sugar, baking soda, baking powder, salt and cayenne in a bowl.

Fry bacon, drain and set aside.

Steam kale for a minute or two, drain, cut finely and set aside to let cool.

Beat egg, oil and buttermilk together.

Make a well in the dry ingredients, add the buttermilk mixture and stir just to combine. Add reserved kale and bacon, cheddar, bell pepper and chives, and stir lightly—do *not* overmix.

Bake about 35 minutes. If desired, halfway through baking, sprinkle with coarse salt and rosemary leaves.

MAKES 4 TO 6 SERVINGS

Kale Quinoa Cakes with Sweet Potato & Black Beans

¾ cup (180 mL) raw quinoa (white or red), well rinsed

1½ cups (350 mL) water with a pinch or two of salt

3 cups (700 mL) loosely packed kale

1 egg, lightly beaten

1 cup (250 mL) cooked black beans

1 cup (250 mL) mashed cooked sweet potato

⅓ cup (80 mL) minced red onion

½ tsp (2.5 mL) ground coriander

½ tsp (2.5 mL) ground cumin

½ tsp (2.5 mL) salt

A few grindings of pepper

A handful each of chopped cilantro and parsley

Zest of 1 lime or lemon

*vegan if egg-less variation is made

These kale quinoa cakes are easy to make and cost about three dollars each in high-end stores and delis. You can make an entire batch for about that much if you grow your own kale. Serve with a lemon or lime wedge plus Kale Cilantro Chimichurri (see page 109), salsa or chutney, and also a little yoghurt or sour cream if you like. If you're using leftover cooked quinoa, you'll need about 3 cups (700 mL). Quinoa cakes will keep well in the fridge for up to three days. Make them smaller for appetizers, adjusting cooking time to suit.

Cook quinoa in salted water. Bring almost to a boil, then cover the pot and simmer about 20 minutes until quinoa is tender and water is absorbed. Transfer to a large bowl and allow to cool. Preheat oven to 350F (175C).

Steam kale quickly in just a tiny bit of water for 2 minutes. Squeeze with your hands to remove as much liquid as possible, then chop fine. Add kale to the quinoa along with everything else. Mix using a wooden spoon or your hands. Refrigerate mixture for about 30 minutes.

Shape mixture into about fifteen 3-in (7.5-cm) patties, wetting your hands periodically to prevent sticking. Or, for perfectly round patties, press the mixture into a ring mold. Arrange on a greased pan—if you have parchment paper, first line the pan with it and lightly spritz it with oil.

Bake for about 15 minutes—cakes should hold together and be slightly browned on the bottom. Flip and bake about 5 to 10 minutes more. Remove from oven and serve hot or at room temperature.

MAKES ABOUT FIFTEEN 3-INCH/7.5-CM CAKES

FRUITY IDEA

Add ½ cup (125 mL) currants and 1 Tbsp (15 mL) orange zest to the quinoa mixture.

VEGAN WRAP VARIATION

Omit the egg. Instead of shaping into patties and baking, spoon mixture into large Portuguese kale leaves, top with salsa, and you have quick kale wraps. Lettuce leaves work, too!

Crispy Kale Herb Canapés with Old Nippy

1 cup (250 mL) butter, softened

8 oz (225 g) Old Nippy or Imperial cheese, at room temperature

½ tsp (2.5 mL) ground pepper

½ tsp (2.5 mL) Worcestershire sauce

¼ tsp (1 mL) sea salt

1 tsp (5 mL) dried dill weed

1 tsp (5 mL) each finely minced thyme and rosemary leaves

1½ cups (350 mL) unbleached flour

4 cups (1 L) Rice Krispies cereal

½ cup (125 mL) dried kale (see sidebar on page 64)

*vegetarian if anchovy-free Worcestershire sauce is used; gluten free if gluten-free cereal, gluten-free Worcestershire sauce and gluten-free flour are used

You will have to buy...wait for it...Rice Krispies to make these addictive "cookies" for snacks or cocktail parties (do people still have those?) Snap, crackle, you-know-what. Yes, yes, there's lots of butter in these. But they are sooooooo good, and the recipe makes many, many cookies, and you can just eat one...can't you?

Preheat oven to 350F (175C) and place oven rack in middle position.

In a large mixing bowl, cream butter and cheese thoroughly. Mix in seasonings, herbs and flour. Add Rice Krispies and dried kale mixing well with your hands until the dough hangs together.

Roll into 1-in (2.5-cm) balls and place on a parchment-paper-lined baking sheet. Flatten cookies with a wet fork, and bake for about 15 to 20 minutes until very lightly browned.

Cool on a rack and serve—they are best eaten right away.

MAKES ABOUT 5 DOZEN CANAPÉS

Pizza with Kale Buds, Lemon & Olives

12-in (30-cm) unbaked pizza crust

5 tsp (25 mL) olive oil, divided

1 cup (250 mL) packed kale buds

1 Tbsp (15 mL) freshly squeezed lemon juice (grate zest from lemon before cutting it)

½ cup (125 mL) crumbled goat's cheese

1 Tbsp (15 mL) grated lemon zest

2 tsp (10 mL) minced rosemary

¼ cup (60 mL) chopped pitted olives

Salt to taste

A few grindings of pepper

Kale flowers for garnish

*gluten free if gluten-free crust is used

A glass of Pinot Noir or amber ale makes beautiful music with this quick, aromatic pizza. This recipe calls for an unbaked pizza crust, but you could make your own (it's easy, see page 94). Instead of goat's cheese, feta works well, and manouri or kefalotyri are wonderful if you are in a Greek mood! Sharon is a big fan of the canned, anchovy-stuffed olives from Spain, widely available in delis and specialty grocery stores. Otherwise, use whatever pitted olives you fancy.

Place oven rack near the top of the oven and preheat to 450F (230C).

Arrange pizza crust on a preheated pizza stone or parchment-paper-lined cookie sheet. Brush crust with a little of the olive oil.

Steam kale buds for 1 minute—they should still be crisp. Drain, coarsely chop and scatter onto pizza crust. Drizzle lemon juice over pizza, then sprinkle with goat's cheese.

Combine lemon zest and rosemary in a small bowl and scatter mixture over pizza, along with olives.

Sprinkle pizza with salt and pepper, and drizzle remaining olive oil lightly over all.

Bake about 10 minutes or until pizza is lightly browned.

Once cooked, top with kale flowers if you have some available in your garden.

MAKES 1 TO 2 SERVINGS

HINTS

Use kitchen scissors to cut pizza—they work very well and the pizza does not slide as it is cut.

Sharon likes to make her pizzas on the small side—that way, the toppings toward the middle aren't still soggy when the edge of the crust is getting overly browned. Experiment!

(Pretty Much) No-Knead Pizza Dough

2 cups (475 mL) bread flour or
unbleached white flour

½ tsp (2.5 mL) fast-acting yeast

½ tsp (2.5 mL) sea salt

½ tsp (2.5 mL) sugar

Up to 1¼ cups (300 mL)
warmish water

1 Tbsp (15 mL) olive oil

A FEW NOTES ON THIS DOUGH

In hot weather (or a hot kitchen), start this dough as late as one o'clock in the afternoon and the dough will rise in time for dinner. Otherwise, start it in the morning.

If you happen to have some buttermilk in the fridge, replace up to a third of the water with it. If you have recently made your own Greek yoghurt or paneer (page 191), you can replace up to half the water with the leftover whey, which makes the pizza crust more tender.

Do not be afraid to make your own pizza dough—reading this recipe might take longer than throwing a few things together, then just letting the mixture sit while you do absolutely nothing to it for about six to eight hours. Homemade pizza is so satisfying, costs almost nothing and is dead easy. As well, the homemade version is free of "dough conditioners" and other sketchy additives, along with the overdose of sodium that seems to go hand in hand with frozen pizza. If you don't use all the dough, keep it tightly covered in the fridge and use it in the next few days.

In a medium bowl, combine the flour, yeast, salt and sugar, and mix well. Add about half the water, then the olive oil, then—gradually—the remaining water. Depending on how fresh the flour is, you will probably need close to the amount of water specified, but add it slowly, mixing with a knife. The dough should not be smooth but rather raggy. Cover the bowl with plastic wrap or a clean tea towel and an upside-down plate to keep air out.

When the dough has doubled in size, gently fold it (don't punch it!) and let it sit with a towel over it, still in the bowl. Let it rest for about 20 minutes.

Sharon uses a parchment-lined heavy cookie sheet for her pizza; other cooks favour a pizza stone or a pan especially made for pizza.

On a floured board, place the dough (divided, if you wish, or use it all for one big pizza) and shape and roll it into a crust of the thickness you like. Brush with a little olive oil, cover with desired toppings and bake—usually at around 450F (230C) or even hotter, with the oven rack in the upper third of the oven—for about 10 to 15 minutes. Do not overbake.

MAKES 2 OR 3 SMALLER OR 1 LARGE PIZZA

Tuscan-style Arugula Pizza with Kale Petals

 *

¼ cup (60 mL) chopped raisins

¼ cup (60 mL) good white wine

Pizza crust (for homemade, see No-Knead Pizza Dough, page 94)

2 Tbsp (30 mL) olive oil, divided

2 cups (475 mL) lightly packed arugula leaves, washed and left a little damp

¼ cup (60 mL) pine nuts

½ cup (125 mL) freshly grated Romano cheese

Salt

A few grindings of pepper

A shower of kale or arugula flowers for garnish

*gluten free if gluten-free crust is used

Sharon says: Jesse, my eldest, is a pizza aficionado and takes pains to replicate the conditions in wood-fired pizza ovens used in Italy that reach ridiculously high temperatures, even 1000F. Jesse uses a burning-hot cast-iron frying pan and the broiler. During the summer of 2013—on the hottest day of the year—we kept the good old stove at full tilt while Jesse kept bringing on the pizzas, eight of them, which we devoured, along with quite a lot of wine. Cooking this pizza as described below is much easier (and cooler for the cook!), but it's best to make the pizzas on the small side (about 8 in/20 cm in diameter; they don't need to be round though). Otherwise the edges are overcooked while the centre is soggy. In any case, homemade pizza is easy, so cheap and a treat.

An hour before you want to make the pizza, soak the chopped raisins in the wine in a small bowl and cover with a plate.

Place the oven rack near the top of the oven and preheat to 450F (230C).

Roll or stretch out pizza crust, and place on a parchment-paper-lined pizza pan or cookie sheet.

Brush lightly with a little of the olive oil. Distribute arugula leaves relatively evenly, and top with the soaked raisins and pine nuts. Sprinkle with cheese, then salt and pepper. Drizzle remaining olive oil over pizza.

Bake for about 8 to 10 minutes until edges are lightly browned.

Decorate with some kale flowers (if using).

MAKES 1 TO 2 SERVINGS

SHRUBS, RUBS, PESTOS & SAUCY STUFF

Michelle's Kale Ginger Shrub

2 cups (475 mL) kale

2 Tbsp (30 mL) minced ginger root

2 cups (475 mL) cane sugar

2 cups (475 mL) apple cider vinegar

Not only is Michelle Nelson famous among friends for making fabulous shrubs—concentrated syrups, made from fruit and vinegar, for adding to drinks—she is somewhat legendary for her incredible stew made from rabbits she raises ethically with her partner, Chris Mull (see pages 191 and 195). This refreshing shrub has a slightly botanical undertone from the kale, offset by some bite from the ginger.

In a canning jar large enough to hold all of the ingredients, muddle (crush) the kale, using a muddler or blunt wooden spoon; doing so causes the cell walls in the kale to break down.

Add ginger, stir in sugar and let sit in the fridge, covered, for 24 to 48 hours.

Add vinegar, then let sit for a week at room temperature.

After a week, strain out the solid ingredients. At this point, you can start mixing beverages with your shrub, or let it sit for another week to let the fermentation add more complexity of flavour.

MAKES ABOUT 3 CUPS (700 ML)

WHAT'S A SHRUB, ANYWAY?

As Michelle puts it, shrubs are concentrated drinking syrups made from a perhaps unlikely combination of fruit and vinegar. Mixed with sparkling water, and sometimes with spirits, these fermented preserves are a refreshing combination of sweet and tangy, and are remarkably thirst-quenching.

The basic ingredients are very simple: fruit, sugar and vinegar. Apple cider vinegar is the best, but some shrubs work with other subtle vinegars. Avoid white vinegar. The shrub-making process takes one to two weeks and includes a period during which naturally occurring organisms in the fruit and vinegar ferment to create a cohesive combination of flavours. The result is an interesting and unusual way to preserve summer's bounty. The shrub will continue to ferment slowly in the jar on the countertop for several weeks, or will keep in the fridge for several months.

Use shrubs to replace vinegar in salad dressings and sauces in which you would like extra flavour and zing.

Fennel Huckleberry Shrub

4 cups (1L) huckleberries (or blackberries)

½ cup (125 mL) herb fennel foliage

2 cups (475 mL) sugar

2 cups (475 mL) champagne vinegar

Forage for huckleberries and use herb fennel—one of those plants that we both love to grow for its versatility, beauty and benefits to the garden (see page 42)—to make this tangy and tart shrub.

In a large canning jar muddle (crush) the berries, using a muddler or blunt wooden spoon. Add fennel, stir in sugar and let sit in the fridge covered for 24 to 48 hours.

Add vinegar, then let sit for a week at room temperature.

After a week, strain out the solid ingredients. At this point, you can start mixing beverages with your shrub, or let it sit for another week to let the fermentation add more complexity of flavour.

MAKES ABOUT 4 CUPS (1 L)

Strawberry Rosemary Shrub

2 cups (475 mL) strawberries

2 Tbsp (30 mL) rosemary leaves

2 cups (475 mL) cane sugar

2 cups (475 mL) apple cider vinegar

What could be more summery than the combo of garden-fresh strawberries and rosemary, that Mediterranean wonder-herb?

In a large canning jar, muddle the berries. Stir in rosemary and sugar and let sit in the fridge, covered, for 24 to 48 hours.

Strain out berries and return rosemary to the retained liquid. Add vinegar and then let sit for a week at room temperature.

At this point, you can start mixing beverages with your shrub, or let it sit for another week to let the fermentation add more complexity of flavour.

MAKES ABOUT 3 CUPS (700 ML)

Three Shrub Cocktails

To make shrubs into cocktails, simply mix with sparkling water and add spirits...or you can skip the booze for a refreshing alcohol-free beverage. See pages 96 and 97 for Shrub recipes.

Kale Ginger

A wedge of lemon

2 slices ginger root

1 oz (30 mL) Michelle's Kale Ginger Shrub

1 oz (30 mL) rum

Sparkling water

A pretty kale leaf for garnish

Muddle the wedge of lemon and slices of ginger with a wooden spoon in a tall glass.

Add the Kale Ginger Shrub and rum (if using), then top up with sparkling water.

Garnish with a kale leaf.

MAKES 1 COCKTAIL

Strawberry Rosemary

1 oz (30 mL) Strawberry Rosemary Shrub

1 oz (30 mL) tequila

Sparkling water

A stem of rosemary for garnish

Add the Strawberry Rosemary Shrub and tequila (if using) to a tall glass, then top up with sparkling water.

Garnish with rosemary.

MAKES 1 COCKTAIL

Fennel Huckleberry

1 oz (30 mL) Fennel Huckleberry Shrub (or more to taste)

1 oz (30 mL) vodka

Sparkling water

A gorgeous herb fennel stem or flower for garnish

Add the Fennel Huckleberry Shrub and vodka (if using) to a tall glass, then top up with sparkling water.

Garnish with herb fennel.

MAKES 1 COCKTAIL

Mint Mojito Magic

VE **GF**

10–12 mint leaves

1 tsp (5 mL) superfine or granulated sugar

Juice of ½ lime (or more to taste)

Ice

1–2 oz (30–60 mL) white rum

Soda water

A slice of lime or a mint leaf for garnish

We are both big fans of talented writer, gardener and shutterbug Christina Symons, food (and sometimes kale) photographer for this book and the first *Book of Kale.* Thank you, Christina! While she and partner John Gillespie are both firmly rooted in their own Eden—an incredible edible garden on BC's Sunshine Coast (which we totally envy—how do they keep it so pretty and tidy?), their partnership extends also to the kitchen and workshop. Visit their website, EverydayEden.com, or check out their inspiring books *Everyday Eden* and *Sow Simple* for hundreds of eco-project ideas and many a smashing garden-cocktail suggestion just like this one.

In a tall glass, using the back side of a spoon, crush the mint leaves against the sugar, mixing firmly until the sugar and mint are well muddled. The aroma of the mint at this point should be arresting. If it's not, add more mint leaves and keep muddling.

Add lime juice, ice and rum. Stir gently and top with soda water.

Garnish with a slice of lime or a mint leaf—or both.

MAKES 1 COCKTAIL (OR MOCKTAIL IF YOU SKIP THE RUM)

CHRISTINA SAYS…

The key to making great classic mojitos is to use fresh spearmint leaves. Don't use dried mint or, even worse, mint liquor. If you have other flavours of mint growing in your garden, be sure to experiment. Chocolate mint mojitos, anyone?

Those lucky souls who travel the Caribbean sometimes scoff at North American mojitos and say they don't taste "quite right." Try replacing the sugar with a liberal dose of cane-sugar juice (not easy to find but worth the pursuit) and skip the soda water. You may also need to add more mint. Finally, a dash of Angostura bitters will add authentic flavour. You can also make a virgin (alcohol-free) mojito by substituting white grape-juice concentrate for the rum.

Mediterranean Rub with Fennel Seeds & Rosemary

4 garlic cloves, chopped

3 Tbsp (45 mL) fennel seeds

2 heaping Tbsp (30 mL) minced rosemary

1 tsp (5 mL) fancy salt (such as Maldon)

1 tsp (5 mL) grated lemon zest

½ tsp (2.5 mL) freshly ground pepper

1 Tbsp (15 mL) olive oil

1 Tbsp (15 mL) balsamic vinegar

If you have a mini food processor, spice grinder or smoothie maker with a sharp blade, use it to make this fragrant rub to season anything you want to roast or sizzle on the barbecue. If not, just chop everything as fine as possible. If you have time, apply the wet rub the night before or even just a couple of hours before. Store the rubbed meat or veggie in a big freezer bag in the fridge. Remove it about half an hour before you begin cooking. If you're making a big dinner, you probably will want to double this recipe—go ahead and freeze what you don't use.

Whiz everything together, or chop the dry ingredients finely, then add oil and vinegar.

Slather all over whatever you are cooking. If you can, leave it to marinate for a night or at least a couple of hours before baking or barbecuing.

MAKES ABOUT ½ CUP (125 ML)

SPICE UP YOUR WHOLE SPICES...

...by grinding them yourself. Use a mortar and pestle, a suribachi or a spice grinder (or even an old coffee grinder that has been well wiped out). Grinding your spices as you need them gives them a huge step up in flavour—it's similar to the difference between pre-ground coffee and beans that you grind right before brewing. The volatile oils disappear quickly from anything ground, so take that extra minute or two and taste the delicious difference.

Six Superfood Pestos

Naked Pumpkin Seed & Kale Blossom Pesto

½ cup (125 mL) kale blossoms, plus a few extra for garnish

1 cup (250 mL) arugula leaves

¼ cup (60 mL) raw naked pumpkin seeds

¼ cup (60 mL) olive oil

Salt to taste

2 Tbsp (30 mL) pumpkin-seed oil (optional)

1 Tbsp (15 mL) lime juice (or some of your favourite vinegar)

A few shreds of nori

This novel pesto comes from amazing bee-advocate and author Lori Weidenhammer, a.k.a. Madame Beespeaker, who advises:

The spicy heat of the arugula in this recipe is tempered by the sweetness of the kale blossoms. You can put the pesto on crackers, crostini, pasta, cooked quinoa, or any way you use traditional pesto. Make sure the pumpkin seeds and oil are fresh.

Remove any woody stems from the kale blossoms and arugula leaves.

Put all the ingredients in the food processor and pulse just until well mixed but the mixture still has some texture.

Garnish with kale blossoms and shreds of nori.

MAKES ABOUT 1 CUP (250 ML)

ON EATING KALE BLOSSOMS...

We couldn't resist sharing this story from Madame Beespeaker Lori Weidenhammer, who is currently working with Carol on her own book about gardening for bees. We are excited about that! In the meantime, over to you, Madame Beespeaker, for your inspiring kale tale:

In early May, the kale plants in community plots start to get very tall and burst into glorious yellow bloom. The bumblebees, mason bees and honeybees love them. Some of the more exuberant plants start to fall over into the aisles of the community garden, or lean onto other people's plots. This inevitably leads to a polite email from the garden manager telling the members to tidy up the kale plants. "Don't cut off all the blossoms," I plead. "Please save some for the bees! Plus, you can eat the flowers! You can put them in salads, pesto and mango smoothies." I made the argument that since we were having a spring heat wave, the kale plants would shade tender seedlings, preventing them from getting scorched. I started feeding kale blossoms to every man, woman and child who passed our garden bed. The elementary-school students I work with got really excited about snacking on kale blossoms: "It's like broccoli, only better. I can't stop eating them!"

Spring Bud Pesto

A large handful of kale buds

4 sorrel leaves

3 young lovage leaves, chopped

2 garlic cloves, roughly chopped

1 cup (250 mL) chopped parsley

½ cup (125 mL) chopped chives

2 Tbsp (30 mL) finely minced rosemary leaves

¼ cup (60 mL) walnuts

3 Tbsp (45 mL) olive oil

2 Tbsp (30 mL) white wine

½ tsp (2.5 mL) salt

Zest of 1 lemon

If you aren't growing lovage, try to find a fellow gardener who is, because you can't find it in stores. Otherwise, omit it. But take this opportunity to sow a lovage seed or dig in a plant where you have room for a sizable addition—lovage is big in both structure and benefits for your garden. This herb attracts the good guys, such as those little ladybugs that can keep the aphids off your other plants, including that all-important kale crop. Tip: You can freeze this spring-y pesto in a mini-muffin pan or ice-cube trays. When frozen solid, transfer to freezer bags for use on pasta, in soups, on toast with creamy cheese…add it to whatever needs a bit of spring zing.

Combine everything in the food processor. Pulse until smooth, or to the consistency you prefer.

MAKES ABOUT 2 CUPS (475 ML)

Arugula Kale Pesto

½ cup (125 mL) walnuts

2–3 garlic cloves, chopped

2 cups (475 mL) packed arugula leaves

1 cup (250 mL) tightly packed young kale

¼ cup (60 mL) freshly grated Parmigiano or Romano cheese

½ cup (125 mL) olive oil

Juice of 1 good-sized lime

Salt to taste

A few grindings of pepper

Packs an arugula-y punch; great on gnocchi, perfect with pasta, piquant on pizza, bravissimo on bruschetta…or use as a dip for veggies, especially contrasting ones like carrots, cauliflower, radishes and strips of pale green bulb fennel. If you have walnut oil, use half and half with the olive oil to change it up.

Chop walnuts and toast them in a dry pan over medium heat, stirring and shaking the pan, for about 5 to 8 minutes until fragrant.

Place walnuts and all other ingredients in a food processor and pulse until very fine. Check for seasonings. Enjoy!

MAKES ABOUT 2 CUPS (475 ML)

Double Walnut Sage Pesto

½ cup (125 mL) walnuts

⅓ cup (80 mL) chopped parsley

3 Tbsp (45 mL) smallish sage leaves

2 large garlic cloves, roughly chopped

Pinch of cayenne

1 Tbsp (15 mL) balsamic vinegar

¼ cup (60 mL) olive oil

¼ cup (60 mL) walnut oil

½ tsp (2.5 mL) salt

A few grindings of pepper

½ cup (125 mL) grated Parmigiano or Romano cheese

Use this pesto on any kind of pasta or as a topping for bruschetta, or brush it on chicken toward the end of barbecuing or roasting. Divine.

Toast walnuts in a small cast-iron frying pan over low heat, shaking the pan—don't take your eyes off them because they burn very quickly.

Place walnuts, parsley, sage, garlic, cayenne and vinegar in a food processor. Pulse until finely chopped. Drizzle in oils; blend well. Transfer to a large serving bowl. Stir in salt, pepper and cheese.

MAKE ABOUT 1½ CUPS (350 ML)

Presto Garlic Scape Pesto

½ lb (225 g) garlic scapes

½ cup (125 mL) olive oil (or more)

⅓ cup (80 mL) pine nuts, walnuts or almonds

Juice of 1 large or 2 small limes

A few grindings of pepper

⅔ cup (160 mL) grated Parmigiano or Romano cheese

When you've collected the scapes for this recipe, before using them snap off the hard part of the stem as you would for asparagus. You can save the tough parts to use in soup stock (see page 138).

Cut scapes into 1-in (5-cm) sections. Combine everything but the cheese in a food processor or blender, adding extra oil as needed to make a creamy consistency. Stir in cheese. Great on bruschetta, with hot pasta, in pasta salads or with chicken, fish or meats!

MAKES ABOUT 2 CUPS (475 ML)

Parsley Pesto for Pasta

3 cups (700 mL) loosely packed parsley, most stems removed

A handful of fresh basil leaves (optional)

1 cup (250 mL) kale in chiffonade

½ cup (125 mL) walnuts

½ cup (125 mL) freshly grated Parmigiano or Romano

½ cup (125 mL) ricotta cheese

⅓ cup (80 mL) olive oil

½ tsp (2.5 mL) salt

A little lemon zest

A few grindings of pepper

A snap to whip up, this pesto is lighter than regular versions because of the ricotta. To serve, toss pesto with hot pasta and add a little of the cooking water to thin it a bit if needed.

Place all ingredients in a food processor and blend until very smooth—if pesto is too thick, add a little cold water.

MAKES ABOUT 2 CUPS (475 ML)

Onion Confit with Thyme

2 Tbsp (30 mL) olive oil

3 medium red onions, thinly sliced (about 3 cups/700 mL)

¼ cup (60 mL) sugar

4 garlic cloves, skin on, smacked with the side of a knife (see sidebar on page 158)

⅓ cup (80 mL) red wine vinegar

1 Tbsp (15 mL) minced thyme leaves

¼ cup (60 mL) water

Kosher salt

Heaven on a bagel with kale and creamy cheese of any sort, whether it be soy or dairy (and maybe with a thin slice of lox on top) or on our BKT (see page 70). It also works well with chicken or fish. Keeps in the fridge for at least a couple of weeks and could be preserved by canning if you wanted to make more of it.

Heat oil in a large skillet over medium heat. Add onions and sugar, and cook, stirring frequently, until onions are deeply caramelized—about 35 to 45 minutes.

Add garlic, vinegar, thyme and water. Simmer, stirring occasionally, until juices thicken—about 3 minutes.

Season with salt. Discard garlic.

MAKES ABOUT 2 CUPS (475 ML)

Garlic Scape Refrigerator Pickles with Dill

1 tsp (5 mL) dill seeds

A few stems of dill weed (if available)

12–20 garlic scapes, depending on their thickness

1 dried chili pepper

Scant 1 cup (250 mL) apple cider vinegar

⅔ cup (160 mL) water

1 heaping Tbsp (15 mL) coarse kosher or sea salt

1 Tbsp (15 mL) sugar

1 Tbsp (15 mL) honey

Carol says: When I snipped the scapes off most of my garlic plants in early July to make pickles, I left some to bloom for the bees—they are crazy about these spherical flowers typical of the Allium family. Plus, I was curious to see if the bulbs would be skimpy when the scapes weren't snipped. The answer is yes! Those bulbs were about a third smaller than those from scape-scalped plants. It's worth gathering scapes for two reasons: they are a big bonus in the kitchen for pesto, omelettes, salads, stir-fries and pickles, and removing them from the plants allows garlic bulbs to plump up.

These easy pickles are unprocessed and last in the fridge for up to six months but will likely be eaten up long before that. Pick scapes on the young and fairly thin side. Use the tenderest part of the scape and save the tougher bits for garlicky soup stock (see page 138). Scapes tend to curl, making them easy to fit into the jar, especially if they are younger. If you prefer "ruler-straight" pickles, use the straight part instead and save the curvy swirls for pesto. Add a bit o' finely minced scapes to dips, egg salad, or even a Caesar (drink or salad), or just gobble them the way they are. Double, triple or quadruple this recipe if you have lots of scapes.

Sterilize a 2-cup (475-mL) canning jar: fill a quarter full with water and microwave on high for 3 to 4 minutes or until very hot. Remove (use tongs or oven mitts) to counter.

Place the dill seeds and weed in the jar first. Follow with the scapes, twisting them in a circle if they are going that way. If they snap, don't worry about it. Add the chili to the jar when it is half full.

Heat the vinegar, water, salt, sugar and honey in a small pan. Bring to a boil, then simmer for a few minutes until sugar and salt have dissolved.

Pour hot mixture into the jar—cover the scapes completely. Seal jar tightly. Cool, then store pickles in the refrigerator for 6 to 8 weeks before eating them…before that, the flavour won't be as intense.

MAKES ONE 2-CUP (475-ML) JAR

Green Harissa

1 Tbsp (15 mL) caraway seeds

1 Tbsp (15 mL) coriander seeds

2 jalapeño peppers, deveined, seeded and chopped

1 poblano pepper, deveined, seeded and chopped

1 small red Thai, habanero or Scotch bonnet pepper, deveined, seeded (using gloves or extreme care), chopped

2 garlic cloves, chopped

½ cup (125 mL) cilantro leaves, stems and roots

⅓ cup (80 mL) freshly squeezed lime juice

½ tsp (2.5 mL) sea or Maldon salt

Use only a little harissa—not a lot—as a pre-barbecue schmear for chicken, fish or meat, or in mashed zucchini dips or other Middle Eastern mezes. A reddish harissa paste from Tunisia in a tube is widely available in supermarkets (see the introduction to our Kale with Chickpeas, Squash & Merguez Sausage recipe on page 194). The peppers in store-bought harissa are the Baldouti, Meski and Beldi varieties, the likes of which you are unlikely to find fresh. If you like to live on the wild side, use hot hot hot peppers in this recipe. Otherwise stick to the jalapeños and a small hot pepper, or half. Fresh poblanos add zing and are sometimes available—they're a deep chocolaty green and just a little spicy. If you can't find them, add one more jalapeño. When cutting hot peppers, do not touch your eyes and either wear rubber gloves or wash your hands well after handling the peppers.

Using a mortar and pestle, suribachi or spice grinder, grind the caraway and coriander seeds (see sidebar on grinding, page 101).

Place the spices, peppers, garlic and cilantro in the bowl of a food processor, and pulse a few times until the mixture is nicely chopped. If you'd rather, you can use your mortar and pestle or suribachi and have your hands do the work rather than a food processor.

Transfer mixture to a small bowl; stir in the lime juice and salt and taste for seasoning.

MAKES ABOUT 1 CUP (250 ML)

Kale Cilantro Chimichurri

5 garlic cloves, roughly chopped

1 large jalapeño or medium poblano pepper, roughly chopped

1½ cups (350 mL) roughly chopped cilantro leaves, stems and roots

1 cup (250 mL) roughly chopped parsley leaves and tender stems

⅓ cup (80 mL) oregano leaves

½ cup (125 mL) roughly chopped chives or 1 large shallot, chopped

½ cup (125 mL) roughly chopped kale

⅓ cup (80 mL) good red wine vinegar

1 tsp (5 mL) brown sugar

1 tsp (5 mL) good salt

½ cup (125 mL) olive oil

Bright, green and cha-cha-cha, chimichurri hails from Argentina where they slather it on giant grilled steaks. It also works well as a marinade for just about anything on the barbecue—meat, tofu and vegetables—and as a way to use up that wonderfully healthy oregano that we always seem to have a lot of in the summer garden. Use chimichurri as a marinade (and maybe start it soaking up the flavour the day before), then as a sauce. Measure herbs after chopping them—you need lots. The oil goes in at the end, so it doesn't become a green slurry.

Place everything but the oil in a food processor and pulse lightly. Do not overprocess—the herbs should still be semi-distinct and not puréed.

Transfer mixture to a bowl, and stir in the oil. If the mixture is too thick to stir, add a little red or white wine. Store, covered, in the fridge for up to 3 days.

MAKES ABOUT 2 CUPS (475 ML)

MARINATE SAFELY

To marinate meat or chicken, reserve and refrigerate ½ cup (125 mL) chimichurri to serve with the meal. Use the rest as a marinade. Simply slather the chimichurri onto the meat or chicken, place in a freezer bag and then store in the fridge, turning the bag frequently so that the sauce really penetrates. Try to do this the day before cooking for optimum taste, but if you want the meat or chicken for dinner tonight, marinating it for 3 hours should do the trick. It will not be as intensely flavoured, though, as it would be if marinated overnight.

Grill meat or chicken, then serve with the reserved chimichurri.

Lovage Sauce

3 Tbsp (45 mL) butter

12–14 young lovage
leaves, minced

1 Tbsp (15 mL) flour

¼ cup (60 mL) dry white wine

⅔ cup (160 mL) cream, heated

2 tsp (10 mL) Dijon mustard

Salt to taste

A few grindings of pepper

*gluten free if gluten-free
flour and mustard are used

An aromatic sauce for halibut or sole, or try it napped onto steamed new potatoes, baby carrots and steamed beets, or alongside a vegetable pie. Go with heavy cream or light depending on your mood.

In small heavy saucepan, melt the butter over medium-low heat. Add the lovage and sauté for 3 minutes or so.

Whisk in the flour and stir with a wooden spoon to make a roux—about 3 minutes.

Add the wine and cook while whisking for 1 minute, then add the cream, mustard, salt and pepper. Cook, stirring constantly, until sauce is thickened—just a few minutes.

MAKES ABOUT 1 CUP (250 ML)

Browned Butter & Sage (BB&S)

½ cup (125 mL) unsalted butter

3 Tbsp (45 mL) sage leaves in chiffonade

French chefs call brown butter *beurre noisette*. It doesn't contain nuts, but if the butter is cooked to the correct degree of brownness, it smells a little nutty or like butterscotch. As you cook the butter, the water evaporates and you'll see specks of milk solids turn slowly to a light-brown colour. Do not be intimidated—this is dead easy to make! Just don't do it while multi-tasking.

Melt butter in a large heavy saucepan over medium heat. Cook, shaking pan and stirring occasionally, until butter solids begin to turn light brown—about 3 minutes.

Add chopped sage to the pan and stir-fry for 1 to 2 minutes, until sage is a little crispy and butter is a little deeper brown. Quickly remove pan from heat and transfer the mixture to a bowl—otherwise it will keep cooking in the pan and burn.

MAKES ABOUT ½ CUP (125 ML)

WHAT TO DO WITH BB&S

Dress salad greens from the garden—baby kale, arugula, endive, escarole, radicchio, lettuce or anything else tender and leafy—with this warm BB&S and a little lemon juice or balsamic vinegar for a wilted salad. Before making the browned butter, sauté and slice a little prosciutto or pancetta if you like, which will add flavour and substance to your greens.

Toss cooked pasta with BB&S. Throw in some capers, chopped kale or parsley, or all three.

Sauté scallops in a little plain butter; remove them to a warm plate or scallop shell when done to your liking. Add a bit more butter to the pan and make BB&S as described above. Place scallops on a bed of fresh or wilted kale in chiffonade, and dress them with the BB&S and a squeeze of lemon.

Dish up absolutely any kind of potatoes—boiled, mashed, fried—or baked sweet potatoes with BB&S. The flavours are meant for each other.

Top scrambled, poached or fried eggs with a little BB&S. Try poached eggs served on steamed asparagus and topped with BB&S.

Add a dash of maple syrup and a sprinkle of cinnamon to BB&S; toss with chunks of roasted butternut squash.

Chive Blossom Vinegar

About 12 chive blossoms

White wine vinegar

Tiny completely closed rosebuds from an organic garden (optional)

If you add rosebuds to the vinegar, it has a faintly flowery yet chive-y flavour. Use it in anything that calls for a tasty vinegar, such as the many salad recipes in this book where we suggest white wine vinegar. You can also spritz a little on roast chicken or fish.

Gather chive blossoms, preferably in the morning, give them a rinse and loosely pack into a 1-cup (250-mL) canning jar until about two-thirds full.

Fill with white wine vinegar, ensuring that all blossoms are covered.

Cap the jar, place in a dark cupboard and leave it for 2 to 3 weeks. The flowers will lose their colour and the vinegar will turn pink.

Strain the vinegar and discard the spent blossoms or add them to your compost. Now add the rosebuds (if using) to the vinegar. Just 2 or 3 will add a mild rose flavour.

Store wherever you keep vinegar; use within 6 months.

MAKES 1 CUP (250 ML)

CHIVE JIBES

Carol says: I don't mean to make fun of Sharon, but... when it came time to narrow down what superedibles we want you to grow along with your masses of kale, I said "chives!" and she retorted that her chives lasted for only a month before going to seed. Sharon was astonished to hear that I pick loads of chives every single day from spring right through to very hard frost. The trick with chives is to continually cut them down so that they keep growing. I swear they sprout up at least an inch every day if you keep trimming them!

Creamy Basil Vinaigrette

2 garlic cloves, chopped

1 cup (250 mL) tightly packed basil leaves

½ cup (125 mL) buttermilk

2 Tbsp (30 mL) white wine vinegar

1 Tbsp (15 mL) balsamic vinegar

1 Tbsp (15 mL) Dijon mustard

1 Tbsp (15 mL) honey

½ tsp (2.5 mL) cracked pepper

½ tsp (2.5 mL) salt

A generous handful of parsley, roughly chopped

A generous handful of chives, roughly chopped

⅔ cup (160 mL) olive or grapeseed oil

Tangy and a snap to put together once ingredients are assembled. Feel free to add other soft herbs from your garden. This vinaigrette is luscious as a dressing for a quick kale salad or poured over sliced tomatoes, poached salmon, steamed or sautéed zucchini, potatoes, beans—we could go on! Try slathering it onto Portuguese kale leaves, crunchy wedges of iceberg lettuce, poached eggs or a BLT (or BKT—see page 70).

Combine everything except the oil in a food processor or blender equipped with a feed tube. Slowly drizzle in the olive oil while processing so that the dressing emulsifies.

Keeps for 3 to 4 days, refrigerated.

MAKES ABOUT 2 CUPS (475 ML)

Arlene's Husband's Favourite Vinaigrette

 *

1 garlic clove, minced

⅔ cup (160 mL) olive or grapeseed oil

¼ cup (60 mL) apple cider vinegar

1 Tbsp (15 mL) finely minced oregano leaves

1 tsp (5 mL) dry mustard

1 tsp (5 mL) salt

1 tsp (5 mL) sugar

½ tsp (2.5 mL) pepper

"This is the only dressing his highness will tolerate," says Arlene. His name is Gerry, and he and Arlene live in Kamloops and started one of the first greenhouse-greens operations many years ago. Sharon met Arlene on the telephone while working for West Coast Seeds—the rest is history. About this recipe, Arlene says, "I usually leave the garlic out if I have choir practice or students, which means almost every time I make it!" We say: Arlene, go ahead and put the garlic in—students, choir or come what may!

Place all ingredients in a covered container and shake well. Pour over greens or use as a marinade (see Chive Grilled Potatoes on page 163).

MAKES ABOUT 1 CUP (250 ML)

SALADS

Sexist Slaw with Kale

About 1 lb (454 g) green cabbage, tough outer leaves and core removed

1–2 garlic cloves, minced

1 small onion, quartered and thinly sliced

2 cups (475 mL) kale in fine chiffonade

1½ cups (350 mL) cottage cheese (do not use lowfat or nonfat type)

½ cup (125 mL) chopped flat-leaf parsley

⅓ cup (80 mL) mayonnaise

½ tsp (2.5 mL) salt

Juice and zest of half a lemon

A few grindings of pepper

If you have a mandoline, this salad will take less than five minutes to make. Based on a recipe called "Men's Favorite Salad" from a 1960s issue of *Gourmet*, evidently, men could not resist it, "licking the plate clean." We added kale (of course), lemon zest and a lot more lemon juice than the original recipe that called for one skimpy teaspoon—seriously, in all that salad? Okay, it's for men, but we like it too. Make it during summer when cabbage is tender and sweet. And don't "discard" the outer leaves and core of the cabbage as the original recipe advised—yikes—compost them!

Using a very sharp knife, cut cabbage in quarters, then eighths. Slice very thinly crosswise. If using a mandoline, use the fine shredding blade. You should have about 6 cups (1.4 L) shredded cabbage. Transfer to a bowl and add everything else.

Mix well and let stand at least 1 hour before dishing out aggressively.

MAKES 6 TO 8 "MAN-SIZED" SERVINGS

Hood River Kale Salad

8 cups (2 L) finely chopped kale

1 bunch green onions, chopped

1 large red bell pepper, chopped

1 cup (250 mL) toasted pecans, chopped

4 Tbsp (60 mL) olive oil

2 Tbsp (30 mL) rice vinegar

2 Tbsp (30 mL) honey

1 cup (250 mL) crumbled feta

Jacquie Barone and her husband, Pasquale, raised a family of two daughters, all the while owning and operating the famous Hood River Hotel (complete with restaurant and deli) in Hood River, Oregon—so they were a little busy. Jacquie says this salad keeps for many days in a container fitted with a tight lid.

Combine kale, green onions, bell pepper and pecans in a large bowl.

Whisk together oil, vinegar and honey; pour over salad and toss.

Sprinkle with the feta when serving.

MAKES 4 TO 6 SERVINGS

Garden Bay Kale Slaw

8 cups (2 L) kale—preferably a mixture of kale types—in chiffonade

¼ cup (60 mL) or more pine nuts

3 Tbsp (45 mL) olive oil

2 Tbsp (30 mL) rice or apple cider vinegar

Scant 1 Tbsp (15 mL) maple syrup

Salt to taste

A few grindings of pepper

Not another slaw, you say? We like to use the word. This was created at Carol's place and the family ate it up in about five seconds. Top this off with a few kale flowers—but remember to leave some of the yellow blossoms in your garden for the bees.

Place kale in a large bowl.

Toast pine nuts in a small cast-iron frying pan over low heat, shaking the pan—don't take your eyes off them because they burn very quickly.

Whisk together remaining ingredients and pour over salad. Toss, top with the toasted pine nuts, and serve.

MAKES 6 SERVINGS

Chiffonade of Kale with Salty Sweet Walnuts

2 Tbsp (30 mL) butter
or olive oil

½ cup (125 mL) walnut halves

2 Tbsp (30 mL) maple syrup

Coarse salt

8 cups (2 L) kale in chiffonade

1 cup (250 mL) crumbled feta

3 Tbsp (45 mL) olive oil

2 Tbsp (30 mL) balsamic vinegar

A few grindings of pepper

This salad was a big hit at the Sunshine Coast Botanical Garden when we agreed to do a cooking demonstration in the lovely reception hall. We are not Food Channel cooks, so it was fun having attendees coach us as we forgot one recipe ingredient after another. If you can, pay a visit to this remarkable community-created garden on Mason Road in Sechelt, BC. In addition to having a lot of rare and semi-rare trees (the property was formerly a tree nursery), there is a bountiful vegetable garden maintained by volunteers…and the produce goes to the local food bank. Plus, the community grows a ton of kale in the garden! In this salad, use assorted types of kale if you have them.

In a heavy sauté pan, melt butter over medium-low heat. Add the walnuts and sauté, stirring and shaking the pan often, until they give off a fragrance and become lightly toasted. Do not walk away from the stove—walnuts burn easily! Add the maple syrup (it will sizzle a little), stirring to coat the nuts thoroughly, then remove from heat. Sprinkle salt on the walnuts—not too much, whatever suits your salt preference. Allow the nuts to cool a little.

Place the kale in a serving bowl. Add the feta and walnuts.

Drizzle with olive oil and toss gently to coat the kale.

Add balsamic vinegar and pepper, toss again and serve.

MAKES 4 TO 6 SERVINGS

Kale Tahini Salad

¼ cup (60 mL) tahini

2 tsp (10 mL) miso

1 Tbsp (15 mL) lemon juice

1 Tbsp (15 mL) Bragg Liquid
Aminos or soy sauce

2 garlic cloves, roughly chopped

A few grindings of pepper

2 pinches cayenne

2 tsp (10 mL) apple cider vinegar

2 tsp (10 mL) honey

2 Tbsp (30 mL) water

6 cups (1.4 L) kale in chiffonade

*gluten free if gluten-free miso,
soy sauce or liquid aminos are used

Uber-healthy, the dressing has lots of ingredients but only takes a few minutes to make and you don't even have to dirty a food processor or blender—unless you want to. (It'll take you longer to wash the blender than it does to make the whole works by hand—just use a small whisk or spoon.) Add finely chopped parsley if you want more green. Let the dressing mellow in the fridge for at least an hour before serving. Bits of fresh Medjool dates and a handful of chopped tangerines or clementines in season would be nice, too. The tasting panel was split on whether ginger should be added to this simple salad—if you love it, go ahead and add a smattering of finely minced chopped ginger. But if you don't, this salad is fine just the way it is.

In a small mixing bowl, blend the tahini with the miso. Add lemon juice and Bragg Liquid Aminos, and stir a little more—the mixture will become emulsified. Add garlic, pepper, cayenne, vinegar and honey, and stir again. Add the water a bit at a time, beating between additions.

Let the dressing mellow in the fridge for at least an hour before serving over the kale chiffonade.

MAKES 4 SERVINGS

The recipe makes about ¾ cup (180 mL) tahini dressing—probably too much for the kale chiffonade—but it's a great dip for veggies, especially carrots from the garden! It's also fantastic on grilled salmon—just slather it on after turning the fish halfway through the cooking process.

Kale with Ginger Marinated Daikon

 *

6 cups (1.4 L) kale in chiffonade

½ hothouse or homegrown cucumber, or a couple of Saudi-style cucumbers, finely sliced

1 red bell pepper, halved, then finely sliced

1 orange or yellow bell pepper, halved, then finely sliced

A handful each of mint and basil leaves in chiffonade

½ cup (125 mL) thin slices daikon (peel and halve lengthwise before slicing)

⅓ cup (80 mL) freshly squeezed lime juice

1 Tbsp (15 mL) grated ginger root

1 scant Tbsp (15 mL) palm, brown or Demerara sugar

2 Tbsp (30 mL) grapeseed or other vegetable oil

1 Tbsp (15 mL) rice wine vinegar

2 tsp (10 mL) sesame oil

2 tsp (10 mL) soy sauce

Salt to taste

A few grindings of pepper

*gluten free if gluten-free soy sauce is used

A cooling mélange, good on its own or with seafood of any kind. Look for palm sugar at an Asian specialty shop or substitute another type of sugar. The clean flavours of the ginger and cucumber are perfect foils for the kale, while the daikon adds bite. Here in Vancouver, BC, daikon—the very long, white radish—is easily found. If you live in a daikon-less locale, substitute regular radishes. You can, of course, grow your own daikon or a smaller type of long white radish called White Icicle, which has a mild flavour.

Combine kale, cucumber, peppers and herbs in a serving bowl. Place the sliced daikon in a separate bowl.

Whisk together the rest of the ingredients, pour over the daikon and let it marinate in the fridge for 30 minutes.

Toss kale and daikon mixtures together.

Allow salad to sit for another 5 minutes before serving.

MAKES 4 TO 6 SERVINGS

Kale & Jackfruit in Thai Curry Mayo

2 cups (454 g) rotini, fusilli or other wiggly pasta

2×19-oz (540-mL) cans jackfruit

1 cup (250 mL) mayonnaise

½ cup (125 mL) sour cream or yoghurt

2 Tbsp (30 mL) Thai red curry paste or to taste

2 tsp (10 mL) good curry powder

2 cups (475 mL) kale in chiffonade

¼ cup (60 mL) chopped Thai or other basil leaves, plus leaves for garnish

¼ cup (60 mL) finely minced cilantro leaves, stems and roots, plus leaves for garnish

⅓ cup (80 mL) lightly toasted pine nuts (optional)

*gluten free if gluten-free pasta is used

Sharon says: My dear friend Cherryl Reed served a version of this unusual pasta salad on her boat, *The Arasheena*, a lovely ferro-cement motor sailer that reminded me of a pirate ship. I occasionally slaved in the galley and, boy, was it hot! Jackfruit, used in Thai and various South Asian cuisines and available at Asian supermarkets or other specialty stores, is musty/musky and sweet at the same time (nothing like durian, which stinks like smelly socks) and has a meaty texture. This dish is a guaranteed hit at potlucks or anywhere else, and people just can't figure out what's in it. Add some pine nuts if you want a little more crunch. The recipe makes lots but if you take it anywhere to share, it'll disappear.

Cook the pasta al dente, according to directions. Drain, briefly rinse, drain again and transfer to a large bowl.

Chop the jackfruit into bite-sized pieces and discard all but ¼ cup (60 mL) jackfruit syrup.

Combine mayonnaise, sour cream, curry paste and curry powder. Mix into the pasta, add the jackfruit, reserved syrup and kale, and stir well.

Fold in chopped basil and minced cilantro. Garnish with herb leaves and toasted pine nuts (if using).

Refrigerate for at least 1 hour before serving to allow flavours to meld and kale to be tenderized.

This salad keeps well in the fridge for a few days, but it's unlikely any will be left over.

MAKES 8 TO 10 SERVINGS

Minted Kale with Peas & Blue Cheese

½ cup (125 mL) finely minced shallots

2 Tbsp (30 mL) butter

Scant ¼ cup (60 mL) rice wine vinegar

2 Tbsp (30 mL) oil

1 Tbsp (15 mL) Dijon mustard

2 tsp (10 mL) brown sugar

4 cups (1 L) packed kale in chiffonade

1 cup (250 mL) loosely packed mint leaves in fine chiffonade

¼ cup (60 mL) thinly sliced sweet onion

1 cup (250 mL) fresh peas or chopped snap peas (or frozen peas thawed just before using)

¼ cup (60 mL) mild blue cheese or ½ cup (125 mL) goat's cheese

A few grindings of pepper

Elizabeth, a customer at the University of British Columbia Botanical Garden, where Sharon works on Saturdays, shared this recipe that she created after eating it day after day in a restaurant in San Francisco and craving it after she left. Make the dressing first…it's a cooked one. Vary the recipe by adding arugula or other greens, but it definitely requires the sturdiness of kale to stand up. You can use thawed frozen peas or even chopped fresh snap peas, but if you use your own homegrown freshly shelled peas, look out—you might just perish from pleasure. Choose Cambozola or Roquefort or a "mild gorgonzola"—an oxymoron? If you're not a fan of blue cheese, substitute goat's cheese.

Sauté shallots in butter until softened. Add rice vinegar and cook down for a few minutes, stirring frequently. Add oil while whisking, then add the mustard and brown sugar. Cook until mixture is thick, remove from heat and allow to cool.

Put kale, mint and onion in a mixing bowl and toss. Add dressing and toss again. Top with peas and cheese, and add a few grindings of pepper. Toss just before serving.

MAKES 3 TO 4 SERVINGS

Summer Salad of Baby Kale, Arugula & Berries

⅓ cup (80 mL) halved or very coarsely chopped filberts (hazelnuts)

6 cups (1.4 L) kale in chiffonade

3 cups (700 mL) arugula leaves

¼ cup (60 mL) chopped parsley

A small handful of basil leaves, roughly chopped

1 cup (250 mL) raspberries, blackberries, blueberries, wild berries or a mix

4 Tbsp (60 mL) olive oil

2 Tbsp (30 mL) red wine or balsamic vinegar

1 Tbsp (15 mL) honey or maple syrup

½ tsp (2.5 mL) dry mustard

A dash of salt

A few grindings of pepper

½ cup (125 mL) coarsely crumbled firm goat's cheese (optional)

*vegan if optional goat's cheese is omitted and if maple syrup is used rather than honey

A whopping whack of phytonutrients in a salad that is pretty, quick and easy. Make it July through September, when your own berries (or wild ones) are plentiful and your basil is thriving. Goat's cheese is optional but makes the salad more luxurious. You can prepare the salad ahead, but to keep it from becoming goopy, add the cheese just before serving. Substitute almonds if filberts are not available.

In a small heavy frying pan, lightly toast filberts on low heat, shaking and stirring frequently until they throw off a fragrance and are slightly toasty. Remove from pan and set aside to cool.

Place kale, arugula, parsley and basil in a serving bowl and toss mixture lightly. Add berries and incorporate them ever so lightly so they remain whole.

Combine oil, vinegar, honey, mustard, salt and pepper in a jar; shake well. Drizzle over salad.

Top salad with toasted filberts and goat's cheese (if using).

MAKES 6 TO 8 SERVINGS

Arugula Flower Power Salad

1 fennel bulb, quartered lengthwise and thinly sliced

3 cups (700 mL) loosely packed arugula leaves

½ cup (125 mL) chopped basil leaves

½ cup (125 mL) chopped chives

½ cup (125 mL) chopped parsley

¼ cup (60 mL) olive oil

2 Tbsp (30 mL) excellent wine vinegar

2 tsp (10 mL) Dijon mustard

1 tsp (5 mL) honey

½ tsp (2.5 mL) salt

A few grindings of pepper

Arugula, kale, borage, nasturtium and calendula flowers

*gluten free if gluten-free mustard is used

The simplicity of this salad belies its complex flavours. Plus, you will feel energized after eating it! Arugula flowers have an exquisitely spicy yet sweet and floral taste. Toss them into the bowl—along with a handful of kale blooms. You can also use borage, nasturtium or calendula flowers, assuming they are organically grown.

In a large bowl, combine fennel, arugula, basil, chives and parsley.

In a small bowl, whisk together oil, vinegar, mustard, honey, salt and pepper.

Drizzle the vinaigrette over the salad. Garnish with flowers.

MAKES 4 SERVINGS

WHAT'S THE DIFFERENCE BETWEEN BULB AND HERB FENNEL?

Long ago, "wild" herbaceous fennel developed a bulbous bottom—the licorice-y bulb fennel (*finocchio* in Italian) we know and love and pay dearly for at farmers' markets. Unlike herb fennel, bulb fennel can be a bit of a challenge to grow. It's another of those plants that "resents transplanting" (see page 35), so must be seeded in situ, then thinned out and treated well. Otherwise, the plant will bolt and will not form a bulb, or perhaps just a wimpy one. We're not saying you can't grow bulb fennel, just that it requires high maintenance compared to the herb form. For more information on herb fennel, see page 42.

Nectarine, Tomato & Feta Salad with Purple Ruffles

3 large nectarines

About 3 large tomatoes or the same volume of cherry-sized tomatoes

½ medium-sized purple onion, thinly sliced

⅔ cup (160 mL) crumbled feta

Lots of chopped purple basil leaves, plus extra leaves for garnish

1 Tbsp (15 mL) olive oil

2 tsp (10 mL) balsamic vinegar

A few grindings of pepper

Pinch of salt

Like getting your own entire bowl of fruit salsa to gorge on, and an excellent reason to grow Purple Ruffles basil. You can sub the nectarines with freestone peaches if you like. Using your own tomatoes—"salad" size like Chadwick's Cherry, Sungold, Black Cherry, Green Grape…or any other smallish variety you grow—will make the salad extra special.

Halve nectarines, remove pits, and cut into bite-sized chunks. Transfer to a bowl.

Cut large tomatoes into chunks or halve little tomatoes, and place in same bowl. Add onion, feta and basil and gently combine. Drizzle olive oil over salad ingredients and stir to coat, then add the vinegar, pepper and salt. Garnish with basil leaves and serve immediately.

MAKES 4 SERVINGS

Arugula Kale Salad à la Suellen

 *

¼ cup (60 mL) freshly squeezed orange juice

1 Tbsp (15 mL) finely minced shallot

3 Tbsp (45 mL) olive oil

1 Tbsp (15 mL) balsamic vinegar

1 Tbsp (15 mL) maple syrup

1 tsp (5 mL) grainy mustard

½ tsp (2.5 mL) sea salt

A few generous grindings of pepper

4 cups (1 L) loosely packed arugula leaves

2 cups (475 mL) kale in chiffonade

1 cup (250 mL) lightly toasted, roughly chopped pecans

½ cup (125 mL) crumbled goat's cheese

8 firm strawberries, thinly sliced

*gluten free if gluten-free mustard is used

Sharon says: This is adapted from an old standby from my friend Suellen—formerly my boss at The Fitness Group where my healthy "seed muffins" were a big hit in the cappuccino bar I managed. When Suellen lived in Vancouver, our visits involved reading recipes from magazines to each other until we became ravenous, then jumping into the kitchen and cooking for hours. Now living in Santa Fe, Suellen continues to inspire with her Artist of the Everyday blog, as well as her artful recipe ideas.

In a small bowl, whisk together the orange juice, shallot, oil, vinegar, maple syrup, mustard, salt and pepper.

Place arugula and kale in a bowl (glass looks nice). Anoint with the vinaigrette and toss lightly, adding just enough vinaigrette to make the leaves glisten. Add the pecans and mix just to incorporate. Top with cheese and strawberries, and toss the salad at the table.

MAKES 4 SERVINGS

Many-Celeried Lemony Snicket Kale

2 Tbsp (30 mL) butter, preferably unsalted

2 Tbsp (30 mL) olive oil, divided

20 whole almonds

Salt to taste

A few grindings of pepper

1 small lemon

3 cups (700 mL) kale in chiffonade

2 cups (475 mL) sliced celery stalks from the heart (cut crosswise at an angle)

½ cup (125 mL) chopped celery leaves

½ cup (125 mL) chopped parsley

1 tsp (5 mL) lovage seeds or ¼ tsp (1 mL) celery seeds

Chopped leaves from a few sprigs of tarragon (optional)

2 tsp (10 mL) Demerara sugar

2 Tbsp (30 mL) lemon juice

1 tsp (5 mL) horseradish sauce

1 Tbsp (15 mL) tarragon or white wine vinegar

*vegan if butter is replaced with olive oil

Best use organic celery to make this tangy salad. We won't go on here about that devilish "Dirty Dozen" dripping in pesticides, as we don't want you to completely lose your appetite. You'll need a sharp knife to cut the lemon, and a mandoline for slicing the celery would be dandy; that way you can make it super thin. Use an assortment of kale, including some purple types for colour, such as Red Russian or Redbor.

Melt the butter in a smallish heavy pan, add 2 tsp (10 mL) of the oil and turn the heat to medium-low. Add the almonds and fry them, shaking the pan and stirring often, until they're lightly browned. Sprinkle with salt and pepper and shake or stir a few more times. Remove almonds with slotted spoon and place on a cutting board to cool. Set pan aside (don't wash it). When almonds are cool, chop them very coarsely.

Using your sharpest knife, remove the skin and white pith of the lemon. Cut the lemon in half lengthwise. Slice each half as thinly as possible.

Chop the kale and combine in a bowl with the celery, celery leaves, lemon slices, parsley, lovage seeds and tarragon.

Return pan to medium heat. Sprinkle sugar in the pan and stir for about 1 minute. Add the lemon juice, horseradish and vinegar, and stir well, scraping up caramelized bits.

Pour the warm pan mixture over the salad, then drizzle with the remaining olive oil and toss. Taste for seasoning, then let the salad rest for about 10 minutes.

Strew chopped almonds over the salad and serve.

MAKES 4 TO 6 SERVINGS

Arlene's Kale, Cauliflower & Sweet Potato Salad

1 sweet potato, cut into small cubes

2 cups (475 mL) small cauliflower florets

1 ripe but firm avocado, diced

1 red pepper, sliced into narrow strips

About 6 cups (1.4 L) kale in chiffonade

½ cup (125 mL) chopped chives or 4 green onions, chopped

¼ cup (60 mL) minced parsley

2 Tbsp (30 mL) olive oil

2 Tbsp (30 mL) red wine vinegar

2 tsp (10 mL) minced tarragon leaves

2 tsp (10 mL) minced thyme leaves

Juice of 1 lime

Salt to taste

A few grindings of pepper

Sharon's good friend Arlene Soloman lives in Kamloops, BC. Sharon met Arlene while working at West Coast Seeds. Arlene had called there looking for a video on growing greens for market production…back in the mid-1990s. Go-big-or-go-home Arlene took on the project fully, along with her husband and business partners. Their huge greenhouse supplied local restaurants and stores with ultra-fresh organic greens for many years. Arlene went on to create the herb garden for the chef's training program at Thompson Rivers University, as well as an ambitious medicine-wheel zero-mile-diet garden for a resort in Chase, BC. The yellow section of the wheel featured Sun Cherry yellow tomatoes, yellow zucchini, Hungarian yellow peppers and Teddy Bear sunflowers. And the green section featured…do we really need to say it? With regard to this colourful salad, Arlene says you can add chickpeas to up the protein, and/or garnish with toasted cashews.

Steam the sweet potato for about 5 minutes until cooked al dente—you don't want it to go mushy in the salad.

Steam cauliflower florets for just a few minutes to the tender-crisp stage. Rinse with cold water and drain.

Transfer sweet potato and cauliflower to a serving bowl and add avocado, red pepper, kale, chives and parsley.

Place remaining ingredients in a jar and shake, or whisk them together in a small bowl. Pour vinaigrette over salad, mix well and serve.

MAKES 4 TO 6 SERVINGS

Cool Quinoa Kale Salad

1½ cups (350 mL) quinoa, well rinsed

3 cups (700 mL) water, plus a pinch of salt

1 English or regular cucumber

1 large orange

4 cups (1 L) chopped kale

2 shallots, finely minced

1 red pepper, diced

1 cup (250 mL) finely chopped parsley

½ cup (125 mL) chopped dried cranberries

½ cup (125 mL) roughly chopped raisins

½ cup (125 mL) halved seedless grapes

Juice of 1 lemon

¼ cup (60 mL) raspberry vinaigrette

Firefighter Ryan Chinbo contributed this distinctive, healthy and juicy offering. He and co-workers at the District of North Vancouver Fire & Rescue, Station #1 in Lynn Valley, BC (some of whom are vegans), frequently prepare vegetarian and vegan dishes. You could add other berries in season—raspberries or strawberries would work well. Ryan cools the quinoa in the freezer while chopping the other ingredients, possibly because the fire bell might start dinging at any moment, so he has to work quickly. How exciting!

Cook quinoa in salted water. Bring almost to a boil, then cover the pot and simmer about 20 minutes until quinoa is tender and water is absorbed.

Dice cucumber. If using regular cucumber, cut in half and remove seeds first.

Peel and remove pith from orange, and dice.

Steam kale for 2 to 3 minutes, drain well and finely chop.

Place cooled quinoa and all other ingredients except the lemon juice and vinaigrette in a large bowl. Sprinkle lemon juice over all, dress with vinaigrette and toss well.

MAKES 4 SERVINGS

Garden Harvest Feast

1 cup (250 mL) quinoa, rinsed well

2 cups (475 mL) water, plus a pinch of salt

1 perfectly ripe avocado, cubed

2 cups (475 mL) kale in chiffonade

2 cups (475 mL) chopped spinach, Swiss chard or a mix

1 cup (250 mL) cooked black beans

1 cup (250 mL) organic corn niblets cut from a cob, or frozen corn niblets

½ cup (125 mL) snipped chives

½ cup (125 mL) chopped mint leaves

¼ cup (60 mL) chopped cilantro leaves and stems

A few chive blossoms, torn into little florets

A handful of arugula leaves

3 Tbsp (45 mL) olive oil

2 tsp (10 mL) rice or apple cider vinegar

Juice of 1 lime, 1 lemon and 1 orange

Salt to taste

A few grindings of pepper

When posted on *The Book of Kale*'s Facebook page, this dish was viewed 1,200 times in just hours. Called "Saturday Morning's Breakfast," it was in truth breakfast and lunch for several days. It's a playful salad to which you can add whatever—pretty much anything from your refrigerator produce drawer and what's ready to snip in your garden. Originally a June feast, this recipe contains many ingredients from the late-spring garden. If made in July or August, throw in fresh basil. This salad keeps for several days when chilled; however, it's best to add the tender greens like spinach, chard or arugula just before serving. Along with the chive florets, you could toss in a few yellow kale flowers, blue borage blossoms, calendula petals and/or nasturtiums if they're growing in your garden, and your salad will transform into a veritable work of food art.

Cook quinoa in salted water. Bring almost to a boil, then cover the pot and simmer about 20 minutes until quinoa is tender and water is absorbed. Transfer to a large bowl to cool.

When cool, combine quinoa with the avocado, kale, spinach, beans corn, herbs and arugula.

In another bowl, whisk together the oil, vinegar, citrus juices, salt and pepper. Pour dressing over the salad, mix well and serve.

MAKES 4 TO 6 SERVINGS

Herb Salad with Fennel, Chervil & Shiso

½ cup (125 mL) chopped tender herb fennel foliage

¼ cup (60 mL) purple basil leaves in chiffonade

¼ cup (60 mL) regular basil leaves in chiffonade

¼ cup (60 mL) snipped chives

2 Tbsp (30 mL) chervil

2–3 shiso leaves (preferably purple)

Lots of kale flowers

2 tsp (10 mL) white wine vinegar

1 Tbsp (15 mL) olive oil

2 tsp (10 mL) honey

2 pinches of salt

A few grindings of pepper

Large perfect leaves of kale (ideally Rainbow Lacinato)

* vegan if maple syrup is used rather than honey

Meant to be a smallish, appetite-stimulating taste, this salad is challenging because chervil is at its best in cool weather, and basil thrives in the heat. However, you may get lucky (see sidebar below), and if not, the salad will be fine without the chervil. *Perilla frutescens* (shiso leaf) is used in Japanese cooking and grows easily and attractively in warm weather, often self-seeding. If you wonder what that little plastic leaf is in your takeout sushi, it's an imitation shiso leaf. We love the dark purple variety with pink blossoms, and the bees love it too. This salad looks very pretty in glass salad bowls.

Combine herbs and kale flowers in a bowl. Whisk together vinegar, oil, honey, salt and pepper, drizzle mixture over the herbs and toss lightly. Serve over kale leaves.

MAKES 2 TO 3 APPETIZER SERVINGS

CHERVIL CHATTER

Sharon says: Carol seems to have bad luck growing this aromatic herb, yet it grows easily for me. It self-seeds and is pretty and delicate. Chervil grows well in part shade and cooler temperatures; in my (messy, rarely gets weeded) garden, it thrives from February through the first occurrence of fairly intense heat in May, when it shoots up and goes to seed. In the fall it grows again, until a hard frost.

Carol says: I trust Sharon on this one, but my chervil plants are usually a cranky red colour, which she tells me happens when they get too hot. I tried planting the seeds in little pots, but Sharon told me that chervil resents transplanting. Next time I try to grow this very cantankerous herb, I will sow the seeds directly somewhere cool and damp—maybe in the shadier "grotto" where I grow ferns outside a basement window.

Sharon says: Though it's not included as one of our hardy, dependable workhorse herbs, you really should give chervil a go. It is one of the ingredients in fines herbes (see page 86), a staple in the cooking of Provence, France. Its cross-between-mild-licorice-and-parsley flavour complements fish, chicken, eggs, salads and other dishes.

Goats in Boats

3 garlic cloves, skin on

2 cups (475 mL) kale

¾ cup (180 mL) goat's cheese

2 tsp (10 mL) honey

1 tsp (5 mL) minced thyme leaves, plus a few thyme sprigs for garnish

Salt to taste

A few grindings of pepper

1 navel or other common type of orange

2 blood oranges

4 medium-sized Belgian endives

A composed winter salad, made when oranges are in season—heaven when you use your own kale that has been kissed by frost to make it even sweeter. Use restraint with the thyme: just a whiff in the kale mixture or the delicate flavours will be overwhelmed. If you don't have thyme in the garden, use a few finely minced rosemary leaves. If you don't have either of those, borrow from a neighbour this time, but get some growing in the garden (see pages 54 and 58)!

Boil the garlic cloves in a small saucepan of water for 5–6 minutes until tender; drain and allow to cool a little. Peel the garlic and transfer to food processor. Add kale leaves, goat's cheese, honey, thyme, salt and pepper. Pulse 4 or 5 times until kale is pulverized.

Halve the regular orange; squeeze the juice to make about ½ cup (125 mL). Drizzle orange juice slowly through feed tube of processor to thin the kale mixture, stopping when it's creamy but not runny. Taste for seasoning, remembering that the flavour will intensify, so don't go overboard.

Using a sharp knife, peel the blood oranges, removing a thin layer of the membrane. Carefully separate oranges into sections.

Trim endives and separate leaves. Arrange on a platter or individual plates, fanned out like flower petals, in a line or in whatever pattern strikes your fancy. Place orange sections atop the endive leaves. Drizzle with the kale mixture, making a pool or two on the platter or plates as well. Garnish with leaves from the thyme sprigs.

MAKES 4 SERVINGS

Salade d'Hiver

VG **GF**

About 6 cups (1.4 L) kale in chiffonade

1 oz (about 30 g) piece of frozen Stilton or other blue cheese

1 sweet apple (skin on)

½ cup (125 mL) chopped walnuts

2 Tbsp (30 mL) olive oil

While visiting last Christmas, Veronica (see page 85) wanted to introduce her mother, Mary, to kale and brought a lovely bouquet of Tuscan kale. Veronica writes:

"Let's have a kale salad," says I, and I began to cut the kale into thin strips. "Do you have any walnuts, Mom?" My mother produced walnuts she'd gathered from a tree in the neighbour's yard. "How about a strong cheese?"

She replied, "Blue, in the freezer, it never goes bad there."

I was mortified to see a very expensive block of Stilton cheese had been frozen. Unfazed, Mom handed me a microplane grater that worked like a charm—fluffy shavings of cheese fell on the strips of kale. I found a Golden Delicious apple and used the grater to create a pulpy juice that acted as a dressing for the kale and Stilton. We tossed in a handful of the walnuts and…perfection! We had a simple winter salad that had appeared like stone soup.

Put kale in a serving bowl.

Using the fine holes of a box grater (or a microplane), grate the frozen cheese over the kale, and toss a few times.

Grate the apple, skin on, onto the salad and toss again, then scatter the walnuts over.

Drizzle with a little olive oil and serve.

MAKES 2 TO 3 SERVINGS

Warm Potato Salad with Kale & Crema di Balsamico

About 2 lb (1 kg) medium-sized new potatoes (ideally homegrown)

8 cups (2 L) water

1 Tbsp (15 mL) salt

3 Tbsp (45 mL) olive oil, divided

1 Tbsp (15 mL) butter

⅓ cup (80 mL) minced shallots

1 large garlic clove, minced

2 Tbsp (30 mL) crema di balsamico (see sidebar page 77)

2 tsp (10 mL) grainy mustard

½ tsp (2.5 mL) salt or to taste

A few generous grindings of pepper

1½ cups (350 mL) kale in chiffonade

1½ cups (350 mL) mixed soft herbs—parsley, mint, chives, oregano, chervil, basil or whatever is in season

*gluten free if gluten-free mustard is used

The method of cooking the potatoes is adapted from *Cook's Illustrated*. With this technique, the slices remain intact and there's no need to handle hot potatoes. We suggest using soft herbs, but if you use any stronger-flavoured woody herbs like thyme or rosemary, go easy—add just a few finely chopped leaves so as not to overwhelm the salad.

Slice potatoes (skin on) about ¼ in (0.5 cm) thick. Bring water to a boil and add 1 Tbsp (15 mL) salt (that's a lot of salt, but you won't taste it) and potatoes, and cook for about 4 minutes or until they are al dente when pierced with a fork. Drain potatoes, reserving ¼ cup (60 mL) of the cooking water. Set potatoes aside to cool a little.

Heat 1 Tbsp (15 mL) of the oil with the butter in a small heavy-bottomed skillet over low heat. Add shallots and stir-fry until they are soft and aromatic—about 4 to 5 minutes. Add the garlic and cook another minute or so. Add the crema di balsamico, mustard, salt, pepper, remaining olive oil and reserved cooking water. Cook mixture down for another few minutes, then remove pan from heat.

In a large bowl, toss together kale and herbs, then add potatoes and the warm dressing, being mindful to not disturb potato slices. Gently and carefully transfer to a large low platter or pasta bowl, and serve immediately.

MAKES 4 SERVINGS

SOUPS

Making Stock (Carol's Soup Tirade)

Use any amount of fresh or previously washed and frozen "kitchen scraps," from the list on the opposite page.

Poultry or meat, including bones (optional)

Water

Salt or soy sauce

If you include bones, add a splash of vinegar to the stock to draw the calcium from them.

*vegan if prepared without optional chicken or meat scraps; gluten free if gluten-free soy sauce or liquid aminos are used

Growing our own means we don't want to waste one darned leaf when harvesting from our gardens, so in Carol's kitchen, any morsel too rough-looking for other recipes is rinsed and frozen for soup stock. When the house gets chilly come fall, a simmering pot of stock on the stovetop keeps the kitchen snug and everyone who enters is fed with soul-satisfying, immune-boosting broth.

But... you might be saying... aren't you supposed to avoid putting anything from the brassica family into soup stock if you really want it to taste good? Some cookbooks do advise against adding brassicas to stock, but don't worry. Kale is great in stock if it and any other brassicas constitute only about a third of the ingredients in your pot. You can also throw in the outer leaves of cabbage, chard or broccoli. Don't waste a speck of the vitamin-loaded, disease-fighting brassicas!

Place all ingredients except seasonings in a large pot, and fill it to a few inches from the top with cold water. Bring to a vigorous boil and then simmer for up to 2 hours.

Add seasonings to taste.

When the stock is aromatic and flavourful, turn off the heat. Cooking longer will not improve the taste and can diminish it.

Cool for a few hours and then strain so that you are left with a clear golden liquid. If the stock contained meat, after refrigerating stock overnight, remove any fat from the top.

Once cooled, refrigerate for up to 5 days or freeze in bottles, leaving a good couple of inches of head space to allow for expansion.

STOCK UP!

Throughout the winter, use stock as a nourishing liquid when making rice or quinoa dishes, sauces and gravies, in addition to using it as a base for your favourite consommé or chowder.

Sharon says: Sometimes Carol gets on a bit of a tirade about not wasting one scruffy kale leaf. Okay, it might be the healthiest vegetable on the planet, but if you don't have time to make stock, it's *okay* to just put your vegetable scraps in the compost! That kale nourishment will just come around again in your next garden crop.

STOCK OPTIONS

When choosing from this list, try to keep a balance between brassicas, oniony elements and other milder vegetables:

- Every precious pinch of kale deemed too rough or tough for serving—leaves, stems, green seedpods, even flowers.
- Garlic stalks, scapes, bulbils and cloves, peel and all—any bit of the garlic plant adds flavour and healthy benefits.
- Sorrel—add just a little for extra antioxidants and taste.
- Chives—cut down any tough stems and flowers in your garden so that your chives renew themselves with fresh growth for salads and garnishes.
- Leathery layers from leeks—when washing leeks, separate the layers, as they can trap soil.
- Onion skins and ends—they may look rough but these kitchen cast-offs add fabulous flavour as well as appetizing colour to broth.
- Peelings—save the skins of your organic carrots or potatoes; just make sure you scrub prior to paring, as the peelings are hard to wash!
- Tomato ends—if you will be turning the stock into Mediterranean-inspired minestrone, add all the tomato leftovers on hand (plus any basil scraps); if you're going for Japanese udon soup, use just a few.
- Celery and/or lovage—use up any stringy celery leavings or throw in a leaf or two of lovage (but no more, as it's strong-tasting).
- Pea pods and green-bean ends.
- Carrot, turnip, beet, kohlrabi and radish tops.
- Corn cobs—after you've cut off the niblets, chop the cob and pitch it in.
- Going-to-seed parsley, parcel (also called leaf celery), cilantro, arugula, chervil or any other bolting salad green—collect seeds to sow another crop, and then rinse and chop up the plant.
- Pre-infestation veggies—if you see the white cabbage butterfly moving in on your garden brassicas during the summer months, snip off a bunch of the leaves in advance of their becoming infested and freeze what you can't use right away. Eventually, the caterpillars will disappear and new leaves will pop up on your mostly picked plants. Meanwhile, you've stocked up your freezer for winter.
- Chickweed, wild sorrel and (just a few) dandelion greens—yes, you can eat the edible weeds from your organic garden—we do!

Udon Soup Bar

Soup stock

Salt (or Bragg Liquid Aminos or soy sauce)

Udon or Asian-style rice noodles

A selection of the following:

Kale in chiffonade (lots of this!)

Kale microgreens

Sliced vegetables such as broccoli, carrots, peas, peppers and mushrooms

Chives, chopped

Green onion, chopped

Parsley, chopped

Chervil, chopped

Shiso, chopped

Garlic scapes and/or greens, chopped

Thyme leaves (just a few)

Oregano leaves (just a few)

Sliced precooked chicken or other meat, or chicken or turkey sausage

Bragg Liquid Aminos or soy sauce

Sesame oil

Chili flakes

*vegan if prepared with vegetarian stock and without optional meat; gluten free if gluten-free rice noodles and gluten-free soy sauce or liquid aminos are used

Once you have a rich soup stock on hand, it's easy to dish up dinner in a flash. A quick and healthy meal that kids love is an udon soup bar. Just line up your choice of ingredients on a counter, heat and season the stock, and boil noodles for a nourishing and fun family feast. Let everyone fill a bowl with their choice of ingredients, then ladle on the hot stock, which will par-cook the vegetables in the bowl so that they are tender and warm but still crispy and fresh-tasting.

Slowly heat up a large pot of stock while you wash and chop the vegetables, herbs and cooked meat, and display them smorgasbord-style. Season the stock to just the right degree of saltiness.

When everything is almost ready, cook noodles according to package directions in a separate pot of stock (for rich-tasting noodles) or water.

Have ready large soup bowls, soup spoons and chopsticks. Encourage all your soup enthusiasts to fill a bowl with their choice of ingredients, ladle steaming stock over top and season as they like with Bragg Liquid Aminos or soy sauce, sesame oil and chili flakes. Dinner is served!

2 CUPS (475 ML) STOCK AND 2 CUPS (475 ML) INGREDIENTS MAKES ONE HEARTY DINNER

If small children are dishing up, allow a little extra time for them pick out the ingredients they want, then ladle on the hot stock for them and set their bowls aside to cool for a few minutes before they dig in.

Kail Yard Soup

2 Tbsp (30 mL) vegetable oil or butter

1 large onion, chopped

2 large or 3 medium floury potatoes, peeled and chopped

6 cups (1.4 L) rich soup stock

About 4 cups (1 L) chopped kale

Salt to taste

A few grindings of pepper

Grated cheese (optional)

*vegan if oil is used instead of butter, vegetarian soup stock is used and optional cheese is omitted

For a simple soup, Scottish folk in days of old would have harvested the tatties (potatoes), as well as the kale, from their kail yard (food garden). By floury potatoes we mean keeper-type potatoes like Russet or Yukon Gold, not "new" potatoes. If you want to be authentic, use Winterbor or another curly Scottish variety of kale. Barley might have been used in soup like this to thicken it and make it stretch enough to feed big families. With some bread cooked over the fire and homemade ale, this soup would have constituted many a meal. A wee dram, anyone? The broth makes it—so try to use homemade rich stock of some kind, whether it be vegetable, chicken or other beastie. In those days, it would likely have been mutton broth. To tart it up, grate a little hard cheese or Scottish cheddar over the soup before serving.

Heat the oil in a heavy-bottomed stockpot on medium heat, add the onion, stirring, and stir-fry for a few minutes.

Add the potatoes, and stir-fry a little more.

Pour in the stock, turn down the heat, half-cover the pot and simmer until potatoes are almost tender—about 10 minutes.

Add the kale and continue to simmer until kale is tender but still green. If the soup appears too thick, add a little water.

Season with salt and pepper. Sprinkle cheese on top (if using).

MAKES 4 SERVINGS

Kale-a-Leekie Soup

2 Tbsp (30 mL) each olive oil and butter

3 cups (700 mL) chopped leeks

2 big or 3 medium potatoes, diced

5 cups (1.2 L) vegetable or chicken stock

3 cups (700 mL) chopped kale

1–2 pinches of cayenne

Juice of 1 lemon

Salt to taste

A few grindings of pepper

Chopped parsley for garnish

*vegan if vegetable stock rather than chicken stock is used and butter is omitted

Easy as can be. Just don't add the kale too soon lest it becomes brackish looking and therefore a bit on the unappetizing side, although it still tastes good. We learned how to clean leeks from watching celebrity chef Jacques Pépin cut them almost through lengthwise, then run cold water over the opened-up leeks to wash away any soil between the layers.

In a heavy-bottomed soup pot, heat oil and butter over medium heat. Add leeks and sauté for about 5 minutes, stirring often, until leeks are slightly transparent. Add potatoes and continue to sauté another 5 minutes, stirring. Pour in the stock, cover the pot and bring mixture almost to a boil; turn heat to low. Simmer until potatoes are tender, about 10 more minutes.

Add the kale, cayenne pepper and lemon juice, as well as a little water should the soup seem too thick. Continue to simmer just until kale is tender.

Season with salt and pepper. Serve the soup sprinkled with chopped parsley.

MAKES 3 TO 4 SERVINGS

Garlicky Kale Zucchini Zuppa

2 Tbsp (30 mL) olive oil

10 garlic cloves, roughly chopped

1 large sweet onion, chopped

8 cups (2 L) vegetable or chicken stock

8 cups (2 L) puréed fresh tomatoes (with or without skins; see page 171) or canned tomatoes

¼ cup (60 mL) basil purée (from 1½ cups/350 mL fresh basil plus a little olive oil)

1 Tbsp (15 mL) chopped oregano leaves

1 Tbsp (15 mL) thyme leaves

¼ cup (60 mL) tomato paste with garlic (optional)

3–4 small to medium zucchini, sliced into small pieces

4 cups (1 L) chopped kale

1 cup (250 mL) chopped parsley

1 cup (250 mL) cooked white beans, rinsed

Salt to taste

A few grindings of pepper

½ cup (125 mL) cooked quinoa (optional)

Grated cheese and chopped chives for garnish

*vegan if vegetable stock is used and cheese is omitted

This thick and nourishing soup feeds Carol's family three nights in a row during a busy week. There are a couple of secrets to this soup: (1) Do *not* skimp on the basil or garlic (and, yes, we really do use 10 big cloves) and (2) drizzle each bowl with fresh high-quality olive oil and top with freshly ground black pepper and some grated Parmigiano, Asiago or cheddar cheese.

In a large pot, heat olive oil and sauté garlic and onion until soft but not brown.

Add the stock, puréed tomatoes, basil purée, oregano and thyme. Bring mixture to a boil and then simmer for 5 minutes. Taste to see if the broth is flavourful enough. This will depend on the richness of the stock and ripeness of the tomatoes. If it needs more flavour, whisk ¼ cup (60 mL) tomato paste into a cup of the hot broth and then add the mixture to the pot. Taste again and add more paste if needed.

Add zucchini, kale, parsley and cooked beans. Simmer, allowing soup to bubble gently, for 5 minutes. Season with salt and pepper.

If you want to add cooked quinoa, toss it into the pot now and heat through, but only if all the soup will be eaten that day. If you're planning to have leftovers, add the quinoa to each bowl of soup when served.

Serve each bowl sprinkled with chives, pepper, grated cheese and a drizzle of olive oil.

DINNER FOR A CROWD

PITCH IN YOUR HEELS

By heels, we mean the ends of hard cheeses, such as Parmigiano or other cheeses suitable for grating, that have accumulated in your fridge and now are too dry to grate. The good news is you can add them to soups—particularly minestrone, vegetable soups or the recipe above (but not udon or other Asian-inspired recipes).

Chickpea Purée with Kale Buds

VE * **GF**

3 Tbsp (45 mL) oil

3–4 garlic cloves, roughly chopped

1 large or 2 small onions, chopped

Generous splash of good white wine

2×19-oz (540-mL) cans chickpeas, drained and rinsed

6 cups (1.4 L) vegetable or chicken stock

Kale buds—6 per bowl

Minced herbs—thyme, parsley, mint, chives—for garnish

Salt to taste

A few grindings of pepper

Freshly squeezed lemon juice

*vegan if vegetable stock is used

Here's how to use those darling buds of May (or April or June). If you want, you can cook your own dried chickpeas, in which case you'll need about 1⅓ cups (330 mL) water, plus an extra hour or so to cook them. The wine isn't imperative but makes the dish fancier. Like many soups, this one tastes better if made a day before serving, but wait until the last minute to steam the kale buds.

Heat oil in a heavy pot over medium heat. Sauté garlic and onions for about 10 minutes—do not allow them to brown. Stir frequently until onions are translucent. Add wine, turn up the heat a little, and cook for 3 to 4 minutes, then add chickpeas and stock. Bring mixture almost to a boil, cover, and simmer for about 30 minutes. Remove from heat.

If you're serving the soup now, it's time to harvest the kale buds and fresh herbs. Give them a brief rinse. Finely chop herbs and ensure that the kale buds are in bite-sized pieces.

Purée the soup (see our sidebar on Puréeing Soups Safely on page 148). If you prefer, leave some of the soup unblended so it has a bit of texture. Before serving, reheat and add seasonings.

Gently steam kale buds for a few minutes (use the cooking water if you want to thin the soup a titch), then run under very cold water to stop the cooking process and keep them bright green.

Ladle out the soup, float the kale buds on top, strew with chopped herbs and drizzle lemon juice over all.

MAKES 4 SERVINGS

Uprising Breads Kale & Lentil Dahl

2 cups (475 mL) orange lentils

3 or 4 garlic cloves, chopped

Small knob of ginger root, minced

3 Tbsp (45 mL) olive oil

2 tsp (10 mL) cumin seeds

Pinch or 2 of chili flakes

1 large onion, chopped

½ tsp (2.5 mL) ground cardamom

Scant 1 Tbsp (15 mL) ground turmeric

8 cups (2 L) vegetable stock

14-oz (398-mL) can tomatoes, chopped, or a couple of chopped tomatoes

2 large sweet potatoes or yams, diced (about 1 lb/454 g)

4 cups (1 L) chopped kale

Juice of 1 lemon

Scant 1 tsp (5 mL) salt or to taste

½ tsp (2.5 mL) ground pepper

½ cup (125 mL) chopped cilantro for garnish

Make sure you go outside (maybe to harvest the cilantro?) while this soup is cooking so you can come back inside and inhale the aroma of your kitchen! No need to peel the sweet potatoes. This is our favourite soup at Uprising Breads Bakery, a long-standing institution on the east side of Vancouver, BC, where they use spinach instead of kale and offer all kinds of excellent bread and baked goodies. Use a little ginger or a lot, depending on how you feel about ginger.

Rinse lentils 3 times, put in a bowl and cover with water; set aside.

In a soup pot over low heat, fry garlic and ginger in the olive oil with cumin seeds and chili flakes for 3 to 4 minutes. Add onion and sauté until softened.

Add cardamom and turmeric, and stir-fry a little longer, then pour in the vegetable stock and tomatoes. Simmer for 15 minutes.

Add the lentils and sweet potatoes and continue to cook until both are almost tender—about 15 to 20 minutes.

Toss in the kale and simmer for 5 to 6 minutes more, or until kale is tender but still green.

Add lemon juice, salt and pepper.

Garnish with chopped cilantro.

MAKES 16 CUPS (4 L)

Roasted Garlic & Carrot Soup with Brie

2 Tbsp (30 mL) butter or oil

4 cups (1 L) roughly chopped carrots

12–18 garlic cloves, skin on

6 cups (1.4 L) chicken or vegetable stock, or water

1 Tbsp (15 mL) tomato paste

2 pinches cayenne

Salt to taste

A few grindings of pepper

Scant 4 oz (about 100 g) brie cheese, in small pieces

½ cup (125 mL) cream

Finely chopped parsley for garnish

*vegetarian if vegetable stock or water is used instead of chicken stock

Use young carrots for this soup and not yucky old bulk ones. Don't you hate it when a recipe calls for "1 Tbsp tomato paste"? We did until finding tomato paste in a squeeze tube that lasts in the fridge for ages. Phytonutrients like alpha- and beta-carotene, as well as lutein and several anthocyanins in the carrots, need fat to be absorbed properly by the body, and this soup does a dandy job of fulfilling that requirement. To cut calories, you can use light rather than heavy cream, or take the dog out for an extra long walk.

Heat oven to 450F (230C) and melt the butter on a lipped cookie sheet or baking pan. Add carrots and garlic cloves, and use a wooden spoon to coat them with the butter. Return pan to the oven; roast vegetables for 15 minutes or until lightly browned, shaking the pan and stirring once in a while.

Remove garlic skins.

Transfer carrots and garlic to a heavy lidded saucepan. Add stock, tomato paste, cayenne and a little salt and pepper. Bring mixture to a boil, then half-cover the pot and simmer for about 20 minutes until carrots are tender. Add the brie pieces, then remove saucepan from heat. Purée the soup (see our sidebar on Puréeing Soups Safely on page 148). Return it to saucepan and heat gently, add the cream and taste for seasoning. Garnish with parsley and serve in shallow soup bowls, preferably white ones for a pretty presentation.

MAKES 4 TO 6 SERVINGS

Celery Soup with Lovage & Chives

About 6 cups (1.4 L) chopped celery, inner stalks and tender leaves only

Scant 3 Tbsp (45 mL) butter

3 medium-sized firm potatoes such as Yukon Gold, peeled and sliced

2 Tbsp (30 mL) chopped lovage leaves

5 cups (1.2 L) chicken or vegetable stock

2 Tbsp (30 mL) chopped chives, plus extra for garnish

½ tsp (2.5 mL) salt (optional)

A few grindings of pepper

½ cup (125 mL) heavy cream

A few young lovage leaves for garnish

*vegetarian if vegetable stock is used instead of chicken stock

Since the potage is puréed, don't worry about how you chop the veggies.

In a heavy-bottomed pot, sauté the celery stalks in butter over medium-low heat for about 6 to 7 minutes or until slightly soft. Add the celery leaves, potatoes and lovage, and stir-fry for 5 to 6 minutes.

Pour in the stock and bring to a low boil. Turn the heat down and simmer, stirring occasionally, for about 30 minutes or until potatoes are very tender. If the mixture seems too thick, add a little water.

Add 2 Tbsp (30 mL) chopped chives, salt and pepper, and remove pot from heat. Purée the soup (see our sidebar below). Return soup to pot and, when ready to serve, reheat. Ladle soup into bowls, and top (artistically) with a little cream, a lovage leaf and some chopped chives.

MAKES 6 STARTER SERVINGS OR 4 LUNCH OR DINNER SERVINGS

PURÉEING SOUPS SAFELY

When puréeing soups, especially hot ones, be careful, and follow these important safety tips, some of which we had to learn the messy way!

Immersion blender: Basically a stick with a blade on the end, this is the preferred tool for puréeing hot soups. Use it to blend directly in the pot, keeping the blade and blade hood entirely immersed to avoid splattering. Turn the immersion blender on and off only when the blade is completely submerged. Use this tool to purée soups that fill the pot less than halfway—a metal pot taller than it is wide is ideal. If handling the blade for any reason, *always* unplug the tool.

Blender: This tool is fine for liquefying or puréeing thin mixtures. We recommend you allow hot liquids to cool before blending. If you *do* blend hot liquids in a blender, fill it *less than halfway* and vent the lid to allow steam to escape; otherwise the hot liquid could splatter you and your kitchen—dangerous and very messy! Always place a dish towel over the open vent to ensure you are not splashed, start blending at a slow setting and build up speed gradually to the desired level.

Green Bean Soup with Lemon Chive Butter

1 garlic clove, chopped

½ cup (125 mL) chopped chives

⅓ cup (80 mL) unsalted butter

Pinch of salt

Zest and juice of 1 lemon

2 Tbsp (30 mL) unsalted butter

1 onion, chopped

3 generous cups (700 mL, or about 1½ lb/650 g) trimmed, chopped green beans

5 cups (1.2 L) chicken stock or very good rich vegetable stock

½ tsp (2.5 mL) salt or to taste

1 cup (250 mL) whipping cream or light cream

A few grindings of pepper

A few snipped chives for garnish

*vegetarian if vegetable stock is used instead of chicken stock

This soup is a velvety, luxurious proffering for a special meal. If you're not in a soup mood, try the butter alone: put lashings of it onto steamed green (or yellow or purple) beans, enjoy on grilled halibut or salmon, or brush on a chicken before roasting.

To make lemon chive butter, combine garlic, chives, ⅓ cup (80 mL) unsalted butter, salt, and lemon zest and juice in a blender or food processor and process until smooth; set aside.

In a heavy-bottomed pot, melt 2 Tbsp (30 mL) unsalted butter over medium heat, add onion and sauté for about 6 minutes until tender and fragrant. Add the green beans and cook, stirring, for about 5 minutes.

Add the chicken stock and salt. Bring to a boil, reduce heat and simmer until beans are tender, about 15 minutes.

Purée the soup (see sidebar on page 148). Return soup to the pot, add cream, heat thoroughly and season with pepper.

Bring out your best bowls or fancy soup cups. Ladle out the soup, and spoon a little chive butter on top. Garnish with snipped chives.

MAKES 4 SERVINGS

Gail's French Sorrel & Chive Soup

2 Tbsp (30 mL) butter

1 smallish onion, finely chopped

2 cups (475 mL) sorrel leaves in chiffonade

1 very large floury potato or 2 medium-sized, peeled and diced

Scant 4 cups (1 L) water

Salt to taste

A few grindings of pepper

1 egg yolk

2 Tbsp (30 mL) heavy cream

¼ cup (60 mL) very finely snipped chives

Sharon's friend Gail Davidson has an old cookbook, *French Cooking for Pleasure*, published in 1966. Many pages are stained from use; there are child-markings in crayon, as Gail raised four children, mostly as a single mother, while putting herself through law school. How, you might ask, did she have time to make Salmon Coulibac (a many-layered pâté en croûte, croûte made from scratch), Chicken Marengo, Beef Wellington and French Sorrel Soup? No computer, that's how; instead of Facebooking, she was cooking. The next time you say (or think), "I'm too busy to cook," think about Gail and *French Cooking for Pleasure*. Serve her soup with wonderful bread.

Melt butter in a saucepan, add onion and sauté over low heat until softened and sweet, about 8 minutes. Add sorrel and continue to cook for another 3 minutes. Add potatoes, water, salt and pepper. Cover and simmer for about 20 minutes until potatoes are tender; remove saucepan from heat.

If you have a tureen, fill it with boiling water and allow the tureen to heat up for a few minutes. Discard water, and beat egg yolk and cream together in the warmed tureen. Add the soup. Garnish with chives.

MAKES 2 SERVINGS

> **Carol says:** Although Sharon thinks I am a bit of a know-it-all about cutting back chives to keep them growing (see page 112), I didn't realize the same strategy works for French sorrel—a perennial like chives—until I learned this from author Christine Allen while editing her delightful book *A Year at Killara Farm*. In the introduction to her recipe for Salmon Fishcakes with Sorrel Sauce, Christine says, "Sorrel is one of my favourite greens. Lush and vigorous for much of the year, it gives me a few leaves to add to a salad even in the depths of December. As a sauce it complements fish better than any other herb, even tarragon, which is hard to beat."

Pea & Lettuce Potage with Mint

1 medium-large onion, chopped

3 Tbsp (45 mL) butter

⅔ head green leaf lettuce,*
chopped (about 2 packed
cups /450 mL)

3 cups (700 mL) water, divided

3 cups (700 mL) peas, plus a
dozen peas for garnish

3 Tbsp (45 mL) chopped young
mint leaves, plus a few small
mint leaves for garnish

2 pinches of salt

A few grindings of pepper

A dot of butter or good splash
of cream for garnish (optional)

*The lettuce must be green—
not red or any other colour!

This recipe from Diana Batts sounds too simple—as well as odd—to be amazing, but it is. Says Miss D. about the soup:

> *Twenty years ago, my granny, Poppy Davenport, and I were taken for a delicious meal by her wonderful neighbours Sir Lewis and Lady Elspeth Robertson. The table at La Potinière in East Lothian near Edinburgh, Scotland, was booked a year in advance, because the restaurant was such a busy place! I fell in love with this Potage Saint-Germain and am still amazed that the owners generously shared the recipe. It is always a hit at dinner parties.*

In a medium heavy-bottomed pot, sauté onion in butter over low heat. Do not brown. Add the lettuce, and sauté for 1 minute while stirring. Add half the water and simmer for 20 minutes. Purée lettuce mixture (see our sidebar on Puréeing Soups Safely on page 148) and transfer to a bowl.

Using the same pot, bring remaining water to a boil. Add the peas and cook for 3 to 4 minutes.

Purée peas, cooking water and mint. Combine with lettuce mixture in pot. Season with salt and pepper, and keep warm.

Serve the soup as is, or dotted with butter or drizzled with a little heavy cream (if using). Garnish with the remaining peas and a small mint leaf or two.

MAKES 4 SERVINGS

Fresh Tomato Soup with Beaucoup de Basil

3 Tbsp (45 mL) olive oil

2 Tbsp (30 mL) butter

2 medium or 1 big yellow onion, chopped

6 garlic cloves, roughly chopped

⅓ cup (80 mL) dry white wine*

½ cup (125 mL) water

About 8 cups (2 L) chopped skinless ripe tomatoes

1 tsp (5 mL) kosher or other good salt

½ tsp (2.5 mL) pepper

1 cup (250 mL) basil leaves, plus more for garnish

⅓ cup (80 mL) heavy cream (optional), plus more for garnish

*No plonk, a.k.a. swill

*vegan if optional cream is omitted and butter is replaced with additional olive oil

You are going to blend this soup one way or another, so don't worry about cutting veggies finely. You can leave the skins on but we find it oddly satisfying to skin the tomatoes (see sidebar on page 171). Almost as good without the cream, just not as rich so you can eat more.

Heat olive oil and butter in a heavy-bottomed stockpot over medium-high heat. Add onion and cook, stirring frequently, for about 8 minutes or until onion is translucent but not brown.

Add garlic, turn down the heat a little, and cook for another 3 minutes. Pour in the wine, cook for another 5 minutes, then add the water, tomatoes, salt and pepper. Simmer for another 5 or so minutes, then remove from heat.

If you prefer your soup with chunky bits, remove a cupful and set aside.

Purée the soup (see our sidebar on Puréeing Soups Safely on page 148). If the soup is still warm, let it cool—this is important to do before adding the basil or it might turn an unappetizing colour.

Add the basil, blend for 1 or 2 seconds, then stir in any soup that was reserved.

Pour the cream (if using) into a small bowl, and add a ladleful of the tomato mixture to the bowl. Stir lightly, then pour into the pot—warming the cream first prevents it from curdling when added to the soup. Gently heat the soup but don't let it boil.

Strew with basil leaves and perhaps an extra drizzle of cream.

MAKES 4 TO 6 SERVINGS

A SEEDY NOTE

If your tomatoes contain a lot of seeds, you might want to remove most or at least some of them, as they contribute a bitter flavour to the soup.

Cucumber Herb Gazpacho with Bunny Tails

About 1 cup (250 mL) cubed English cucumber (about ½ smallish cucumber)

2 tsp (10 mL) very good olive oil

Pinch of salt

1 Tbsp (15 mL) fresh lemon juice

A few gratings of lemon zest

1 Tbsp (15 mL) minced chives

2 mint leaves, plus more for garnish

2 new fennel "bunny tails," plus fennel florets or foliage for garnish

Thinly sliced red bell pepper for garnish

A cooling, tonic soup brightened by fresh lemon juice, made in minutes. If you tell kids that the new growth on fennel is a "bunny tail," they might even eat this soup, especially if you let them harvest the tails! Add or vary herbs as they are available in the garden, but avoid strong woody ones like thyme and rosemary, which would overpower the cucumber. The quantity is for one serving—multiply by how many folks will be imbibing.

Put the cucumber, oil, salt, and lemon juice and zest into a food processor or blender, and process until smooth.

Add the chives, mint and fennel, and pulse once or twice so that the herbs remain a little bit distinct.

Chill for at least 2 hours. Garnish with a few small mint leaves, fennel florets or foliage and bell pepper.

MAKES ABOUT 1 CUP (250 ML)

Cold Hot-Pink Soup with Purple Basil

3 cups (700 mL) chopped firm seedless watermelon, divided

1 cup (250 mL) chopped seeded ripe tomatoes

1 small jalapeño, seeded, white ribs removed

Juice of 1 good-sized lime

3 Tbsp (45 mL) very good olive oil

1 Tbsp (15 mL) rice vinegar

¼ cup (60 mL) roughly chopped sweet onion (Walla Walla or Vidalia are good choices)

¼ cup (60 mL) roughly chopped cilantro leaves, stems and roots

Pinch of cayenne

⅓ cup (80 mL) crumbled goat's cheese (optional)

Small piece of raw beet, grated very finely, for garnish

Purple basil leaves for garnish

*vegan if optional cheese is omitted

Fancy, good for you, easy. Almost everything goes into the blender—and feel free to add a little more or a little less of anything. If the limes are miserly with their juice, use two. Great for summer lunch on the terrace (Sharon's been watching too many British dramas), for company as a starter or between courses. Or just make it for yourself and eat the whole thing. Watermelon and tomato seem strange bedfellows but they are not—you'll see. You can leave out the cheese but the creaminess adds…creaminess and smoothes out the flavours.

Put 1 cup (250 mL) of the chopped watermelon, tomatoes, jalapeño, lime juice, olive oil and rice vinegar into the blender or food processor. Pulse until smoothish, add the onion, cilantro and cayenne, and pulse 2 or 3 times.

Transfer to a bowl or glass serving dish and fold in the rest of the watermelon pieces.

Garnish with goat's cheese (if using), a smidgen of grated beet and purple basil leaves.

MAKES 4 STARTER SERVINGS, MORE AS AN AMUSE-BOUCHE

VEGETABLE DISHES & SIDES

Five Yummy Ways to Sauté Kale & Garlic

Take note that if your kale has been frozen in the garden, it will become tender after less time in the skillet. And if the weather is chilly and you just don't feel like salad tonight, here are five fabulous recipes for sautéed kale with garlic.

GF ## Pancetta, Garlic & Herbs

2 Tbsp (30 mL) olive oil

⅓ cup (80 mL) diced pancetta

1 shallot, minced

Garlic cloves, chopped

2 tsp (10 mL) chopped thyme leaves

2 tsp (10 mL) chopped rosemary leaves

1 bay leaf

8 cups (2 L) chopped kale, rinsed but not dried

2 tsp (10 mL) balsamic vinegar

⅓ cup (80 mL) stock or water

Scant ½ tsp (2.5 mL) salt

A few grindings of pepper

¼ cup (60 mL) chopped parsley for garnish

Deep, rich and green, with the earthy punch of aromatic herbs. The pairing of kale with pancetta is a classic, but you can substitute bacon for the pancetta if you prefer. Use as many or as few garlic cloves as you like.

Heat olive oil in a large skillet fitted with a lid, over medium heat. Fry the pancetta, stirring frequently, until cooked through; add shallot and continue to sauté over medium-low heat for about 2 minutes.

Add the garlic, thyme, rosemary and bay leaf and sauté for another 3 or so minutes, then increase the heat to medium-high.

Add the kale and stir-fry for about 3 minutes until well coated with pan ingredients. Add the vinegar, stock, salt and pepper. Cover the pan, lower the heat a little and continue to cook—kale should be gently bubbling—until it is tender, about 8 minutes. Transfer to a serving dish, garnish with chopped parsley and serve.

MAKES 4 SERVINGS

VE **GF**

Thai-style with Turmeric

2 Tbsp (30 mL) coconut oil

1 shallot, minced

1 jalapeño pepper, pith and seeds removed, minced

2 Tbsp (30 mL) finely minced ginger root

1 tsp (5 mL) ground turmeric

3 garlic cloves, minced

8 cups (2 L) chopped kale

1 red bell pepper, quartered, seeded and thinly sliced

½ cup (125 mL) coconut milk

Try this one paired with steamed jasmine rice. Oh, and we're sorry about the half cup of coconut milk…see if you can find the small tomato paste-sized can…or you can add up to a whole cup of coconut milk if you'd like it more "stewy."

In a large skillet, melt coconut oil over medium heat. Sauté the shallot, pepper, ginger and turmeric for 3 minutes or until vegetables have softened.

Add garlic and stir-fry for another minute or so, taking care not to burn the garlic. Add kale and continue to stir-fry for another few minutes until it is well coated.

Pour in the coconut milk, continue to sauté until kale is tender, and serve.

MAKES 4 SERVINGS

VE **GF**

Mellow Garlic

1 good-sized garlic head, separated into cloves

Water to cover garlic

2 Tbsp (30 mL) coconut oil

8 cups (2 L) kale in chiffonade

2 Tbsp (30 mL) maple syrup (or a little extra)

¼ tsp (1 mL) salt

2 pinches of cayenne

Juice of ½ lemon

When precooked, garlic loses its bite and becomes sweeter and gentler. This is a good recipe for those new to kale—and a favourite of children.

In a small deep saucepan, cover garlic cloves with water. Bring to a boil, lower heat to medium and keep at a low boil for about 10 minutes, or until garlic cloves have softened. Remove them to drain, and set aside the water. When garlic cloves are cool enough to handle, peel them and chop coarsely; set aside.

In a large skillet, melt the coconut oil over medium-high heat; add the kale and stir-fry for about 8 minutes until kale is almost tender.

Add maple syrup, salt, cayenne and ¼ cup (60 mL) of the garlic water. Stir mixture a few more times, then cover and steam for about 5 minutes. When kale is very tender, squeeze the lemon juice over, stir again and transfer to a serving dish.

MAKES 4 SERVINGS

Tuscan-style with Pine Nuts & Raisins

⅓ cup (80 mL) white wine

¼ cup (60 mL) roughly chopped soft organic raisins

¼ cup (60 mL) pine nuts

2 Tbsp (30 mL) olive oil

3 garlic cloves, chopped

8 cups (2 L) Tuscan kale (Lacinato) in chiffonade

¼ tsp (1 mL) salt

A few grindings of pepper

A riff on the classic spinach dish, this sauté—perfect for a cold night when the kale has been kissed by frost—goes well with something hot and roasted and some potato and celery root mash, and maybe a glass of Chianti. The raisins need to be soaked in wine for half an hour, so attend to that first.

In a small bowl, combine the white wine and the raisins. Let stand for about 30 minutes. Drain the raisins, reserving the wine.

Meanwhile, in a small heavy pan, toast the pine nuts over low heat, shaking the pan frequently and stirring, for about 5 minutes or until lightly toasted. Don't leave the stove. Quickly remove pine nuts from the pan once they are toasted—if left in the pan they will burn.

In a heavy skillet, heat the olive oil over medium heat. Add the garlic and stir-fry quickly—don't let the garlic burn—about 30 seconds. Add the kale and stir-fry again for 3 to 4 minutes until leaves are well coated. Add the soaked raisins, salt and pepper, and stir-fry lightly for another minute.

Pour reserved wine over the kale, and sauté until tender—about 5 more minutes. If the pan gets dry, add a little water. Transfer to a serving dish, sprinkle with pine nuts and serve.

MAKES 4 SERVINGS

SMACK THAT GARLIC!

Sharon says: It's hard to know how to describe it, but I do it all the time—put my heaviest chef's knife on its side on top of a garlic clove and smack it. Jacques Pépin suggests you cut the root end off first. Then, when you press your knife on the clove and smack, the garlic easily comes away from the skin. When Pépin does this, he uses such a heavy knife that he simply gives it an elegant nudge with his fist. In my kitchen, it's definitely more of an out-and-out smack, and the usual next step is to chop or mince or finely mince the garlic for whatever I'm making that day.

Roasted Garlic & Baby Portobellos

1 garlic head

3 Tbsp (45 mL) olive oil, divided

1½ cups (350 mL) sliced baby portobellos or crimini mushrooms

8 cups (2 L) chopped kale

¼ cup (60 mL) white wine

¼ cup (60 mL) freshly grated Parmigiano

Super savoury. Make extra roasted garlic and freeze it for use another day, or you can bake the garlic ahead of time when you have the oven on for something else.

Preheat oven to 400F (205C).

Remove most of the skin and slice off the very top of the garlic. Place it in a small ovenproof dish, drizzle with 1 tsp (5 mL) of the olive oil, and bake until soft—about 25 minutes. Transfer garlic to a chopping board and let it cool a little until you can handle it. Squeeze out the garlic from each clove into a little dish and set aside.

In a large skillet over medium heat, heat olive oil—wait until it shimmers—and then add mushrooms. Stir-fry them for about 5 minutes. Add the kale, and continue to stir-fry for another few minutes.

Pour in the wine, cover the pan and steam over medium-low heat for about 8 minutes or until kale is tender. Transfer to a serving dish, strew the cheese over all, and serve.

MAKES 4 SERVINGS

My Big Fat Greek Beans with Kale

1 lb (454 g) dried giant beans, butter beans or giant limas

2×28-oz (796 mL) cans of tomatoes

1 cup (250 mL) olive oil

3 garlic cloves, roughly chopped

2 tsp (10 mL) salt or to taste

½ cup (125 mL) chopped fresh dill or 1 Tbsp (15 mL) dried dill

4 cups (1 L) chopped kale

1 lemon

Vaya, long-time clerk at the Parthenon Supermarket in Kitsilano in Vancouver, BC, has a distinctive way of greeting customers whenever they stand at the deli counter to buy feta cheese or olives. She says in the most endearing way, "Tell me!" So you tell her what you would like. Usually it's feta or olives. But sometimes it's a recipe or a recommendation of a product. Regarding elephant beans, "gigantes," butter beans...only the giant from *Jack in the Beanstalk* knows the real name. If you can't find them in a deli or specialty store, seek out the largest lima beans.

This dish calls for a lot of olive oil, but (a) you are not eating the whole thing (it serves about 12), and (b) Vaya says, "You must use the olive *oil*." This is the way she pronounces it—olive *oil*. The better the oil and the better the tomatoes, the better the dish will be. It improves if you let it sit for an hour or so before serving and is even tastier (of course) the next day.

Rinse the beans carefully and drain. Cover with lots of cold water and let them soak overnight—they do not need to be refrigerated.

The next day, drain the beans and put them in a heavy pot with lid (oven and stove-proof.) Preheat oven to 350F (175C). Add enough water to cover beans completely. Bring beans to a boil on the stove, reduce heat to low, cover and simmer until almost tender but not quite—about 25 minutes. Bigger beans will take a little longer. Add tomatoes, olive oil, garlic, salt and dill, mixing well.

Bake, uncovered, for about 1½ hours, stirring every 20 minutes or so. Depending on the freshness of the beans, they will soak up more or less liquid, so add water if necessary. When the beans are almost done and your kitchen smells like a taverna on Corfu, mix in the kale, cover and bake another 15 minutes.

Squeeze a little lemon juice on top when dishing it up.

MAKES 10 TO 12 SERVINGS

Sneaky Rice

4½ cups (1.1 L) stock

2 cups (475 mL) brown basmati rice

1–2 Tbsp (15–30 mL) butter

Zest of 1 large lemon

Juice of 1 large lemon

½ tsp (2.5 mL) salt (double if stock is not salted)

A few grindings of pepper

2 cups (475 mL) finely minced kale, chives and parsley

¼ cup (60 mL) finely minced thyme and oregano leaves

*vegetarian if vegetable stock is used

This quick lemony rice has been a staple over the years in Carol's kitchen. Her dear friend Susan Martin shared the idea with her when they were both busy bringing up a lot of kids, and Carol kept stuffing more and more greens into this rice dish to see how many she could get in before the kids started noticing. It's fine to be a bit flexible about what minced leaves are added; just know that you can stuff in a lot more of the milder fresh greens—kale, chives, parsley, dill—than the stronger-tasting thyme and oregano. If you're rushing to make this on a rainy day and just don't feel like picking greens, a good tablespoon of dried dill—as Susan adds—is very tasty too.

Bring stock to a boil in a rice maker or (Carol's preference) large cast-iron pot with a tight-fitting lid. Rinse the rice in a colander and add to stock. Return to a boil.

Add butter, lemon zest and juice, salt and pepper, and stir well. Taste stock for correct saltiness and add a pinch or two more salt if needed.

Now fold in the kale and herbs. Cover pot tightly and, when boiling again, lower heat and simmer for about 35 minutes.

Check that the rice is done. If it seems a little dry, sprinkle a little stock or water over it, cover, and simmer for a few more minutes.

MAKES ABOUT 6 CUPS (1.4 L)

Warm Lentil Salad with Kale

1 lb (454 g) French lentils

1 medium onion, peeled

3 whole cloves

1 garlic clove

2 bay leaves

Sprig of thyme

2 tsp (10 mL) sugar

3 Tbsp (45 mL) red wine vinegar, divided

2 cups (475 mL) vegetable or chicken stock

4 cups (1 L) kale in chiffonade

4 Tbsp (60 mL) butter

Salt to taste

A few grindings of pepper

A handful of parsley for garnish, chopped

* vegetarian if vegetable stock is used

Great with grilled fish or soup and dense, crusty bread, this substantial fall or winter fare calls for French lentils, such as the beluga or Du Puy varieties, grown in the volcanic soil in the Auvergne region. Unusually, the vinaigrette is made with browned butter rather than oil. Substitute olive oil if you'd rather have a cold salad, and add the kale raw, lightly massaged. If you grow your own kale, the recipe won't cost more than three dollars, so you can splurge on some excellent red wine vinegar.

Rinse lentils 2 or 3 times, and discard any tiny rocks (you don't want anyone to break a tooth).

Poke the onion in 3 places with something pointy and sharp, and insert the cloves into the holes.

Place the lentils, clove-studded onion, garlic, bay leaves, thyme, sugar and 1 tsp (5 mL) of the wine vinegar in a heavy pot. Add the stock, then enough water to cover the lentils by a little over 1 inch (2.5 cm). Bring mixture to a boil over medium heat, lower heat, cover pan and simmer until lentils are almost tender, about 20 to 25 minutes.

Add kale and a little water if the pan seems too dry. Cover and simmer for another 5 minutes. Kale should still have some texture and be green, and pan should be almost dry but not quite. Remove from heat, and discard onion and cloves, garlic, bay leaves and sprig of thyme—this is what French people do to give simple lentils a certain *je ne sais quoi*.

In a little frying pan, carefully brown butter over medium heat—watch it like a hawk so it doesn't burn. Stir in the rest of the wine vinegar and salt and pepper to taste, then pour the mixture over the lentils and toss lightly. Eat salad warm or at room temperature, garnished with chopped parsley.

MAKES 4 TO 6 SERVINGS

Chive Grilled Potatoes

8 medium-sized new potatoes

Salted water for boiling

½ cup (125 mL) finely chopped or snipped chives, plus extra for garnish

¼ cup (60 mL) Arlene's Husband's Favourite Vinaigrette (see page 114) or vinaigrette of your choice

A shake of good salt

A few grindings of pepper

The beauty of this recipe is its simplicity. Add these scrumptious grilled potatoes to virtually any meal to make it heartier. If you want, double the vinaigrette mixture and brush it onto some raw slabs of zucchini or halved peppers or tomatoes, and toss them on the grill too. Give the hot-off-the-grill vegetables a final slathering of the vinaigrette mixture.

Parboil whole potatoes in salted water until al dente, about 10 to 15 minutes. Drain, saving cooking water for use in soup.

Halve the potatoes. Stir the chopped chives into the vinaigrette and thoroughly brush the mixture onto the potatoes.

Grill the potatoes over medium heat, cut side down, until they are golden and grill marked, probably about 10 minutes.

Put potatoes in a serving bowl. Brush them again with the vinaigrette mixture. Garnish with chopped chives. Season with salt and pepper to taste. Serve immediately.

MAKES 4 SIDE DISH SERVINGS

Garlicky Yukon Golds with Cheese & Chives

3 large or 5 medium Yukon Gold potatoes, scrubbed, unpeeled

6–8 garlic cloves, skin on

¾ cup (180 mL) grated cheese or mascarpone

½ cup (125 mL) milk

⅓ cup (80 mL) finely snipped chives, plus more for garnish

Salt to taste

A few grindings of pepper

This is one of those hearty "just one more spoonful" side dishes for cool fall evenings; maybe serve it with a glass of Gewürztraminer. Depending on your mood at the time, choose the cheese accordingly: Jarlsberg will give this dish a touch of smooth and nutty; Gruyère or Emmental will make it richer and nuttier still. Go for white cheddar if you want tang, Gorgonzola for supertang. If you want smooth, go for the mascarpone…it's a little expensive but worth it.

Cut potatoes into 2-inch (5-cm) chunks; boil in salted water for about 10 minutes or until al dente.

Add the garlic cloves and cook for another 5 minutes or so until potatoes are tender and garlic is soft. Drain, saving cooking water for use in soup.

Peel the garlic and add it and remaining ingredients to potatoes. Mash mixture or put through a potato ricer.

Place in a serving dish and garnish with lots more chives.

MAKES 3 TO 4 SERVINGS

Mashed Sweets with Rutabaga, Sage & Rosemary

2 Tbsp (30 mL) butter

1 Tbsp (15 mL) olive oil

2 large onions, peeled, halved and thinly sliced

8–10 sage leaves, finely chopped, plus a few more for garnish

2 tsp (10 mL) minced rosemary leaves, plus a sprig for garnish

5–6 medium sweet potatoes

1 medium rutabaga

1 tsp (5 mL) salt

½ cup (125 mL) milk or light cream, heated

⅔ cup (160 mL) grated cheese

½ tsp (2.5 mL) salt

A few grindings of pepper

2 cups (475 mL) unopened kale buds

The sweetness of caramelized onions and sweet potatoes contrasts with the musky earthiness of the rutabaga. Add a little richness from the cheese and some brassica "bite" from the kale buds, and this dish tastes very…complete! Enjoy in fall or winter when rutabagas are in season and have been kissed by frost before harvesting. If you don't have sage growing in the garden, use a little more rosemary and maybe thyme, but please don't use dried herbs of any sort or it'll taste like run-of-the-mill turkey stuffing. Speaking of which, this makes an ideal side dish for Thanksgiving or any other turkey-worthy occasion. Choose any cheese you love—from Edam to Asiago to Jarlsberg, or even Parmigiano.

In a large skillet, heat butter and olive oil. When mixture begins to shimmer, add onions and turn heat to medium-low. Sauté, stirring frequently, until onions are beginning to caramelize, about 8 minutes. Stir in sage and rosemary; continue to sauté for another 5 to 6 minutes until onions are lightly browned and very tender. Set skillet aside and keep warm.

Peel and roughly chop the sweet potatoes and rutabaga into 1-in (2.5-cm) chunks. Cover with water, add 1 tsp (5 mL) salt, bring to a boil and cook until veggies are very tender, about 20 minutes.

Drain the pot, and add contents to the skillet, along with the milk, cheese, ½ tsp (2.5 mL) salt and pepper. Mash; cover and keep warm.

Using a steamer or covered pot with a little water in the bottom, steam kale buds for about 3 minutes until al dente.

Transfer the mashed vegetable mixture to a heated serving bowl or platter. Place steamed kale buds on top, and garnish with a few sage leaves and a sprig of rosemary.

MAKES 6 SERVINGS

Garlicky Roast Potatoes & Kale

3 Tbsp (45 mL) olive oil, plus extra to taste

½ tsp (2.5 mL) chili flakes

1 lb (454 g) red nugget potatoes

8 cups (2 L) kale in long ribbons

4 large garlic cloves

2 tsp (10 mL) Cape Herb & Spice Lamb Seasoning (3 or 4 generous grindings)*

*You can substitute a mixture of black pepper, sea salt, minced rosemary leaves and lemon zest

VARIATIONS ON THE THEME

Substitute the following or a mixture of them for the potatoes:

- Sweet potatoes
- Sweet or regular onions, cut in quarters
- Beets, cut in quarters
- Carrots or parsnips
- Mushrooms, preferably shiitake, crimini or portobellos—for this variation, roast the mushrooms for 10 minutes before adding the kale

This offering was created by Georgina Flynn, a librarian at the McGill Burnaby Public Library. She uses Cape Herb & Spice Lamb Seasoning (from South Africa) "in one of those pepper-grinder things" she buys at Donald's Market, a neighbourhood institution on Vancouver's east side. Cape Herb has an online presence, or you can make your own facsimile of this seasoning. It's well worth the few steps, including "massaging" the kale, to achieve garlicky deliciousness! Georgina says, "You can do this with one hand, and sip a glass of wine with the other. This feels wonderful and produces a heavenly aroma, so you can channel Nigella Lawson and enjoy the sensual experience."

Position oven rack toward bottom of oven and preheat to 425F (220C).

Place 3 Tbsp (45 mL) olive oil and chili flakes in a large shallow roasting pan to allow oil to become infused with chili flavour.

Wash, scrub and dry potatoes, then chop into 1-inch (2.5-cm) chunks. Transfer potatoes to the roasting pan and stir until well coated with oil. Roast for 20 minutes, stirring and shaking the pan halfway through.

Place the kale ribbons in a mixing bowl and drizzle with more olive oil. Shred garlic using a garlic press or microplane, distributing garlic over the kale, then grind or sprinkle on seasoning. Now comes the fun part: massage the leaves for a few minutes.

Remove potatoes from oven. Loosen any that are stuck to the pan, add the massaged kale and give everything a good stir. Return to oven and roast for another 20 minutes or so, shaking or stirring once or twice, until potatoes are lightly browned and the kale is a bit crispy.

MAKES 4 SERVINGS

WHY WE LOVE COOKING IN CAST IRON

Cast-iron pots and pans are handsome, heat evenly and are reasonably priced, especially when you consider that, if treated properly, they can (and do) last over several lifetimes. They can be used on the stovetop, in the oven and even over a fire, and are really the original non-stick pan without any worrisome chemical coatings. We think cast-iron cookware is the most environmentally friendly, especially when it's already 50 years old and handed down from a mother-in-law (as in Carol's case) or found still as solid as ever in a second-hand store.

SEASONING YOUR CAST-IRON PAN

Some folks complain that food sticks to their cast-iron cookware. If so, it has not been seasoned properly. Here's how to do that:

1. Wash the pan with soapy water, as cast iron comes with a coating to prevent rust.

2. Dry the pan thoroughly, then rub with a light coat of oil—vegetable oils, shortening or lard, or even coconut oil. Use your hands to do this.

3. Next, rub most of the oil off using a clean rag or paper towel.

4. Place the cast-iron pan upside down in a cold oven—use a cookie sheet or a piece of foil big enough to catch any oil that may drip, but there will not be much. Turn the oven up to 450F (230C), and heat the pan for around 30 minutes. Ideally, do this in the spring or summer when you can have your doors and windows open, as this process will generate some smoke, just as when your apple pie leaks juice all over the oven floor.

5. Turn the oven off, and leave the pan where it is until cooled. You could repeat the whole process several times to ensure that your pan is properly seasoned.

CLEANING CAST-IRON PANS

1. Don't use dish soap to clean the pan. Just rub it with a little salt and then wipe, or simply wipe the pan.

2. If you cooked fish in the pan and want to get rid of the smell, rub the pan with half a lemon, pour boiling water over it and dry thoroughly. Place on the stovetop on low heat and rub a little oil into the pan, letting it heat up for 10 to 15 minutes. Some people like to do this every so often after cleaning to keep the seasoning of the pan in top shape.

Kale with Buckwheat Noodles & Roasted Beets

3 medium beets

3 Tbsp (45 mL) olive oil, divided

A light sprinkling of salt

A few grindings of pepper

⅔ cup (160 mL) fresh orange juice (from 1 or 2 oranges), divided

½ cup (125 mL) walnuts

8 oz (225 g) buckwheat noodles (about 3 cups/700 mL cooked and drained)

6 cups (1.4 mL) chopped kale

½ cup (125 mL) snipped or finely chopped chives

8–10 young mint leaves, finely chopped

A handful of parsley, finely chopped

1 garlic clove, minced

3 Tbsp (45 mL) rice vinegar

3 Tbsp (45 mL) tahini

Okay, not all our recipes are going to be quick and easy—this one will take a little time and requires roasting beets. Apologies, dear reader, for asking you to cook a few beets in a hot oven; see if you can also use that heat to roast whole garlic heads to use at another time, or bake a few sweet or regular potatoes, or pizza. If the beets are new—and that's when they're the best—they shouldn't take long to roast.

Preheat oven to 425F (220C).

Trim beets, halve them and slice into sticks the size of skinny french fries. In an ovenproof dish, toss beets with 1 Tbsp (15 mL) of the olive oil, and sprinkle with salt and pepper. Roast for 15 minutes, remove from oven and drizzle ¼ cup (60 mL) of the orange juice over beets. Roast for another 10 to 15 minutes until beets are cooked through and lightly caramelized. Set aside to cool.

While beets are cooking, lightly toast the walnuts in a small cast-iron or other heavy-bottomed pan. Remove from heat, transfer to a cutting board and chop coarsely.

Cook buckwheat noodles according to package directions—usually for about 5 minutes in a big pot of boiling water with a little salt added. Drain, rinse briefly with cold water, drain again and transfer to a large bowl.

Add the reserved beets, kale, chives, mint and parsley.

In a small bowl, combine the garlic, vinegar and tahini with the remaining olive oil and orange juice. Pour over salad and mix well.

Refrigerate for 1 hour or so, and serve.

MAKES 6 SERVINGS

Forbidden Rice Tabbouleh

1 cup (250 mL) black rice

2 cups (475 mL) water, slightly salted

½ cup (125 mL) chopped walnuts

2 cups (475 mL) finely chopped parsley

1 cup (250 mL) thinly sliced green onions

1 cup (250 mL) finely chopped kale

About ½ cup (125 mL) finely chopped mint leaves

A couple of handfuls of snap peas, lightly steamed and halved

1 orange bell pepper, quartered, seeds and white parts removed, thinly sliced

¼ cup (60 mL) olive oil

3 Tbsp (45 mL) fresh lime juice

1 Tbsp (15 mL) maple syrup

Pinch of cayenne

Salt to taste

A few grindings of pepper

Once, black rice—also known as forbidden or purple rice—was exclusively for Chinese emperors. Brimming with antioxidants and rich in "royal-purple" anthocyanin, black rice has a nutty flavour and takes about as long as brown rice to cook if you soak it for a few hours before. Use a red pepper if you can't find an orange one—this is one colourful salad, easily thrown together and very good for what ails you. Consider serving this salad as part of a vegetarian feast with Pea & Lettuce Potage with Mint (see page 151).

Soak the rice for at least 2 hours or even overnight. Drain, rinse once, then cook as you would brown rice in salted water until tender but still firm, about 35 to 40 minutes.

Drain rice if necessary and fluff with a fork, then transfer to an open platter to cool.

Toast the chopped walnuts in a dry pan over medium heat, stirring and shaking the pan, for about 5 minutes until fragrant—do not leave the stove, as nuts burn easily.

Add the parsley, green onions, kale, mint, peas and bell pepper to the rice, and combine lightly.

Put the oil, lime juice, maple syrup, cayenne, salt and pepper in a jar and shake well, or whisk in a small bowl.

Pour the dressing over the rice mixture, and toss well. Serve.

MAKES 4 SERVINGS

Fennel Gratin with Potatoes & Petite Parasols

*

This recipe calls for little "umbrellas"—fennel umbels that are immature and laden with pollen—to garnish the gratin. Choose small and tender tops and remove the tougher "spokes" of the umbrella.

2 fennel bulbs, trimmed

2 cups (475 mL) water

½ tsp (2.5 mL) salt

4 or 5 garlic cloves, skin on, halved

4 Tbsp (60 mL) butter, divided

2 Tbsp (30 mL) flour

½ tsp (2.5 mL) freshly grated nutmeg

2 cups (475 mL) whole milk, heated

2 cups (475 mL) grated Gruyère cheese, divided

¼ tsp (1 mL) ground pepper

½ tsp (2.5 mL) salt

2 pinches of cayenne

4 medium potatoes (preferably Yukon Gold or Russet)

1 medium to large yellow onion

½ cup (125 mL) panko or bread crumbs

1 tsp (5 mL) dried fennel seeds

6–10 herb fennel "umbrellas" with pollen (seeds not yet formed)

*gluten free if gluten-free flour and gluten-free panko or bread crumbs are used

Oil a large-ish ovenproof baking dish.

Remove core from and thinly slice fennel bulbs. Bring water and salt to a boil in a medium saucepan, add fennel and garlic cloves, cover pan, lower heat and steam for about 5 minutes. Drain and set aside. When garlic cools, remove skins and mash pulp with a fork.

To make the cheese sauce, melt 2 Tbsp (30 mL) of the butter over medium heat in a smallish heavy-bottomed saucepan. Whisk in flour and cook for a few minutes. Add nutmeg and lower heat. Whisk in hot milk little by little until sauce thickens. Add 1½ cups (350 mL) of the cheese (the rest goes in the topping), mashed garlic, pepper, salt and cayenne; stir until ingredients are well combined and sauce is smooth.

Peel potatoes, halve lengthwise and slice very thinly.

Cut onion in half, and slice thinly.

Position oven rack in the middle of oven and preheat to 350F (175C).

Place half of the potatoes relatively evenly in the bottom of the baking dish. Strew half the onion slices on top of the potatoes, then arrange half the fennel slices on top of the onions. Pour half the cheese sauce over everything. Repeat the layering a second time, ending with the remaining cheese sauce.

Combine remaining cheese, panko, fennel seeds and fennel umbrellas in a food chopper or processor. Cover the gratin with the panko mixture and pat it down. Dot with remaining butter. Bake for about 1 hour or until all the veggies are tender (test with a knife) and the top is nicely browned. Allow the gratin to rest for 15 minutes before serving.

MAKES 6 SERVINGS

Green Beans with Tomatoes & Mint

1 small onion, minced

2 Tbsp (30 mL) olive oil

2 bay leaves, ripped in half (optional)

2 garlic cloves, roughly chopped

12 oz (340 g) green beans, trimmed

2 cups (475 mL) canned tomatoes, squished with your hands

At least ⅓ cup (80 mL) chopped mint leaves

Salt to taste

A few grindings of pepper

Prepare this dish as part of a Provençal potluck (you have a lot of these, don't you?) or any time, especially when you have your own beans and mint. If you have sun-ripened tomatoes and don't mind cooking them, use them instead. However, since you're going to stew the dish for a fairly long time, canned is fine too. If you do use fresh tomatoes, take time to remove the skins; you can snap the beans in half or leave them whole.

Sauté onion in oil on medium-low heat in a heavy lidded pot, covered skillet or frying pan for about 5 minutes.

Add the bay leaves (if using), garlic and beans. Cover, turn heat down a little and continue to cook for about 10 more minutes, stirring occasionally.

Add the tomatoes and half the chopped mint; cover and cook at a high simmer for about 15 minutes until beans are tender but still green.

Add salt and pepper to taste, along with the rest of the mint. Allow to sit at least 1 hour before serving to allow the flavours to meld. Serve warm or at room temperature.

MAKES 4 SERVINGS

TECHNIQUES FOR SKINNING TOMATOES

METHOD 1

On the stove, in a saucepan boil enough water to cover 3 or 4 tomatoes at a time. Reduce heat but keep water barely at a boil. Remove cores from the tomatoes and make a few shallow slits in their skins with a sharp knife.

Pop the tomatoes a few at a time into the boiling water and leave them for 10 seconds. Using a slotted spoon, transfer them to a bowl of very cold water and leave for 15 seconds. The skins should slip off easily. If not, repeat the boiling- and cold-water steps.

METHOD 2

Remove cores from the tomatoes and make a few shallow slits in their skins with a sharp knife. Place the tomatoes in a heatproof bowl. Pour boiling water over them, let sit for 10 to 15 seconds, transfer to a bowl of very cold water and leave for 15 seconds. The skins should slip off easily. If not, repeat the boiling- and cold-water steps.

Roasted Tomato Cobbler with Thyme

About 3 lb (1.5 kg) tomatoes

A little salt

A few thyme leaves for the tomatoes

2–3 garlic cloves, sliced into little shards

Olive oil

½ large sweet onion

1 cup (250 mL) flour

2 tsp (10 mL) sugar

½ tsp (2.5 mL) baking powder

½ tsp (2.5 mL) salt

1 cup (250 mL) grated cheese

⅓–½ cup (80–125 mL) melted butter

2 tsp (10 mL) finely chopped thyme leaves or more

Inspiration for this recipe came from the Smitten Kitchen blog's rhubarb strawberry dish, which is stupendous. For the tomatoes, grow or seek out "salad" tomatoes; for example, "on the vine" selections like Campari. In a pinch, use small Roma tomatoes sliced in half lengthwise. You can use a lot of garlic on the tomatoes or just a little shard or two. Try replacing the thyme with oregano and use feta in the topping to make the dish Greek-ish. A combination of cheddar and Parmigiano works well in this recipe, but any firm cheese will do. Since the oven will be on for a few hours, you could dry some kale or slow-roast whole garlic heads or anything else so as not to waste electricity. Sharon suggests pairing this dish with Sexist Slaw with Kale (see page 116).

Preheat oven to 250F (120C).

Halve the tomatoes and arrange cut side up on parchment-paper-lined cookie sheets. Sprinkle with salt and put a few thyme leaves in each half, as well as a small shard of garlic, pushing the garlic and thyme down into the tomato (this sounds like a lot of work but it's not). Drizzle or spray a little olive oil on top. Slow roast the tomatoes for 2 hours or so until they are quite a bit smaller but still moist.

Transfer tomatoes to an oiled ovenproof dish, laying them out rather evenly. Using a box grater, grate onion on top of tomatoes, spreading onion out as evenly as you can with your hands. Turn oven up to 375F (190C).

Combine flour, sugar, baking powder and salt, and mix lightly with a fork. Add the grated cheese and mix again. Pour in the melted butter, add the 2 tsp (10 mL) of thyme and mix with the fork again. Topping will be on the dry side in small and larger bits. Scatter the topping as evenly as possible over the tomatoes. It will even out as it bakes. Bake for about 30 minutes or until topping is lightly browned.

MAKES 4 TO 6 SERVINGS

Tomato Kale Nirvana

6 medium to large tomatoes
(about 3 in/7.5 cm in diameter)

A little salt

3 Tbsp (45 mL) olive oil

2 garlic cloves, minced

1 carrot, minced

1 small onion, minced

½ cup (125 mL) uncooked
Arborio or converted rice

3 cups (700 mL) chopped kale

½ tsp (2.5 mL) sea salt

A handful of basil leaves,
finely chopped

A few grindings of pepper

Scant ¼ cup (60 mL) panko or
fine bread crumbs

¼ cup (60 mL) freshly grated
Parmigiano

*gluten free if gluten-free panko
or bread crumbs are used

This is a celebration of summer tomatoes, field or homegrown, which are usually abundant in mid to late August and at their most juicy and flavourful. Use different herbs if you like. Include this dish as part of a Mediterranean feast with grilled 'Ronde de Nice' zucchini (round, so the slices don't fall through the grill) and meat, chicken or fish, and beautiful bread to sop up the juices.

Using a serrated knife, cut off the tops of the tomatoes and eat them. Working carefully, scrape out everything from the insides of the tomatoes—Sharon uses her hands to do this—and place in a bowl. (Be careful not to cut right through the side of the tomatoes; if you do, the filling will leak out during the cooking.) Sprinkle a little salt inside the tomatoes and invert them onto a plate.

Using a knife or food processor, chop tomato insides finely. Set aside.

Heat half the olive oil in a heavy skillet over medium heat. When the oil is shimmering, add the garlic, carrot and onion, and sauté for a few minutes.

Toss in the rice and stir-fry for a few more minutes. Add the chopped tomato insides, kale and sea salt. Bring mixture to a gentle boil, reduce heat, cover skillet and simmer, giving ingredients an occasional stir, for about 10 minutes until rice is al dente.

Remove pan from heat and stir in basil and pepper.

Preheat oven to 350F (175C). Place tomatoes in a lightly oiled ovenproof shallow casserole. Carefully stuff them about three-quarters full, leaving room for the rice to expand as it finishes cooking, taking up the luscious juices of the tomatoes.

Combine panko and cheese, spoon a little of the mixture onto each tomato and drizzle evenly with remaining olive oil.

Bake for about 35 minutes until tomatoes are wrinkly and rice is cooked. If you aren't sure, use a tiny teaspoon to test a little of the rice. It should be soft and juicy.

MAKES 6 SIDE DISH SERVINGS

Maria's Sri Lankan Tomato Curry

1 lb (454 g) ripe tomatoes

1 medium red onion, diced

2 Tbsp (30 mL) butter or ghee (clarified butter)

2 tsp (10 mL) vegetable oil

2 tsp (10 mL) mustard seeds

4–6 garlic cloves, chopped

1 tsp (5 mL) ground coriander (see sidebar on grinding, page 101)

½ cup (125 mL) chopped cilantro leaves and roots

½ tsp (2.5 mL) salt

Use fresh, bursting-with-flavour, large, bright red tomatoes. Maria Rajanayagam is a friend of Sharon. This curry is one of many ambrosial dishes she prepared when Sharon was her dinner guest. Cilantro is used more like a vegetable than herb—lots of it makes the dish; try to include roots if you can. Serve this curry over rice.

Remove skins from tomatoes (see sidebar on skinning tomatoes, page 171). Cut tomatoes in large pieces and, if they are particularly juicy and seedy, remove most of the seeds and some of the liquid, but not all of it.

In a heavy pan over medium heat, sauté the onion in the butter and oil for 2 to 3 minutes until onion softens a little. Add the mustard seeds and continue to fry, stirring, until the seeds begin to pop—watch carefully so they don't burn.

Lower the heat, add the garlic and stir-fry for a few minutes until garlic is softened, then add the ground coriander and tomatoes. Cook over medium heat, stirring occasionally, for about 5 minutes—tomatoes should still have some shape.

Add the cilantro and salt, and stir-fry lightly for 1 more minute. Serve.

MAKES 4 SIDE DISH SERVINGS

Warm Zucchini Salad

4–6 small perfect zucchini (about 12 oz/340 g in total)

2 Tbsp (30 mL) butter

1 Tbsp (15 mL) olive oil

1 ripe tomato, peeled, seeded and chopped (see sidebar on page 171)

3 Tbsp (45 mL) heavy cream

Salt to taste

White or black pepper to taste

Lots of chopped basil leaves

Heaven on earth if you use small, fresh (ideally, homegrown) zucchini; if you use your own tomato from the garden, you are going to swoon. Take the time to peel and seed the tomato—doing so makes a difference texture- and richness-wise.

Trim ends from and then slice zucchini as thinly as possible, by hand or using a mandoline. If you want to make the slices long and thin, you could use a peeler or slice the zucchini lengthwise on a mandoline.

Heat butter and oil in a skillet over medium heat, then add zucchini and stir-fry for about 5 minutes until wilted but not brown. Add the chopped tomato and sauté, stirring, for 1 or 2 more minutes until zucchini is cooked through. Pour in the cream, warm briefly, then season with salt and pepper to taste, and garnish with lots of chopped basil. Serve warm or at room temperature.

MAKES 3 TO 4 SIDE DISH SERVINGS

MAINS

Potato-Crusted Kale & Smoked Salmon Tart

2 medium to large
potatoes, grated

¼ cup (60 mL) grated
Parmigiano

1 Tbsp (15 mL) or more chopped
rosemary and thyme leaves

2 Tbsp (30 mL) melted butter
or olive oil

½ tsp (2.5 mL) sea salt

¼ tsp (1 mL) baking soda

Juice of ½ lemon

1 generous cup (250 mL)
chopped leeks

1 shallot, minced

2 Tbsp (30 mL) olive oil

2–4 garlic cloves, minced

4 cups (1 L) chopped kale

3 small or 2 large eggs

½ cup (125 mL) milk or cream

Pinch of freshly grated nutmeg

A few grindings of pepper

Chopped fresh dill (optional)

6 oz (170 g) smoked
salmon in bits

½ cup (125 mL) crumbled
goat's cheese

Here's the story of this sumptuous supper, as told by its creator, Stan Garrod:

In Cafe Talia, on Salt Spring Island, there was a sign that read "gluten-free quiche." The barista told me the crust contained potatoes, oil, rosemary and salt. As a practitioner of food jazz, I figured I could riff on this theme to make something for my wife, Joi, who is avoiding gluten.

Stan used Yukon Gold potatoes, and we recommend these or any other firm potatoes rather than "new" potatoes. Use all milk or all cream to make this dish as rich (or not) as you like. If it's garlic scape time, finely chop two to four scapes and substitute them for the garlic and shallot. Total preparation time, including baking, is just over an hour. Accompany this tart with salad and a glass of Sauvignon Blanc or Chardonnay.

Grate potatoes into a medium-sized bowl. Add Parmigiano, herbs, melted butter, salt, baking soda and lemon juice, and mix with your hands. Press mixture evenly into an oiled pie plate. Bake at 375F (190C) for 15 minutes. Set aside on a rack.

Sauté leeks and shallot in 2 Tbsp (30 mL) olive oil over medium heat, stirring frequently, for about 5 minutes. Add garlic and kale, and continue to stir-fry for another few minutes until kale wilts. Add a splash of water, then cover and steam for 2 minutes. Remove from heat and set aside to cool.

In a medium bowl, beat the eggs with the milk, nutmeg, pepper and dill, if using. Add the slightly cooled kale mixture.

Preheat oven to 350F (175C).

Distribute salmon pieces over the potato crust. Spoon kale mixture on top. Dot with goat's cheese. Bake for 30 to 35 minutes, or until tart appears set. Transfer to a rack and allow tart to cool for at least an hour so it holds together when you cut it.

MAKES 4 TO 6 SERVINGS

BC Bud with Little Ears & Smoked Salmon

GF *

½ lb (225 g) orecchiette (little ears) pasta

1 Tbsp (15 mL) unsalted butter

1 good-sized shallot, minced

1 Tbsp (15 mL) Fennel Huckleberry Shrub (see page 97), sambuca or Pernod, or 2 Tbsp (30 mL) good white wine

½ cup (125 mL) whipping cream

Salt to taste

1 cup (250 mL) kale buds

4 oz (about 100 g) smoked salmon (uncooked), thinly sliced and roughly chopped

A few grindings of pepper

Chopped parsley for garnish

Soft fennel florets or a sprig of foliage for garnish

*gluten free if gluten-free pasta is used

Not that kind of bud, naughty reader. We're talking about those sweet kale buds that grace the tops and sides of our hard-working kale from April through late June. If it's fennel season, harvest a tiny clump of the gorgeous little yellowish florets (before seeds form) or a tiny sprig of the ferny foliage to use for garnish, along with the parsley. The anise-flavoured liqueur will pick up on the fennel. Otherwise, go with the parsley and white wine. If you don't like the idea of eating ears, use another cut pasta such as penne or "little radiators" (*radiatore*).

In a large pot, bring lots of water to a boil, salt it and add the pasta. The pasta ears are small but thick, so they take a little longer to cook than you'd think—up to 12 minutes, maybe. Follow the directions on the package.

While pasta cooks, melt butter in a skillet or saucepan over medium heat. Sauté the shallot for a few minutes, then add the liqueur. Cover and cook over medium heat for about 3 minutes to evaporate the alcohol. Pour in the cream, give the sauce a few stirs, sprinkle in a little salt (remember that the salmon is a little salty) and keep sauce warm on the stove.

Preheat a pasta serving bowl (with a little water in it) in the microwave or by pouring a little boiling water into the bowl, swirling the water around, then pouring it out.

When the pasta approaches doneness but is a minute away from al dente, add the kale buds. Boil for another minute—not much longer. Drain, reserving a little of the cooking water.

Transfer pasta mixture to the heated serving dish. Very gently fold in the smoked salmon pieces and 1 Tbsp (15 mL) or so of the cooking water, and pour the sauce over all.

Add a few grindings of pepper, and garnish with parsley and a few fennel florets or sprigs of foliage. Serve immediately.

MAKES 2 SERVINGS

Salmon Kale Cakes with Fennel & Rosemary

½ cup (125 mL) soft herbs, such as parsley, chervil, chives, basil

1 Tbsp (15 mL) tender fennel foliage

1 Tbsp (15 mL) rosemary leaves

1 egg

Juice of ½ lemon

1 cup (250 mL) kale

½ smallish sweet onion

1 lb (454 g) ground salmon

1 tsp (5 mL) fennel seeds

½ tsp (2.5 mL) salt

A few grindings of pepper

½ cup (125 mL) panko or fine bread crumbs

1 Tbsp (15 mL) grapeseed oil

*gluten free if gluten-free panko or fine bread crumbs are used

Fast and fabulous, these salmon kale cakes are easy to make whenever you have ground salmon on hand. If you don't, you can always use a food processor to mince a cut-up fillet or two, but that will take a little more time. For starter servings, make tiny patties and serve three to a plate with a dab of Lovage Sauce, Chimichurri or Browned Butter & Sage (see pages 109, 110 and 111). Make the patties bigger if you're planning to serve salmon burgers for supper.

Roughly chop the soft herbs, fennel foliage and rosemary leaves. Transfer to a food processor and pulse until finely minced. Add the egg and lemon juice, and pulse again until herbs are even finer and egg well beaten. Rough chop the kale and onion, add to the food processor and pulse until chopped, but do not let the onion turn into mush—it should be in little chunks. Scrape everything into a good-sized mixing bowl.

Add salmon, fennel seeds, salt and pepper. Using a wooden spoon or your hands, mix well. Form the mixture into balls—as big or small as you wish—and roll each one in panko.

Heat a little of the grapeseed oil in a frying pan. Flatten each patty in the hot pan and fry until golden and cooked right through the centre. Add a little oil, as needed, between batches of patties.

MAKES 4 BURGERS OR 12 APPETIZERS

Fillet of Salmon with Chive-onnaise

1 deboned salmon fillet (about 1½ lb/650 g)

⅓ cup (80 mL) mayonnaise

¼ cup (60 mL) minced chives

¼ cup (60 mL) finely minced kale (Sharon says kale is optional, Carol says it's not!)

2 tsp (10 mL) horseradish

½ tsp (2.5 mL) dry mustard

½ tsp (1 mL) ground pepper

Pinch of salt

A variation from "the old days"…everyone and their aunt made it a lot, often with capers, lemon zest, Dijon mustard or what have you. The mayonnaise, when smeared over the up side of a salmon fillet, bakes on, sealing in the moisture and adding *umami* (who knew what that was in the '80s, but we liked it). We've made it with miso and mayonnaise too—you can do chive "misonnaise" if you like, eliminating the mustard and horseradish. But do go easy on the miso or it'll overpower the delicacy of the salmon. Hey, you could even mix finely chopped kale in with the mayonnaise if you want (Carol insists that we say that here…). This recipe lends itself to the barbecue as well—just don't flip the fish. Try this with Warm Potato Salad with Kale & Crema di Balsamico (see page 136).

Position rack toward top of oven and preheat to 425F (220C).

Place salmon fillet on a parchment-paper-lined baking sheet or shallow pan.

Combine all other ingredients in a small bowl and mix well. Using a spoon or a rubber spatula, evenly coat the fillet with mayonnaise mixture, spreading all the way to the edges.

Bake for between 10 and 20 minutes, depending on the thickness of the salmon and how well done you prefer your fish. The mayonnaise mixture should be bubbly and beginning to colour a little. To test for doneness, pierce the thickest part of the salmon with a knife: if it goes clean through, the fish is cooked. If the knife does not pierce the fish readily, or it feels rubbery or looks raw, bake for a few more minutes. For a browner top, turn on the broiler and broil fish for 30 seconds to a minute—do not move away from the stove even for a second!—then remove from oven.

Allow to cool for about 5 minutes, and serve.

MAKES 4 SERVINGS

Green Eggs

1 big bunch Swiss chard with ribs

1 big bunch kale

1 Tbsp (15 mL) oil

1 cup (250 mL) diced onion
and/or leeks

2 garlic cloves, minced, or
2 garlic scapes, finely chopped

½ cup (125 mL) chopped chives

2 Tbsp (30 mL) finely chopped
thyme leaves

6 large eggs

1 cup (250 mL) milk (or nut,
soy or seed milk, sweetened or
unsweetened)

½ tsp (2.5 mL) salt

A few grindings of pepper

½–1 tsp (2.5–5 mL) nutmeg

1 cup (250 mL) grated cheese
(jalapeño Havarti or any fairly
soft cheese)

Here's a way to stuff a lot of greens into a tasty and nourishing meal that works well for brunch, lunch or a simple supper. Once the kale and Swiss chard are washed and chopped, it's a snap to throw everything together and bake it in about 20 minutes. If you grow Portuguese kale, use it here, chopping some of the crispy, tender stems to stir-fry along with the Swiss Chard ribs. To make this recipe truly a one-pot meal, use a large cast-iron pan with a lid so that you can sauté the onions and Swiss Chard ribs and wilt the greens on the stovetop, add the rest of the ingredients, then bake it in the oven. What makes this dish delish is the flavour combination of the nutmeg and cheese—jalapeño Havarti works well because it provides a little added zip. Whichever cheese you choose, however, we know you will like these green eggs here or there, yes, you will like them anywhere.

Preheat oven to 350F (175C).

Wash greens and leave leaves wet. Strip the Swiss chard leaves from ribs and separate. Chop ribs into ½-inch (1-cm) chunks. Chiffonade or chop Swiss chard and kale leaves together. Set leaves aside.

On the stove, heat oil in a good-sized oven-proof skillet with lid, stir-fry diced onion and chopped ribs for about 5 minutes, then spread mixture evenly on bottom of pan.

Toss in the still-moist chopped leaves and sprinkle evenly with garlic, chives and thyme. If the leaves are on the dry side, add 1 Tbsp (15 mL) water. Cook long enough to wilt leaves, which should take 5 minutes or less.

Meanwhile, mix eggs, milk, salt, pepper and half the nutmeg in a blender.

Once the greens are wilted, pour the egg mixture evenly over them. Spread the grated cheese on top and sprinkle the remaining nutmeg evenly over the cheese.

Bake uncovered until the centre is solid, about 20 minutes.

MAKES 4 SERVINGS

Creamy Oven-Baked Eggs with Kale & Chives

GF

1 Tbsp (15 mL) melted butter

½ cup (125 mL) whipping cream

8 fat garlic cloves, unpeeled

1 cup (250 mL) kale in chiffonade

1 Tbsp (15 mL) water

1 small tomato, sliced

1 cup (250 mL) finely chopped chives

½ cup (125 mL) finely chopped parsley

1 tsp (5 mL) minced rosemary, thyme or basil leaves (optional)

¼ cup (60 mL) crumbled goat's cheese

4 generous slices smoked salmon or lox

4 large eggs

Salt

A few grindings of pepper

Baked in individual ramekins, this is comfort food with class. Serve with salad—perhaps Summer Salad of Baby Kale, Arugula & Berries (see page 124)—and/or some buttered triangles of bread toasted in the oven along with the ramekins for the final 5 minutes of cooking time. The pinch of fresh minced rosemary is optional and will give this dish added oomph…or toss in a touch of fresh thyme or basil instead, depending on what you have handy in the garden. If you don't have goat's cheese, Swiss is mellow and delectable in this dish.

Preheat the oven to 475F (245C).

Brush the bottom and halfway up the sides of 4 ramekins with melted butter. Divide whipping cream equally among them.

Place ramekins on a baking pan, along with unpeeled garlic cloves. Bake for 5 minutes.

Meanwhile, steam kale in a small covered pot with water until just wilted. Drain and set aside.

After 5 minutes, remove ramekins and garlic from oven.

Divide steamed kale among the 4 ramekins.

Cool garlic for a minute, peel each garlic clove and slice thickly.

In each ramekin, arrange a slice or two of tomato on top of the kale, along with a quarter of the garlic slices, not quite a quarter of the chives (reserve about 1 Tbsp/15 mL for garnish), and a quarter of the parsley and minced rosemary (if using). Sprinkle a quarter of the crumbled goat's cheese in each ramekin. Top with a slice of lox. Crack 1 egg into each ramekin, and add a dash of salt, a few grindings of pepper and a smattering of the remaining chives.

Return to the oven for about 10 minutes, removing the ramekins when the egg whites are almost set and yolks still runny.

Allow the eggs to settle for a few minutes; ideally the whites will be completely set and yolks runny.

MAKES 4 SERVINGS

Kale Cauliflower Carbonara con Prezzemolo

1 generous Tbsp (15 mL) grapeseed or olive oil

½ smallish red or yellow onion, thinly sliced

2 garlic cloves, minced

2 slices lean pancetta, chopped (about 2 Tbsp/30 mL)

A pinch or 2 of salt

A few grindings of pepper

1 cup (250 mL) kale in chiffonade

1 overflowing cup (250 mL) small cauliflower florets

½ tsp (2.5 mL) red pepper flakes

1 egg beaten with 2 Tbsp (30 mL) water

3 Tbsp (45 mL) light or heavy cream

6 oz (170 g) rotini or other wiggly pasta

½ cup (125 mL) chopped parsley

¼ cup (60 mL) grated Italian hard cheese

*gluten free if gluten-free pasta is used

Light on the bacon…light on the pasta…pretty light on the cream, and coffee cream is okay—no need to use the hard stuff! Sharon is in the habit of drizzling a little olive oil over most pasta she makes. *Grazie* and R.I.P. to the wonderful and hilarious Ruggiero Alberton, part of Sharon's "Italian" family. "He put that s--t on everything," they all used to quip.

In a heavy medium-sized skillet, heat oil over medium heat, add onion and half the minced garlic, and stir-fry for about 4 minutes until onion is softened.

Add remaining garlic, pancetta, salt and pepper. Cook a few minutes longer, then toss in the kale, cauliflower florets and red pepper flakes. Add a little more oil if the pan seems dry, then cover it, lower heat and steam vegetables for about 5 minutes until cauliflower is tender, stirring once or twice. Remove pan from heat.

In a small bowl, whisk together egg mixture and cream, and a little more pepper; set aside.

Bring a medium saucepan of water to a boil, salt it and add pasta. Drain when it's done to your liking, saving a few spoonfuls of cooking water. Place the frying pan back on medium heat, and add pasta and reserved cooking water. Heat while stirring, then add egg mixture, most of the parsley and most of the grated cheese. Serve immediately, garnished with remaining parsley and grated cheese.

MAKES 2 SERVINGS

A FENNEL-Y VARIATION

Substitute chopped bulb fennel (called *finocchio* in Italian) for the cauliflower. If you have any Fennel Huckleberry Shrub (see page 97), Pernod or sambuca, you could add a spoonful to the sautéing onions. Garnish with a few herb fennel flowers if they're in season, along with the parsley.

Zucchini Tomato Basil Gratin

  *

A few slices of slightly stale bread or about 1 cup (250 mL) panko

2–3 garlic cloves, roughly chopped

¼ cup (60 mL) grated Asiago, Parmigiano or other grating-type cheese

A big handful of basil leaves

Thyme leaves (optional—and not too many)

Pinch of cayenne

Salt to taste

A few grindings of pepper

2 lb (1 kg) zucchini—no baseball bats

About 3 Tbsp (45 mL) olive oil

1 lb (454 g) large tomatoes, thinly sliced

Generous ½ cup (125 mL) grated cheese—Emmental, cheddar, feta, goat's cheese or a mixture

*gluten free if gluten-free bread or panko is used

A recipe for the "one that got away," assuming it's not too huge. Zucchini is at its best when picked young, so it's challenging to use largish ones. If you grow Romanesco—an Italian zucchini with scalloped edges—it grows long but doesn't get fat, and can be used at a larger size. Don't mess with any regular-type zucchini the size of a baseball bat, though…mealy and seedy, it makes a good doorstop and that's about it. A word to the wise: cut yourself a big piece of this gratin and hide it for later—once a guest stole into Sharon's kitchen and helped himself to what was left without even asking!

In a food processor, whirl bread, garlic, ¼ cup (60 mL) grated cheese, herbs, cayenne, salt and pepper until mixture has a crumb-like texture.

Preheat oven to 400F (205C).

Oil a heavy gratin dish and sprinkle a very thin layer of the crumb mixture into it. Slice zucchini thinly on the diagonal, either with a knife or a mandoline. Place a layer of overlapping zucchini on top of the crumb mixture. Evenly strew a third of the remaining crumb mixture over the first layer of zucchini. Drizzle with a little olive oil. Make a second layer of zucchini, top with another third of the crumb mixture and drizzle a little more olive oil on top. Add a third layer of zucchini. Place the tomato slices on top, overlapping them. Strew on the rest of the crumb mixture and drizzle again with the remaining olive oil.

Bake for 25 minutes, remove from oven and top with ½ cup (125 mL) grated cheese.

Bake for 15 or 20 more minutes, until gratin is bubbling and cooked through.

Let dish sit for at least half an hour to firm up.

MAKES 4 OR 5 SERVINGS

Kale Pasta with Rosé Sauce

8 oz (225 g) pasta

2 cups (475 mL) chopped kale

¾ cup (180 mL) *passata*

⅓ cup (80 mL) whipping cream

¼ cup (60 mL) grated Parmigiano

A few grindings of pepper

Parsley and/or basil leaves for garnish

*gluten free if gluten-free pasta is used

Decadent yet oh-so-quick. If you are into slow food, move languidly around the kitchen as you cook, and recite a little Dante. In this recipe, the kale is tossed in with the pasta just before it finishes cooking. The sauce is made with *passata*—strained Italian tomatoes, with or without basil, and salt—a cross between canned tomato sauce and tomato paste, but better. It contains no preservatives, so you need to use it up within three or four days (freeze any not used). You can make your own simple tomato sauce if you prefer. The brand of *passata* we usually pick is Mutti from Parma (the address of the manufacturer is on the bottle), which we prefer because its sodium level is much lower than other brands. Look for *passata* on the bottom shelves in the pasta and tomato-sauce aisle of the grocery—below the more expensive sauces displayed at eye level. Rotini, penne or the twisted *cassarece* pasta are best, with lots of nooks and crannies to hold the sauce. Being a butter nut, Sharon likes to add a dab or so of butter to her bowl of pasta, but you do not need to. Or you can splash a dash of olive oil over it, as Carol loves to do.

In a large pasta pot, bring water to a boil. Add salt (to your liking). Cook pasta until it is nearly done—almost al dente but not quite. Add kale, and cook for another 2 to 3 minutes until pasta is al dente.

While the pasta cooks, heat the *passata* in a small pan until it begins to bubble, then turn down heat to low. Add the cream, stir gently and keep rosé sauce warm over very low heat—do not let it boil, because the cream might curdle.

Heat a pasta serving bowl, drain pasta and kale, and transfer to heated bowl. Gently fold in the sauce along with cheese and some pepper. Taste for seasoning—you might need a very little salt but not much.

Garnish with herbs.

MAKES 4 STARTER SERVINGS OR 2 MAIN COURSE SERVINGS

Sweet Million Spaghetti for Kids

 *

3 cups (700 mL) halved cherry tomatoes

2 Tbsp (30 mL) olive oil

2 Tbsp (30 mL) butter

½ small onion

¼ tsp (1 mL) each salt and pepper

2 garlic cloves, chopped

10 cups (2.4 L) water

1 Tbsp (15 mL) salt

220 sticks (yes!) of spaghetti—that's about 7 oz (200 g) spaghetti

A handful of parsley and basil leaves, chopped

A sprig of thyme, leaves removed and chopped

½ cup (125 mL) Parmigiano or other cheese

*gluten free if gluten-free pasta is used

You can make this with Sweet Million or just about any kind of cherry tomatoes—all of them will be good. The sauce is very easy, as you just cook everything together in a pot until it's done. Kids, please ask for help from an adult with the boiling water part, okay? You'll have fun counting out the sticks of spaghetti...we did! Measure the tomatoes after they are cut in half. You can use a few more tomatoes if you want.

Put the tomatoes, oil, butter, onion, salt and pepper in a medium-large-sized frying pan. Cook over medium-low heat for about 25 minutes. Remove onion (it was included just to add flavour—eat it when it's cool if you like). Add garlic, lower heat and allow sauce to simmer while you cook the pasta.

Bring the water and salt to a boil in a big pasta or soup pot. Carefully slide in the spaghetti sticks with the help of an adult and ask them to stir immediately with a long-handled wooden spoon, then give a few stirs occasionally. Don't let it stick to the bottom of the pot. Boil about 8 minutes or whatever the package says. Ask your adult helper to carefully drain and shake pasta to remove water, add spaghetti to the sauce in pan. Keep the pan on the heat turned to the lowest setting so it doesn't cool off.

Now put in the parsley and basil from the garden, and maybe a pinch of thyme. Mix, and taste (blowing on it to cool it first) to see if it needs more salt and pepper. Add half the cheese and mix it in until it gets melty with the sauce and pasta. Dish spaghetti out onto plates or bowls and add a little more cheese on top and maybe a few more chopped fresh herbs.

MAKES 2 TO 4 SERVINGS DEPENDING ON THE AGE OF THE PEOPLE

Kalak Paneer

Chris Mull, partner of Michelle Nelson (of shrub and rabbit-stew fame), contributed this recipe, which is based on the traditional palak paneer of South Asian and Pakistani cuisine. Try serving on top of steamed basmati rice with a sprinkling of cilantro leaves. Roti (Indian flatbread) and raita (a yoghurt-based condiment) are the perfect accompaniments.

Paneer

12 cups (3 L) whole milk

Juice from 2 lemons

Kalak

3 garlic cloves, chopped

1 medium onion, chopped

2 Tbsp (30 mL) grated ginger root

2 dried chilies, chopped (optional)

¼ cup (60 mL) oil

2 tsp (10 mL) ground cumin

1 tsp (5 mL) ground coriander

1 tsp (5 mL) ground turmeric

¾ cup (180 mL) plain Greek-style yoghurt

8–10 cups (1.9–2.4 L) finely chopped kale

1 large tomato, chopped

*vegan if the vegan variation is made

PANEER

Heat milk in a large pot until simmering, stirring often to avoid scalding.

Add lemon juice slowly until milk curdles and separates into curds (solids) and whey (liquid)—this will take anywhere from 2 to 10 minutes.

Wrap curds in cheesecloth and strain, wringing out as much liquid as possible. Cinch the top of the cheesecloth pouch tightly and place it in a sieve or strainer fitted over a bowl to catch the liquid. Put a weight on top (such as a bowl filled with water) and leave to drain for 30 to 45 minutes—the mixture will become firm.

Once the cheese is solid, cut into cubes and set aside.

Either lightly sauté the cubes before adding to the kalak, or use them as they are.

KALAK

In a large shallow pan, sauté garlic, onion, ginger and chilies in the oil until lightly brown. Add cumin, coriander and turmeric, and stir-fry for a few minutes. Stir in yoghurt.

Begin adding the kale a handful at a time while stirring, until it cooks down and becomes soft, about 20 to 25 minutes. Add a little water if the mixture gets too thick or sticks to the pan. At this point, either leave kalak as is or blend in a food processor to achieve the traditional purée.

Mix in the tomato and paneer and heat through.

MAKES 6 SERVINGS

VEGAN VARIATION

Substitute precooked potatoes for the paneer and use soy yoghurt.

Coconut Curried Kale & Butternut Squash

1 medium-sized butternut squash, peeled and cubed

3 Tbsp (45 mL) butter or ghee

2 tsp (10 mL) black mustard seeds

2 tsp (10 mL) cumin seeds

2–4 garlic cloves, chopped

1–2 sliced onions

1 jalapeño pepper, seeded and finely chopped (optional)

1–3 Tbsp (15–45 mL) Thai red curry paste, to taste

2 tsp (10 mL) ground coriander

2 tsp (10 mL) ground turmeric

4–6 cups (1–1.4 L) roughly chopped kale leaves

Water or stock for thinning

14-oz (398-mL) can coconut milk

Salt to taste

Chopped cilantro

*vegan if oil is substituted for butter or ghee

A combination of Indian and Thai elements creates layers of flavour. Amounts of spices are approximate; this is not very spicy, so if you like you can add several pinches of cayenne…just don't rub your eyes afterward! If you are pressed for time or don't have the requisite spices, use a good-quality curry powder such as Dan-D-Pak Special Blend Curry Powder—anywhere from 1 to 2 tablespoons (15–30 mL), depending on how zesty you want it. Accompany with rice or chapati or roti.

Place squash cubes on a lightly oiled or parchment-paper-lined baking sheet. Bake at 350F (175C) for about 15 minutes. Set aside.

Meanwhile, in a large frying pan or skillet with a lid, heat the butter over medium heat. Add the mustard and cumin seeds and fry, stirring, until they begin to pop. Add the garlic and onions, fry a little more, then toss in the jalapeño (if using), curry paste, coriander and turmeric. Continue frying and stirring as lovely aromas swirl around your kitchen.

Add the kale and a little water, cover pan and steam until kale is wilted. Add squash, coconut milk and salt. Cover and simmer, adding a little more water if necessary, for about 15 minutes to allow flavours to meld. Strew with cilantro before serving.

MAKES 4 TO 6 SERVINGS

Szechuan-style Kale with Fried Tofu

VE* GF*

1 Tbsp (15 mL) oil

1 medium onion, halved and thinly sliced

1 Tbsp (15 mL) finely chopped ginger root

2 tsp (10 mL) ground turmeric

4 cups (1 L) chopped kale

¼ cup (60 mL) peanut butter—crunchy or regular

1 tsp (5 mL) sugar

2 tsp (10 mL) chili garlic oil

1 Tbsp (15 mL) sesame oil

1 Tbsp (15 mL) soy sauce

6–8 tofu puffs (halved) or ½ lb (225 g) tofu in thin slices

3 Tbsp (45 mL) water

8 garlic-chive stems with unopened buds or 2 garlic cloves, chopped

1 largish red bell pepper, halved, seeded and cut into very thin strips

1 small jalapeño pepper, seeded and minced

2 cups (475 mL) very fresh mung bean sprouts

A few grindings of pepper

1 Tbsp (15 mL) fish sauce

3 Tbsp (45 mL) lime juice

¼ cup (60 mL) chopped cilantro

*vegan if fish sauce is omitted and gluten free if gluten-free soy sauce and fish sauce are used

Sharon says: I got in trouble for bringing this dish to an early-morning television appearance. I was supposed to make one of the recipes from the first *Book of Kale*, which I did, but the host seemed to prefer this ad hoc mixture I'd thrown into the frying pan. Of course, it would have been appropriate to only make something from the book and not something else too, as my very sweet publicist, Annie, gently hinted. Oh well, live and learn. Hope you like this as much as Steve Darling of *Global TV Morning News* did. Already-fried tofu "puffs" can be purchased at many stores that stock tofu, but purists (not me) might want to fry their own. To make this dish heartier, add cooked buckwheat noodles or soba.

Heat oil in a skillet, add onion and ginger, and stir-fry for about 2 minutes. Add turmeric and stir-fry for a minute. Add kale, stir well, cover and let simmer for about 5 minutes until kale is wilted. If the kale is still damp from being washed, you won't need to add any water to steam the kale; if it's dry, throw in 1 to 2 Tbsp (15–30 mL) water.

While kale is cooking, in a small bowl combine peanut butter, sugar, chili and sesame oils, and soy sauce.

Add the tofu puffs to the kale mixture and heat thoroughly (they are precooked). Add the peanut butter sauce and water. Simmer covered, for about 3 minutes, stirring once or twice. Add the garlic chives or garlic, peppers, bean sprouts, pepper and fish sauce, stir-frying for a few more minutes until bean sprouts soften. Sprinkle with lime juice, strew with cilantro and serve.

MAKES 2 SERVINGS

Kale with Chickpeas, Squash & Merguez Sausage

GF *

1 cup (250 mL) pot barley, quinoa or couscous

1 cup (250 mL) meat, chicken or vegetable stock

1 Tbsp (15 mL) olive oil

4 merguez sausages

1 onion, finely chopped

1 orange squash, about 1½ lbs (650 g)

4 garlic cloves, chopped

1 cup (250 mL) water

1 Tbsp (15 mL) Green Harissa (see page 108) or 1 tsp (5 mL) harissa paste (or more if you like it)

28-oz (540-mL) can excellent plum tomatoes, including juice

4 cups (1 L) chopped kale

2½ cups (600 mL) cooked chickpeas

Additional stock or water

Salt (optional)

*Gluten free if quinoa is used as the grain and gluten-free merguez sausage is used

Hearty as anything when served over barley. If you are not a barley fan, pick some other grain—perhaps quinoa or Israeli or regular couscous. Harissa paste is a Tunisian condiment used in Middle Eastern cooking. You can buy it at most grocery stores, or make your own using our recipe for Green Harissa. We love harissa because, when added to dishes, it makes them taste like someone else did the cooking. Merguez sausage is spicy and made from lamb, among other things. If you can't find it or would rather not use it, substitute chicken, turkey or Italian sausage. Prepare this dish, perhaps with a nice Merlot or Shiraz, in fall or winter when squash is fresh.

Bring barley and stock to a boil in a heavy saucepan. Reduce heat and simmer, covered, until liquid is absorbed and barley is tender, about 40 minutes. (If you are using quinoa or Israeli or regular couscous, cook according to package directions.)

Heat oil in a wide heavy pot. Brown sausages on all sides, then remove to a plate, retaining the juices in the pot and on the plate. Add the onion to the pot and sauté over low heat, stirring frequently, until onion begins to caramelize, about 8 minutes.

Peel, seed and chop squash into 1-in (2.5-cm) chunks. Add squash along with garlic to the pan, turn up the heat to medium, and stir-fry for about 5 minutes. Add water and harissa. Simmer uncovered until squash is al dente. Add tomatoes with their juice and simmer for another 5 minutes. Now add reserved sausage, kale, chickpeas and a little stock or water if mixture seems dry. Continue to simmer until sausage is cooked through. Taste for salt, adding a little if needed.

Serve on the barley.

MAKES 4 SERVINGS

Michelle's Rabbit Stew with Kale

 GF*

1 rabbit (about 3–4 lb/1.4–1.8 kg dressed), jointed

2 bay leaves

2 stalks celery, chopped

1 large onion, whole

2½ tsp (12.5 mL) salt

1 large onion, chopped

5 carrots, chopped

6 cups (1.4 L) chopped kale

¼ cup (60 mL) butter

Scant ¼ cup (60 mL) flour

1 tsp (5 mL) Worcestershire sauce

½ cup (125 mL) chopped parsley

*gluten free if gluten-free flour and gluten-free Worcestershire sauce are used

Just finishing her PhD in conservation biology, Michelle Nelson walks the walk, recently having moved with her partner to Bowen Island, BC, where they raise goats, chickens, quail, rabbits and more, as well as grow food, including lots of kale. Michelle recommends serving the stew "with rustic bread and butter, along with any full-bodied red wine such as the Bordeaux-style blend of Penticton's Perseus Invictus."

Put rabbit meat, bay leaves, celery, whole onion and 2 tsp (10 mL) of the salt in a large stew pot and fill with water to barely cover meat. Simmer until meat falls off the bone, about an hour and a half.

Remove from heat, allow to cool slightly and strain solid ingredients from stock.

Set aside 2 cups (475 mL) stock. Let the meat cool, then remove all bones. Compost remaining solids.

Return meat to stock in stew pot, along with chopped onion and carrots. Simmer for another 15 minutes, add kale and continue to simmer for 5 more minutes.

To thicken the stock, make a roux by heating the butter and flour in a saucepan on medium heat for 2 or 3 minutes. Slowly whisk in the 2 cups (475 mL) reserved stock, remaining salt and Worcestershire sauce.

Simmer for another few minutes. Add thickener to stew pot and allow mixture to bubble on low for about 5 more minutes. Garnish with parsley.

MAKES 4 SERVINGS

Chicken in Fig Jam with Thyme

GF *

3 garlic cloves

1 medium-sized shallot, chopped

⅓ cup (80 mL) apple or orange juice

⅓ cup (80 mL) fig jam

2 Tbsp (30 mL) thyme leaves

2 scant Tbsp (30 mL) balsamic vinegar

1 Tbsp (15 mL) olive oil

2 tsp (10 mL) Worcestershire sauce

2 lb (1 kg) chicken, cut into serving pieces

⅓ cup (80 mL) good red wine

*gluten free if gluten-free Worcestershire sauce is used

If you have a fig tree or know someone who does, you can dry some and use in place of the fig jam, but if you do, heat them up in a little wine so that the food processor can handle them. Also, add a little jam or jelly—grape, blackberry or whatever you have. Barb Coward kindly dehydrated a whole bunch of Desert King figs—green on the outside, pink on the inside—for the first experiment with this recipe. Fresh figs would have been nice to use, but that variety looks terrible when cooked. For a memorable meal, complement this dish with Minted Kale with Peas & Blue Cheese (see page 122) and the best bread you can find to dunk in the juices. Goes great with Rosemary No-Knead Bread (see page 87).

Combine everything but the chicken and wine in a blender or food processor and blend until smooth.

Place chicken pieces in a sealable freezer bag or marinating container with a tight-fitting lid, and pour marinade over. Refrigerate, turning occasionally, and allow chicken to marinate overnight or for a minimum of 3 hours.

Scrape marinade off chicken into a small saucepan. Add wine and bring to a boil, then lower heat and cook down sauce by half.

Meanwhile, either cook chicken on the barbecue or bake it in a 375F (190C) oven until a thermometer inserted in the thickest part of the meat reads 160F (70C), about 45 minutes. Serve with the marinade alongside.

MAKES 2 SERVINGS

Magic Chicken with Kale & Herbs

1 large chicken, cut up, or 8 pieces

¼ cup (60 mL) olive oil

A few grindings of pepper

Scant ¼ cup (60 mL) butter

6 or more garlic cloves, skin on

1 tsp (5 mL) sea salt

1 cup (250 mL) kale leaves in chiffonade

⅔ cup (160 mL) white wine or Marsala

½ cup (125 mL) chopped soft herbs—parsley, chervil, chives, basil

2 Tbsp (30 mL) roughly chopped woody herb leaves—rosemary, thyme, oregano

½ cup (125 mL) heavy cream (optional)

Parsley for garnish

Sharon says: This recipe is from my dear neighbour Karen Luke. We have an ideal arrangement—it's as if our fridges are common property. She'll just walk into my kitchen, open the fridge, see what's interesting, and go ahead and sample it. I do the same in hers. Almost everything Karen cooks is magic…and this dish is particularly so. If you like, you can add cream to the sauce, but it is absolutely not necessary and Karen doesn't bother. She does vary the alcohol—sometimes using Marsala, sometimes white wine; or use a little less white wine and add a glug of brandy. Serve with garlic mashed potatoes and a kale side dish or salad.

Rub the chicken pieces all over with a little of the olive oil—this will help to prevent them from sticking to the pan. Then, dust with black pepper lightly all over.

In a pan large enough to hold all the chicken pieces and that has a lid, heat remaining olive oil on medium-high heat, then add the butter. When it begins to sizzle, add the chicken pieces, lower the heat to medium and sauté, turning frequently, until they become evenly golden. This is just the first cooking and should take about 10 minutes.

Add the garlic cloves and salt, then lower the heat to medium-low. Cover pan and cook, turning the pieces often, for about 35 minutes or until chicken is deeply coloured.

Transfer chicken mixture to a heated dish and keep warm.

Drain most of the fat from the pan, or leave some in the pan if you prefer. Increase heat to medium-high, and add the kale, wine and herbs. Use a wooden spoon to stir the mixture and scrape up any flavourful bits stuck to the bottom of the pan. Taste and adjust seasoning if necessary, or perhaps add a bit more wine. Stir in the cream (if using) and cook liquids down a little.

Serve the chicken napped with the sauce and garnished with a few extra bits of parsley.

MAKES 4 SERVINGS

SWEET TREATS

Coconut Kale Cookies

1½ cups (350 mL) unsweetened flaked coconut

½ cup (125 mL) dried kale flakes (see page 64)

½ cup (125 mL) sugar

½ tsp (2.5 mL) salt

½ cup (125 mL) coconut oil, or butter cut into chunks

1 tsp (5 mL) vanilla

1 egg plus 1 egg yolk

1½ cups (350 mL) flour

½ tsp (2.5 mL) baking powder

Pine nuts or slivered pecans (optional)

*gluten free if gluten-free flour, vanilla and baking powder are used

A food processor whips these cookies up, making them ready to bake in five minutes or less. You could make these into thumbprint cookies, too, and fill with jalapeño jelly or some other not-too-sweet jam. Or add a little finely chopped dried mango to up the tropicalness. Most cookies would contain more sugar, but we prefer them like this. Add more sugar if you like. Don't be afraid to try the gluten-free variation, substituting gluten-free flour and baking powder. Carol does this all the time!

Position rack in the middle of the oven and preheat to 350F (175C).

Mix coconut, kale, sugar and salt in a food processor for about 20 seconds. Add coconut oil and vanilla, and pulse a few times. Now toss in the whole egg plus yolk, and pulse again until mixture is well blended. Add flour and baking powder all at once, then pulse just until combined—do not overmix. If the dough seems too dry to form into a ball, add a little water and pulse lightly.

Using your hands, roll heaping spoonfuls of the dough into balls and arrange on a parchment-paper-lined cookie sheet. You can leave them round, flatten them slightly or use a fork dipped in water to press down lightly as for peanut butter cookies. Poke a few nuts (if using) into each cookie.

Bake for about 20 minutes; remove from cookie sheet to a cooling rack.

MAKES 2 DOZEN 2-IN (5-CM) COOKIES

SHADES OF GREEN

Instead of ½ cup (125 mL) **dried** kale, you can make Coconut Kale Cookies with ½ cup (125 mL) minced **fresh** kale. (Typically, 2 cups/475 mL fresh chopped kale minced in the food processor equals ½ cup/125 mL.)

Dried kale results in a subtle green-ness and a crispier cookie, while the fresh-kale variation will be a gorgeous speckled green, moist and macaroon-like. Try these cookies both ways, depending on whether you have fresh or dried kale on hand.

Kalelicious Chocolate Cake

2¼ cups (530 mL) flour

1½ cups (350 mL) sugar

¾ cup (180 mL) excellent-quality cocoa powder

½ cup (125 mL) dried kale flakes (see page 64)

2 tsp (10 mL) baking soda

½ tsp (2.5 mL) salt

2 eggs

1 cup (250 mL) buttermilk

1 cup (250 mL) good espresso coffee (substitute water if cake is mostly for kids)

1 cup (250 mL) vegetable oil

1½ tsp (7.5 mL) vanilla

The chocolate and coffee give you a small whack of caffeine, so don't eat too much of this cake at night. In a way, you'd never know it contains kale, but it does give the cake a subtle roasty flavour. You can use an electric hand mixer or a stand mixer; either way, it's easy. Feel free to dust with confectioner's sugar or to ice the cake—kale and cream-cheese frosting, anyone? Sharon says: I often halve this recipe if it's for a small family—which in my case is a family of one, as Pocky, my kale-eating dog, can't have any because dogs aren't supposed to eat coffee or chocolate.

Preheat oven to 350F (175C).

Combine dry ingredients in a large bowl. Add remaining ingredients and beat for 3 to 4 minutes until combined.

Pour batter into a greased 10- by 13-inch (25-×32.5-cm) sheet pan. Bake for about 30 minutes, checking after 25 minutes to see if cake is cooked through, testing with a toothpick for doneness. Cool on a rack for about 10 minutes; after about 15 minutes, invert pan to allow cake to slip out.

MAKES 8 SERVINGS

Kale Carrot Walnut Bran Muffins

1 cup (250 mL) bran

1 cup (250 mL) buttermilk

1 large egg, lightly beaten

⅓ cup (80 mL) oil or melted butter

2 Tbsp (30 mL) brown sugar

3 Tbsp (45 mL) honey

¾ cup (180 mL) unbleached flour

1½ tsp (7.5 mL) baking powder

1 tsp (5 mL) baking soda

½ tsp (2.5 mL) cinnamon

¼ tsp (1 mL) salt

1 medium carrot, shredded

1 cup (250 mL) finely minced kale

½ cup (125 mL) chopped apple

½ cup (125 mL) walnuts, lightly toasted and chopped

A small handful of raisins (optional)

Sharon says: I'll never forget my home economics teacher, Miss Miyagishima, telling us we were allowed to stir muffins only 15 times—or else. These muffins are far more flavourful than the ones we made in Grade 7 and way better than Floating Islands, that revolting concoction of beaten egg whites suspended on top of a yolky sauce that made me nauseous…never mind the blue broadcloth (fitted) dress with white dingle balls dangling from the puffed sleeves. In any case, these not-too-sweet muffins are yet another way to get kale into you and your family. If you happen to stir them 16 times, no one will ever know. Grease the muffin pan even if it is a non-stick one, and do not line the pan with paper baking cups, which don't work well for these muffins.

In a medium bowl, mix bran and buttermilk. Let stand for 10 to 15 minutes.

Preheat oven to 400F (205C). Lightly grease muffin cups.

Add egg, oil, brown sugar and honey to bran mixture, mixing lightly.

In a larger bowl, combine flour, baking powder, baking soda, cinnamon and salt.

Fold the wet mixture into the dry one, and add carrot, kale, apple, walnuts and raisins (if using). Barely stir to combine. As with pancake batter, having a few dry spots in this batter is okay.

Spoon batter into muffin cups.

Bake for 15 to 18 minutes, and test muffins for doneness by inserting a toothpick into them.

MAKES 12 MEDIUM-SIZED MUFFINS

Kale Fruit Freezes

1 cup (250 mL) ripe juicy
blackberries

¼ cup (60 mL) honey (decrease
as appropriate)

1 big or 2 small bananas, cut
into chunks

5–6 kale leaves, chopped

Half a 14-oz (398-mL) can
coconut milk

1 cup (250 mL) water

The honey is optional but needed at first when serving to children who are used to very sweet things. Note that the amount of kale can be increased as children adapt to the taste.

Blend all ingredients well. Fill moulds, leaving space for expansion, and freeze.

MAKES ABOUT 10 FRUIT FREEZES (DEPENDING ON SIZE OF MOULD)

KALE IN GUATEMALA

The Compassion Fruit Society, a registered charity based in Vancouver, BC, is establishing the Project Somos Children's Village near Tecpán in Guatemala. This eco-sustainable community will have seven homes, and in each a Guatemalan foster mother will raise up to seven orphaned children as a family. Malnutrition is a major problem there, where 50 percent of children under the age of five are chronically malnourished, partly due to their mono-diet (predominantly corn and beans). To address this problem, the village has installed gardens that produce lush vegetables and fruits. Seen mostly as a decorative plant in Guatemala, kale grows like a weed there (as it does everywhere else!), surpassing a height of six feet. Of course, the plants thrive year round. Heather Knox, founder of Project Somos, has been playing with different recipes that would entice fussy children to gobble up kale. She discovered that frozen fruit pops are the way to go. Blackberries growing on-site mask any hint of green in these treats.

Gluten-free Kale Fruit Loaf

⅔ cup (160 mL) sugar

¼ cup (60 mL) oil

2 eggs

1 cup (250 mL) mashed banana

½ cup (125 mL) any puréed fruit (apples, berries, peaches or whatever you would like to use up)

1 tsp (5 mL) vanilla

2 cups (475 mL) rice flour

2 tsp (10 mL) baking powder

½ tsp (2.5 mL) salt

1 cup (250 mL) ground nuts or seeds—pecans and/or almonds and/or walnuts or whatever nuts and seeds are handy

½ cup (125 mL) dried kale flakes (see page 64)

*gluten free if gluten-free baking powder and vanilla are used

Carol says: When I went gluten free a couple of years ago, I was shocked at the price of most of the ready-made gluten-free goods in stores. I became very motivated to make my own! Some web searching produced this banana bread recipe, which has been adapted and made many times with no flops despite lots of experimentation. Because of the long cooking time, I suggest doubling the recipe to make better use of the oven heat; the double batch fits into the bowl of a stand mixer. As these loaves freeze very well, you can go positively wild and even make two double recipes in a row, while all the ingredients are out, to get four loaves into the oven at once. A wonderful way to use up overripe fruit. Slice the loaves before you freeze them so that you can pull out a piece or two when gluten-free guests drop by.

Preheat oven to 325F (160C). Grease a large loaf pan.

In a large bowl, combine sugar and oil, then beat in the eggs, mashed banana, puréed fruit and vanilla.

In another bowl, combine rice flour, baking powder and salt, then add wet mixture to dry mixture. Beat until dry ingredients are moist.

Add ground nuts and kale. Stir until mixed.

Pour batter into loaf pan. Bake for about 1 hour and 20 minutes.

MAKES 1 LARGE LOAF

Kale Beet Bread

1½ cups (375 mL) finely chopped kale

⅓ cup (80 mL) packed grated beets

½ cup (125 mL) packed grated carrots

3 eggs

⅓ cup (80 mL) white sugar

½ cup (125 mL) packed brown sugar

⅔ cup (160 mL) vegetable oil

½ cup (125 mL) buttermilk

2 tsp (10 mL) vanilla

2 cups (475 mL) flour

1½ tsp (7.5 mL) baking powder

1 tsp (5 mL) baking soda

2 tsp (10 mL) cinnamon

A few gratings of nutmeg

½ tsp (2.5 mL) salt

Like a zucchini or banana bread but with you-know-what instead. You don't need much sugar because the root veggies add an earthy sweetness. This would be good for breakfast, maybe with some cheese and a little fruit, and looks pretty when sliced. You could shake a little icing sugar on top—maybe make a stencil in the shape of a kale leaf?

Position rack in middle of oven and preheat to 350F (175C). Lightly grease 2 loaf pans.

In a medium bowl, combine kale, beets and carrots.

In another bowl, beat the eggs, then beat in the sugars, oil, buttermilk and vanilla.

Sift the remaining ingredients into a large bowl, stir well, and add the egg mixture and veggies, stirring only enough to combine. Batter should be fairly stiff. If it seems too dry, add a splash of buttermilk.

Transfer batter into pans.

Bake for 40 to 45 minutes or until a toothpick or other tester inserted into the loaves comes out clean. Cool on a rack, and turn loaves out of pans after about 15 minutes.

MAKES 2 MEDIUM-SIZED LOAVES

Seedy Gluten-free Scones

1½ cups (350 mL) chickpea flour

1½ cups (350 mL) rice flour

1 cup (250 mL) sugar

3 Tbsp (45 mL) poppy seeds

1 generous Tbsp (15 mL) fennel seeds

1 generous Tbsp (15 mL) lemon zest

1 Tbsp (15 mL) gluten-free baking powder

2½ tsp (12.5 mL) xanthan gum

1 tsp (5 mL) salt

⅔ cup (160 mL) chilled butter, cut into small chunks

1 egg

3 Tbsp (45 mL) lemon juice

⅓ cup (80 mL) plain yoghurt

About 1 Tbsp (15 mL) sugar (or less)

Yes, in addition to a heaping spoonful of seeds from your fennel plant, this recipe is definitely loaded with butter…and we're *not* suggesting you scarf down these decadent scones every single day. But for people who are steadfast about avoiding gluten, this will make up for all those times you've had to take a pass on warm-from-the-oven croissants or the bulging box of doughnuts being shuffled around the office. In fact, your gluten-gorging mates will be eyeing (and salivating over) these treats to the point that you just might want to share some with them—or not.

Preheat oven to 375F (190C).

Combine flours, sugar, seeds, lemon zest, baking powder, xanthan gum and salt in a food processor, mixing well. Add the chunks of chilled butter and pulse until you have very small crumbs.

Whisk egg with the lemon juice. Add to the processor and pulse until well mixed.

Add yoghurt and pulse until the dough comes together. Add more yoghurt if needed for a doughy consistency.

On a rice-floured surface, flatten the dough into a circle (about 8 in/20 cm) and cut into 8 wedges.

Place on an ungreased baking sheet and sprinkle with sugar as desired.

Bake for about 25 minutes until golden brown and cooked right through.

MAKES 8 SCONES

Pears Poached in Merlot with Rosemary Cream

2 cups (475 mL) Merlot or other good red wine

¼ cup (60 mL) brown sugar

6 Tbsp (90 mL) white sugar

Juice of 1 lemon

3 whole cloves

3 firm pears, peeled, halved and cored

⅓ cup (80 mL) whipping cream

1 tsp (5 mL) finely minced rosemary leaves

1 very swift grinding of pepper

Sharon says: I used to make this dish all the time "back in the old days" around Thanksgiving and can't even remember its origin. It is easy considering the appreciative reaction of guests, as poaching fruit seems to have gone out of style. The unsweetened whipped cream with rosemary (and a tiny bite from black pepper) perfectly complements the Merlot-stained pears with their spicy whiff of clove. Do get a decent bottle of Merlot, as you'll have to drink the rest of it. The pears should be on the al dente side but ripe—best just buy the pears the day before, as they're often slightly green at the market but seem to ripen quickly in your fruit bowl.

Pour the wine into a non-reactive skillet. Add the sugars, lemon juice and cloves, bring to a boil and cook for about 4 to 6 minutes or until mixture is slightly thickened. Add the pears and reduce heat to low. Poach the pears in the liquid (they'll add their own as well) for 8 to 10 minutes—don't let them become mushy.

Transfer pears to a plate or storage container. Baste with the marinade several times and turn them over—you want them to become deeply coloured.

Whip the cream lightly, just until it is a little fluffy but not stiff. Fold in the rosemary and pepper.

Serve pears at room temperature or slightly chilled. Pour some remaining marinade over them, and decorate with the whipped cream.

MAKES 6 POLITE SERVINGS

Baked Peaches with Basil Cream

 *

4 ripe but firm peaches, halved, pit removed

2 Tbsp (30 mL) melted butter

2 Tbsp (30 mL) Demerara or raw sugar

¼ tsp (1 mL) good salt

⅔ cup (160 mL) whipping cream

½ tsp (2.5 mL) vanilla

¼ cup (60 mL) packed basil leaves in chiffonade, plus extra leaves for garnish

* gluten free if gluten-free vanilla is used

This dessert—easier than pie—is guaranteed to wow dinner guests or your family. Be sure to use freestone peaches; the other kind will make you crazy trying to remove the pits and halve the peaches without ripping them to smithereens and getting peach juice all over you.

Preheat oven to 425F (220C).

Place peaches cut side up in a pie plate or baking dish lined with parchment paper. Brush with melted butter.

Combine sugar and salt, and sprinkle a little on each peach.

Roast for about 20 minutes or until peaches begin to turn golden brown at the edges.

Remove from heat; transfer peaches to a shallow serving dish or individual bowls or plates, and drizzle any sauce remaining on the parchment paper over top. Allow them to cool for at least 20 minutes.

Beat cream together with vanilla until quite stiff, then fold in the basil. Spoon cream onto peaches, garnish with a few extra basil leaves and experience bliss.

MAKES 4 SERVINGS

CANINE
KALE CUISINE

Kale Doggy Biscotti

1 very packed cup (250 mL) roughly chopped kale

1 egg

1 cup (250 mL) buckwheat flour, plus extra for shaping

1 cup (250 mL) cooked sweet potato

1 tsp (5 mL) baking powder

⅓ cup (80 mL) peanut butter (smooth or crunchy, preferably without salt)

3 Tbsp (45 mL) corn grits or coarse cornmeal

2 tsp (10 mL) nutritional or brewer's yeast (optional)

Dog treats are expensive and can be a bit silly; however now that we have become "dog people," we sometimes get sucked in by the racks of snacks. Instead, try these easy homemade treats. Buckwheat is not a grain and is rich in protein and okay for pooches. The size of the biscotti will depend on the size of the dog—small, medium or large. While we have no evidence for this, we added corn grits, thinking it might help with tooth cleaning. The brewer's yeast is optional, but many dog owners claim it helps discourage fleas! The peanut butter makes the biscotti smell good too. Go ahead…try a little bite.

Preheat oven to 350F (175C).

Put kale in a food processor and pulse a few times. Add egg and pulse again, then add everything else and pulse again. The mixture should be fairly thick and a little sticky.

Refrigerate dough for half an hour.

Turn dough out onto a board sprinkled with a little buckwheat flour and knead lightly.

With your hands, form dough into round flat cookie shapes a little thicker than ¼ inch (1 cm). Place dough on a parchment-paper-lined cookie sheet; using a floured knife, score cookies in quarters (as you would shortbread), or leave them whole if you prefer. You can also roll the dough and cut it with a cookie cutter into shapes—pig, squirrel, postman, gingerbread boy—whatever tickles your fancy or your dog's.

Bake for 15 to 20 minutes depending on size of cookie.

Turn oven down to 200F (90C), and bake cookies 15 to 20 more minutes.

If they are hard, remove cookies from oven; otherwise turn oven off and leave cookies in it for another hour to harden.

To serve, snap the cookies into bite-sized pieces.

MAKES LOTS

IT'S A DOG-EAT-KALE WORLD

Sharon's dog, Pocky, a red miniature pinscher, is a kale-eating canine. Pocky loves to nibble a few kale buds—often as an appetizer before dinner—and we figure they must be good for her. She will also occasionally go out to the garden and nip off low-lying kale leaves.

Add cooked kale to your dog's dinner if you make it yourself. Or, if you don't, why not chop and steam a little to stir into whatever you are serving your dog for dinner. While dogs make their own vitamin C (too bad we can't), there are lots of other good things in kale that are useful for critters. And, for sure, dogs love kale chips…unseasoned, of course. They also might fancy having a chew on a thick kale stem or two (like bones), especially if it's right before dinner and they are hungry as a dog, and eating tender peeled kale stems, cooked or raw.

Patches—who adopted Carol after he was saved by a rescue organization—loves hanging out with family in the garden and knows never to step on the kale. Unlike Sharon's dog, Pocky, Patches likes his kale cooked, preferably simmered in a little bit of homemade stock made without onions (which are not good for dogs), and will always wag his tail for a homemade biscuit.

Bow-Wow Kale Chow

1 lb (454 g) ground turkey or cut-up turkey meat without bones

1 Tbsp (15 mL) vegetable oil

6 medium carrots, diced

3 medium parsnips, diced

1 cup (250 mL) rolled oats

1¼ cups (300 mL) water (or a little more, as needed to cover the stew)

2 cups (475 mL) chopped kale

2 sweet apples

2 Tbsp (30 mL) runny honey

1 Tbsp (15 mL) chopped mixed herbs such as parsley, rosemary and thyme leaves

½ tsp (2.5 mL) ground turmeric

1 tsp (5 mL) ground flaxseed

*gluten free if gluten-free rolled oats are used

This recipe was shared by *Modern Dog* magazine (which Sharon previously thumbed her nose at . . . before becoming a "dog person"). We are glad to see that herbs are good for dogs, turmeric too—in moderation, of course. This chow is intended for dogs who are accustomed to eating "people food;" if you want to introduce a kibble-fed dog to this recipe, you might want to go easy at first, to allow your dog's digestive system to adjust. Pocky has a cast-iron stomach. You can substitute pears for the apples, as pears are very good for dogs too.

In a medium-sized heavy-bottomed saucepan or frying pan with lid, cook the turkey meat in the oil over medium heat, stirring occasionally, until meat is no longer pink.

Add the carrots and parsnips (diced with your dog's size in mind—smaller bits for petite pooches, etc.) and the oats, stir, then pour in the water to just cover the stew. Simmer for about 15 minutes until veggies are al dente. Add kale, then cook for another 5 to 8 minutes until all veggies are tender. Remove from heat.

Peel, core and grate apples, add them to the turkey mixture along with the honey, herbs, turmeric and flaxseed, and stir well. Cool a little before serving—mixture can be warm but, of course, not too hot.

This hearty dog chow keeps for up to 4 days, refrigerated. Feed your dog as much as you usually do. Freeze any extra in ice cube trays or muffin cups.

MAKES ABOUT 8 CUPS (2 L) CHOW

Notes

1. Gerald F. Combs, Jr., "Vitamin K," in *The Vitamins: Fundamental Aspects in Nutrition and Health*, 2nd ed. (San Diego: Academic Press, 1998), 225-44.

2. Talwinder Singh Kahlon, Mei-Chen Chiu and Mary H. Chapman, "Steam Cooking Significantly Improves in Vitro Bile Acid Binding of Collard Greens, Kale, Mustard Greens, Broccoli, Green Bell Pepper, and Cabbage," *Nutrition Research* 28, no. 6 (2008): 351–57

3. Young Jin Moon, Xiaodong Wang, Marilyn E. Morris, "Dietary Flavonoids: Effects on Xenobiotic and Carcinogen Metabolism," *Toxicology in Vitro* 20, no. 2 (2006): 187–210.

4. Ibid.

5. Dean A. Kopsell and David E. Kopsell, "Carotenoids in Vegetables: Biosynthesis, Occurrence, Impacts on Human Health, and Potential for Manipulation," in *Bioactive Foods in Promoting Health: Fruits and Vegetables*, ed. Ronald Ross Watson and Victor R. Preedy (San Diego: Academic Press, 2010), 645–62.

6. "Raw Foods," Lutein Information Bureau, accessed December 2011, http://www.luteininfo.com/whereraw.

7. Kopsell and Kopsell, "Carotenoids in vegetables," 645–62.

8. Elizabeth H. Jeffery and Marcela Araya, "Physiological Effects of Broccoli Consumption," *Phytochemical Reviews* 8, no. 1 (2009): 283–98.

9. Mario G. Ferruzzi and Joshua Blakeslee, "Digestion, Absorption, and Cancer Preventative Activity of Dietary Chlorophyll Derivatives," *Nutrition Research* 27, no. 1 (2007): 1–12.

10. Dr. Joel Fuhrman, MD, who specializes in nutrition-based treatments for obesity and chronic disease, is research director of the Nutritional Research Project and the author of five books. He created the Aggregate Nutrient Density Index (ANDI), which scores foods using the equation H = N/C (health value = nutrients delivered per calorie consumed). The index awards kale absolutely top marks.

Index